SAGE was founded in 1965 by Sara Miller McCune to support the dissemination of usable knowledge by publishing innovative and high-quality research and teaching content. Today, we publish over 900 journals, including those of more than 400 learned societies, more than 800 new books per year, and a growing range of library products including archives, data, case studies, reports, and video. SAGE remains majority-owned by our founder, and after Sara's lifetime will become owned by a charitable trust that secures our continued independence.

Los Angeles | London | New Delhi | Singapore | Washington DC | Melbourne

EMBODYING MOTHERHOOD

EMBODYING MOTHERHOOD
Perspectives from Contemporary India

Anu Aneja and Shubhangi Vaidya

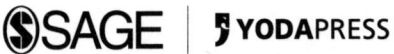

Los Angeles | London | New Delhi
Singapore | Washington DC | Melbourne

Copyright © Anu Aneja and Shubhangi Vaidya, 2016

All rights reserved. No part of this book may be reproduced or utilized in any form or by any means, electronic or mechanical, including photocopying, recording or by any information storage or retrieval system, without permission in writing from the publisher.

First published in 2016 by

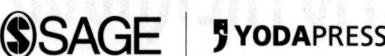

SAGE Publications India Pvt Ltd
B1/I-1 Mohan Cooperative Industrial Area
Mathura Road, New Delhi 110 044, India
www.sagepub.in

YODA Press
268 AC Vasant Kunj
New Delhi 110070
www.yodapress.co.in

SAGE Publications Inc
2455 Teller Road
Thousand Oaks, California 91320, USA

SAGE Publications Ltd
1 Oliver's Yard, 55 City Road
London EC1Y 1SP, United Kingdom

SAGE Publications Asia-Pacific Pte Ltd
3 Church Street
#10-04 Samsung Hub
Singapore 049483

Published by Vivek Mehra for SAGE Publications India Pvt Ltd, typeset in Berkeley 10/12 pt by Zaza Eunice, Hosur, Tamil Nadu, India and printed Chaman Enterprises, New Delhi.

Library of Congress Cataloging-in-Publication Data Available

ISBN: 978-93-515-0893-9 (HB)

SAGE Yoda Team: Sonjuhi Negi, Neha Sharma and Ishita Gupta

To
our mothers,
for embodying us

our children,
for opening up remarkable motherhood chapters in our lives

and to both,
for their faith in our capabilities beyond mothering

Thank you for choosing a SAGE product!
If you have any comment, observation or feedback,
I would like to personally hear from you.

Please write to me at **contactceo@sagepub.in**

Vivek Mehra, Managing Director and CEO, SAGE India.

Bulk Sales

SAGE India offers special discounts
for purchase of books in bulk.
We also make available special imprints
and excerpts from our books on demand.

For orders and enquiries, write to us at

Marketing Department
SAGE Publications India Pvt Ltd
B1/I-1, Mohan Cooperative Industrial Area
Mathura Road, Post Bag 7
New Delhi 110044, India

E-mail us at **marketing@sagepub.in**

Get to know more about SAGE

Be invited to SAGE events, get on our mailing list.
Write today to **marketing@sagepub.in**

This book is also available as an e-book.

Contents

List of Images ix
Acknowledgements xi
Introduction xv

Chapter 1
Disembodied Mothers: Re-writing the maternal metaphor through goddess iconography 1

Chapter 2
Anticipating the Mother's Dream: Maternal subjectivity in psychoanalysis, literature and cinema 33

Chapter 3
'Mere Paas Maa Hai' Reflections on representations of motherhood in Hindi cinema 74

Chapter 4
'More than a Mother': Autism, motherhood discourse and lived experience 107

Chapter 5
Capitalist Encounters: The motherhood pact 134

Chapter 6
Of 'Unfit' Mothers: Disability, stereotypes and contestations 156

Chapter 7
Mapping the Mother in France and India: Discursive revolutions 181

Index 213
About the Authors 219

List of Images

1.1: Saptamatrika	4
1.2: Carving of a Squatting Woman Giving Birth Supported by Two Attendants	6
1.3: Hind Devi	11
1.4: Yama/ Bharat Uddhaar	12
1.5: Shaheed Bhagat Singh	13
1.6: Mother India	14
1.7: Vac Devi	20

Acknowledgements

This book is a labour of love. It was 'conceived' as the result of an ongoing conversation between the authors, both of whom were in the process of thinking through the ideological implications of mothering in terms of the lived realities of their personal lives as well as their academic and intellectual pursuits. In some ways the final product is evidence of our common recognition of the interconnections between these domains, denying a clear-cut separation between the two. Our deep investment in feminist understandings of the experience of mothering has been a way of confronting one crucial aspect of our lives. Equally, it has provided us a lens with which to view and explore its symbolic mutations and re-conceptualizations and to visualize pathways beyond the apparent and commonly shared patriarchal discourses within which we remain embedded. Deeply aware of the essentialist debates within feminist academic discourses, owing to which motherhood continues to occupy a contested space, we wished, at once, to interrogate oppressive and regulatory maternal ideologies and their attendant notions of 'able mothering', as well as to explore liberatory aspects unleashed through revised understandings of the maternal. The dual impulse to question patriarchally constructed motherhood roles and to uncover in altered reconceptions of the maternal a freedom beyond settled perceptions remains at the heart of this enterprise. It is the latter desire that has impelled us to delve into the maternal beyond the merely corporeal, in its various metaphorical embodiments in religious iconography, literature, cinema, psychoanalysis, and beyond.

We would like to acknowledge the contributions of and support offered by the many people who have been an integral part of this process. We are deeply indebted to Arpita Das of Yoda Press for her wholehearted enthusiasm from the very outset of this project. Her faith in the manuscript and her unstinting support through the various phases of the editing process, have been invaluable in sustaining our commitment and ensuring the timely completion of the manuscript. We are also grateful to other members of Arpita's editorial team. For her efficient and meticulous copyediting, her keen eye, and for candidly declaring her pleasure in working with the manuscript, we would like to offer a big thank you to Sonjuhi Negi. For providing assistance in the early part of this process, we thank Nishtha Vadehra. We thank the anonymous reviewer who went through the draft manuscript for generous and encouraging feedback. We are delighted that our work forms a part of the new SAGE Yoda imprint and extend our thanks to SAGE for their support.

For their prompt assistance and their permission to use several of the images that appear in the book, we would like to acknowledge the National Museum, New Delhi; CIViC: Centre for Indian Visual Culture, New Delhi; Patna Museum, Bihar; as well as Christopher Pinney, Priya Paul and Christiane Brosius for sharing images from their respective private collections.

We are thankful to Demeter Press and to the journal *Social Change* (published by SAGE) for allowing us to reprint materials that have previously appeared in their publications. We are grateful to the Indira Gandhi National Open University, and especially the IGNOU Library, for providing us a space within which this research could be accomplished. We deeply appreciate the very willing and personalized support provided by Dr Jaideep Sharma, Head Librarian and Dr Syed Nehal Imam of the IGNOU library, both of whom have always shown an ongoing readiness to help locate valuable resources, and have often gone out of their way to do so. Teaching courses in gender and writing study materials for distance learners has helped us to clarify and refine our ideas and theories. We warmly thank our colleagues in the School of Gender and Development Studies and the School of Interdisciplinary and Trans-Disciplinary Studies, IGNOU, for providing lively, collegial spaces for debate, discussion and mutual learning and for keeping alive ongoing conversations about various gender-related issues. For her valuable and very prompt feedback on parts of the manuscript, we are grateful to Dr Meenakshi Malhotra. We have, over the years, had the great good fortune to interact with eminent scholars, activists and stake-holders in the women's movement and the Disability Rights movement who have enriched our understanding and sensitized us to the often brutal realities experienced by women in general and women with disabilities in particular.

From Shubhangi

I would like to thank Professor Nilika Mehrotra for her sustained support, encouragement and friendship over the years. As my PhD research supervisor at the Jawaharlal Nehru University she opened up the riches of feminist anthropology and disability studies and encouraged me to reflect upon and theorize my experience of mothering a child with disability. Animated conversations with Renu Addlakha over the years have been interesting and enriching and I have learnt much from her. With deep humility I thank the mothers of children with autism who participated in my research and shared their stories. I wish them well for the future and hope that together we can make a more humane world that will be accepting of human diversity and difference.

With deep love and gratitude I pay tribute to the mothering presences in my life. My grandmother, Kamal Vaidya, brought up her two grandchildren with utter devotion and never failed to remind them how much they would miss her when she was gone. You were right, Aai, as always. My mother-in-law, Rajkumari Singh, bore the vicissitudes of life with remarkable courage and fortitude, and is remembered with love and reverence. My mother, the beautiful and brilliant Shobhana Vaidya, was like a 'candle in the wind' whose memories stay aflame in my heart.

I deeply miss the companionship of my husband Sandeep K. Singh who was taken from us far too soon. Our sons Vibhu and Vishu are the light of my life, my raison d'etre. Raising them has been a wondrous journey; I watch with pride and joy as they make their forays into the adult world and forge ahead in their lives. Vibhu has been my rock, my pillar of support in an often turbulent voyage. Vishu, who introduced me to the world of autism has expanded my horizons and enabled me to meet remarkable people. At the top of the list are Merry Barua and her wonderful team at Action for Autism, New Delhi whose work has truly transformed lives.

From Anu

I am indebted to several people who have been by my side while I worked on this book. First and foremost, my husband Neel, my steadfast and resourceful partner who has fearlessly accompanied me on this and every other journey, always unswerving, unfailing through better and through worse; my parents, Sindu and R.P. Aneja for revealing to me, very early on, their delight in 'mothering' girls when not too many seemed familiar with it; my older sister Renu, who mothered me so well before departing; Kamal and Hema, for creating warm, familial spaces of comfort. I am thankful to be able to share with them and with my extended family, spread across cities and continents, common joys and sorrows, and watch the next generation of 'children' find gratifications in shared parenting and re-inventions of 'mothering'.

I am grateful to my sons—Nishant, who held fast in his faith to welcome me into his life, and whom I have been extremely fortunate to love and mother, and Kabeer, who came to me when I most expected him, across the cusp of a half-moon's bay, and brought into view a marvellous new seascape of love and reciprocity. Their enthusiasm, thoughtfulness and faith have constantly shored up my work.

For steering me towards French feminist writing, and various other pleasures of intellectual pursuit, especially those that women are pleased to gift each other, I will remain indebted to my teacher and friend, Christiane Makward. In her generous company I have continued to discover uncommon connotations of mothering.

Working on this book together has been memorable. We shall always cherish the shared moments of excitement and discovery, frustration, doubt and uncertainty, and most especially, laughter and mirth. As we 'birth' this book and finally let it out into the world we can only hope that it will fare well and manage to inscribe for itself a life of its own.

Introduction

Embodying Motherhood homes in on the significant place occupied by the literal and figurative body in motherhood discourse in urban India, in the context of prevailing motherhood ideologies. In ancient religious iconography, the maternal body has been deified and idealized. In a contemporary consumerist culture, it may be commodified or devalued, depending upon its categorization as either an 'able' or a 'disabled' body. In representational discourse, such as literature and cinema, the maternal body is shaped with the help of sign systems at the level of metaphor. Psychoanalysis, with its work on the symbolic, has dwelt at length on the figure of the mother in the unconscious and the central role it plays in unravelling the mysterious working of the psyche. These diverse frameworks present different vistas to arrive at a deeper understanding of the ideological buttresses that shape perceptions and experiences of mothering in a particular cultural context, at a certain point in history. Cutting across the disciplinary boundaries conjured up by the empirical bent of the social sciences and the interpretive slant of representational discourse, the body emerges, fades and re-emerges in these narratives, evincing the shifting effects of patriarchal cultural codifications.

Indian cultural contexts influence and resonate with all of the above discourses in specific ways. In the various chapters of this book, it has been our attempt to employ feminist perspectives to map how patriarchal motherhood ideologies in India get inscribed within these discourses, leading to distinctive narratives of oppression, resistance and revisioning. Feminist discourse has charted out a rich trajectory of the critique of patriarchal constructions of motherhood ideology. At the same time, it enables us to explore affirmative maternal subjectivities through a revised understanding of motherhood. In the context of India, this dual impulse within feminism has taken a particular shape, which reflects specific cultural influences. This book reflects on the nature of motherhood ideology in India, and its critique from a feminist perspective, in an effort to re-vision the embodiment of the maternal as symbolic and experiential. Motherhood has often been reduced to a contractual arrangement that women consent to under circumstances of economic or social compulsions; yet, there has also been an ongoing recognition of deep, visceral satisfactions to be derived from mothering. Located as we are at this crossroads, we try to look beyond the half-way house within which women perform their mothering roles under strict patriarchal surveillance, to imagine the possibility of unfettered maternal agency, subjectivity and freedom of choice—in other words, to follow Susan Suleiman's suggestion and to 'imagine the mother laughing' (1990, 179).

As authors of this book, having a 'background' in different disciplinary areas, we have tried to combine our 'double vision' to fit together at least some of the pieces of the puzzle invoked by feminism's somewhat vexed relationship with mothering. Our particular location as mothers and feminist scholars within an urban-Indian setting has pushed us to look at the implications of this relationship within the specific context of our own environment. In doing so, we have been both guided and bounded by the socio-cultural contexts we describe and analyse. Given India's regional and cultural diversity, class differences and rural-urban divides, there are, of course, huge variations in the way motherhood is represented and understood. Our aim has not been to provide a complete survey of the vast differences that exist in the constructions and performance of motherhood across India; rather, we have selected, as our particular focus, issues concerning mothers in urban India. At the same time, we have tried to contextualize these issues within larger intersectional frameworks, and wherever possible, attempted to show how certain widespread ideological mores influence women across rural/urban, class, caste and regional divides.

Our common desire to make sense of mothering both from a theoretical and an experiential perspective has taken us in various directions—to ancient myth and religion, to psychoanalysis, to literature and cinema, and to socio-economic and cultural frameworks within which women's roles as mothers are defined from the perspective of 'ability' and 'disability'. Through these explorations, certain recurring themes have emerged: the patriarchal 'pact', which forces certain gendered 'performances' of mothering; the privileging of certain motherhood ideologies and conducts; the preference for sons over daughters, and ability over disability; the desexualization of the maternal body, its appropriation as commodity, its being posited as a 'lack', and an ongoing reluctance to grant it the position of subjectivity and agency.

Contemporary constructions of motherhood ideology in India are evidence of both a glorification of an idealized maternal idea as well as the 'deficit' attributed to the maternal body, reflecting deep-seated patriarchal biases whose roots can be traced back in history. This incongruity gives rise to an apparent paradox, which is voiced in the commonly expressed, frustrated response to violence against women: 'Why do we violate women in a country where women are worshipped as mother goddesses?' Such a seeming paradox, however, reveals itself to be its inverse, a parallel whose propositions are consistent with each other. In other words, women are violated not in spite of being worshipped; they are violated *because* the idealization of a desexualized maternal validates the desecration of the irreverent, sexual female body as a pariah, in a cultural context which promotes the splitting up of the maternal object into a divine spirit and a profane body.

Consequently, the notion of 'deficit' runs like a thread throughout our readings of the maternal body. It brings to the fore the embodiment of the mother as lacking/disabled, and the oppression of women stemming from this notion of lack. Most conspicuously, its spectre hangs over the disabled body—whether that of the disabled mother or of the mother of the disabled child. In the case of the former, the very idea of motherhood, associated with care and nurturance, is seen as unattainable by a person who herself requires care. In the case of the latter, her motherhood experience is seen to be blighted or as a failure because she has produced a 'defective' child. In contrast, the 'able' mother is one who attempts to adhere to an idealized image and, since the image is forever elusive, she remains unsuccessful.

This wanting experience of the maternal is the impetus behind the search for a manner of living and doing motherhood differently. However, the concept of an alternate maternal subjectivity is complicated given that motherhood is deeply embedded in larger patriarchal structures that oppress women, and given the rightful feminist wariness about essentialist traps, such as the naturalized association of women with mothering. A huge risk is entailed in assuming that the maternal subject can refute the image of the mother's body as receptacle of male desire, and re-emerge to find ways of experiencing pleasure in maternal identity. A discourse that openly exhibits its desire for pleasureful ways of knowing motherhood will no doubt skirt dangerously close to feminism's old traitor—its exploratory alliances with 'feminine' ways of knowing, and their attendant threats—essentialism and the age-old battle with the Freudian maxim of 'anatomy is destiny.' Yet, as long as women continue to identify as mothers and perform the work of mothering, an ongoing contemplation of the relationship between women and mothering, and strategies of transforming this relationship, must remain on the map. We take this risk based on our recognition that our understanding of motherhood is manufactured by culture to such a degree that it is just possible that in the process of dismantling structures of motherhood, and unearthing the maternal body from under the patriarchal discourses, where it lies interred, we may come upon new ways of 'conceiving' it. What follows below is a brief outline of how we have attempted to pursue some of these trails in the various chapters of this book.

Chapter 1: Disembodied Mothers: Re-writing the maternal metaphor through goddess iconography

Goddess worship is a telling source of the complex envisioning of the maternal in ancient India, and throughout history. Extant images of the mother goddess throw light on the historical association of the maternal with power, divine energy and feminine dominance. At the same time, iconographic representations have also been witness to the patriarchal containing of feminine energy/power in different historical periods. We begin by looking backwards through time in an effort to understand some of these complexities in the mother goddess iconography. This effort helps us trace possible linkages between ancient representations of the Hindu goddess and the sign of the maternal (the maternal metaphor) as it circulates in contemporary times. These linkages between the past and the present times help us trace at least a partial etiology of the historical oppression of women in the context of cultural constructions of the maternal. They also signal possible ways of approaching the past in productive ways so that present-day re-imaginings of the maternal can draw verve from their ancient counterparts, especially in enduring images of resistance. A recognition of the crucial association of specific ancient goddesses with sound and speech opens up the possibility of re-visiting the notion of the contemporary maternal, especially through subversive uses of language, a theme which runs through parts of this book. We present a brief overview of the iconography of major Hindu goddesses associated with the normative maternal idea (including incarnations of Lakshmi and Devi) and its interrogations (in the persona of deities such as Vac/Saraswati and Kali), to show how a gradual process of harnessing the power of the mother goddess is achieved in Indian history. The multiplication of lesser goddesses and a considered prioritization of goddess attributes is evidence of acceptable socio-cultural roles projected for women to emulate. Notwithstanding, the enduring notion of the 'non-maternal mother' as represented through solitary mother goddesses such as Vac/Saraswati and Kali/Durga, whose attributes run counter to the stereotypical self-sacrificing mother, signal resistance to masculine domination and a search for pleasures beyond the constricting spheres of the social and the familial. Employing a feminist perspective, this chapter draws out some of the more affirmative implications of such pleasures made possible by a work on language and its symbolic structures. This emphasis leads us to re-visit, in the subsequent chapter, the significance of maternal imagery in the symbolic realm of the unconscious from the perspective of psychoanalytic theory.

Chapter 2: Anticipating the Mother's Dream: Maternal subjectivity in psychoanalysis, literature and cinema

That the 'dream' of a more pleasurable maternal subjectivity walks dangerously close to the trap of essentialism is a pitfall that feminists have repeatedly grappled with, as previously mentioned. The aim of the second chapter is neither to endorse the promise of maternal pleasure through a revised maternal subjectivity, nor to completely reject such an idea. Rather, it is to ferret out possibilities of other means of visualizing motherhood, outside of its normative constructions in patriarchy. The possibilities of subversive, discursive revisionings of the maternal touched upon in the introductory chapter bring to the fore the significant role played by representation in determining cultural codifications of the maternal. Psychoanalysis, literature and cinema, with their incisive work at the level of the symbolic, become indispensable lenses through which maternal subjectivities can be perceived. These disciplinary realms, linked through the common discourse of representation, foreground, like iconography, the complex projections of the maternal in culture. The feminist critique of mainstream psychoanalytical models (especially as undertaken by French feminists), unlocks the mother from her location as the 'dark continent' of masculist imagination. While the significance of the Oedipal narrative in western psychoanalytical discourse, and its cross-cultural influences, is undeniable, maternal subjectivities in India, dominated by cultural legacies replete with narratives of 'Devi', call for alternative psychoanalytic readings. The invaluable work done in this regard by psychoanalytical theorists such as Sudhir Kakar and Stanley Kurtz may provide culturally relevant models of approaching the maternal idea. At the same time, the primarily masculist orientation of this psychoanalytic theory impels us to interrogate some of its assumptions, and work towards feminist contextualization from the perspective of Indian women. Using the inter-disciplinary lenses offered by psychoanalysis, literature and cinema, this chapter attempts to mark out the track that can lead the mother from being the dreamt to becoming the dreamer. We attempt to do this both through a revised theoretical understanding of the maternal (with the help of contemporary feminist notions of a 'maternal aesthetic') as well as through close readings of selected literary and cinematic examples such as Satyajit Ray's *Devi*, Mahasweta Devi's 'Stanadayini', Manju Kapoor's *A Married Woman* and Deepa Mehta's *Fire*.

Chapter 3: 'Mere Paas Maa Hai': Reflections on representations of motherhood in Hindi cinema

Taking further our analysis of the culturally constructed role of the mother, this chapter mines the rich treasures of mainstream Bollywood cinema whose function is not just 'Entertainment! Entertainment! Entertainment!', as a recent blockbuster film suggests, but also identity-formation through the creation of a popular and acceptable cultural resource that can be accessed and consumed by a mind-bogglingly heterogeneous audience. As ardent cine-goers who are simultaneously constructed by and challenge this discourse, our investment in Hindi cinema is not only scholarly and academic; it is emotive, visceral and organic, rooted in childhood memories and subconscious associations. The chapter engages with a range of films that have shaped popular understandings of the meanings of motherhood as an embodied reality as well as the identification of the emergent nation as mother. The mother imagery in the creation of national consciousness is explored with reference to a range of contexts: Tamil nationalism invoking images of brave mothers as bearers and nurturers of valorous sons; the anxieties of colonial Bengal where the travails of the motherland under colonialism prompt her devoted sons to challenge the British rule; and the 'sarkaari' nationalist rhetoric of unity in diversity, on state-owned television. The defining role of Hindi cinema in narrating the nation is explored through a discussion of iconic films like Mehboob Khan's *Mother India* and Yash Chopra's *Deewar*, which track the transition of the mother nation from an area of hope to one of darkness, as the realities of poverty, corruption and political instability cast their ugly shadows over the anticipation and optimism that independence had promised. In this sense, the story of *Mother India* is also the story of the mothers of India, caught in patriarchal webs that seek to annihilate agency, and create emotional flash-points where unbearable choices must perforce be made. The chapter, like the preceding ones, attempts to establish a link between Motherhood as an ideological system, and mothering as a lived experience wherein real, embodied women struggle to balance precarious existential realities with ponderous cultural rhetoric. The insidious erasure and trivialization of the mother from the discourse of the nation under liberalization and globalization marks the shift from (re)production to consumption, and the ceding of space to the New Global Father who encapsulates the homogenizing discourse of capitalism and the new world order, a theme which is taken up in more detail in Chapter 5. However, concluding on a more optimistic note, we identify interesting new spaces and niches carved out by new filmmakers which reposition the mother in more affirmative and agentic ways. These narratives engage with the realities of contemporary motherhood through explorations of homosexuality, disability, marital strife and other 'liminal' situations, thus adding much needed nuance to the discourse.

Chapter 4: 'More than a Mother': Autism, motherhood discourse and lived experience

This chapter exemplifies the feminist article of faith that the personal is the political, and problematizes the role of the feminist researcher particularly in the context of conducting research with women. As the mother of a child with autism, the author of this chapter is uniquely positioned to access the voices of mothers who find themselves isolated and stigmatized as they attempt to come to grips with what is an extremely complex and challenging condition. However, autism is not just an 'objective' medical label; it is inscribed within multiple layers of discourse that have influenced the way it is diagnosed and treated. The emergence of autism as a recognizable diagnostic category based upon behavioural rather than biological/physiological criteria is located within certain socio-historical contexts in which the categories of normal and abnormal development become salient. In western, industrialized societies, behavioural 'disorders' like autism were associated with social change, marked by changing family patterns and roles, and most significantly, by the changing role of the mother. Psychoanalytical approaches attempted to link 'autistic withdrawal' in a child to a cold and disengaged mothering. The damning term 'refrigerator mother' stigmatized generations of mothers who were made to believe that it was their incompetent mothering that had caused their child to reject the social world, and retreat into an inner world of isolation and aloneness. The debunking of this myth, and the advances in medicine and psychiatry that inform contemporary understandings of autism as a neurological disorder found across classes and cultures has yet not liberated mothers from the blame and opprobrium they routinely face, and this is despite their sustained attempts to challenge these stereotypes by involving themselves fully in the worlds of their children, by becoming 'more than mothers.' The chapter draws upon the author's own experiences as a mother of a child with autism, and from maternal narratives generated during fieldwork with families of children with autism. The mothering ideology that shapes the way these mothers perceive their roles and responsibilities, and their attempts to create meaning out of a disruptive and chaotic situation is illustrated through these narratives. The core themes that emerge are the overwhelming importance of 'mother's love', which is conceptualized as unending, unconditional and unselfish; the primacy of their mothering role above others; and the precedence of the needs of their disabled child. These mothers view themselves as their child's most reliable and stable anchor; the only safe harbour in the stormy sea of life; the 'voice' of the child, which will render her/him intelligible to a world that privileges conformity above difference. Challenging the devaluation and blame they experience for giving birth to disabled children, they attempt to reclaim and redeem their statuses as mothers. They are not passive victims of circumstance but rather draw upon personal, social and cultural capital to make sense of circumstances, and assert their own agency and the personhood of their children. The extension of mothering outside the ambit of the family and the wider social sphere is seen in the engagement and involvement of some mothers of children with disabilities in caring professions like teaching, therapy and advocacy. Extending blood-based kinship to solidarities and support systems based upon shared distress and difficult circumstances, these women become role models for others. The urban space and the neo-liberal social order, which is based upon competition, individualism and consumer culture, paradoxically open up such avenues and mobilizations even as the traditional support system accorded by the joint family dwindles and decays. This sets the stage for the chapter that follows, which examines motherhood under conditions of capitalism with its inherent contradictions and conflicts.

Chapter 5: Capitalist Encounters: The motherhood pact

In the preceding chapter, we see how the ideology and practice of mothering is determined by the specific circumstances of mothering an autistic child. This chapter situates the performance of mothering within the larger context of the dominant economic and social structures prevalent in contemporary urban India. In view of the Indian state's recent impetus towards globalization, it becomes imperative to achieve a deeper comprehension of the effects of capitalist forces on motherhood ideology and practice. Notwithstanding the normative binary associations of 'tradition' with women's oppression, and 'westernization' with women's emancipation, an examination of the performance of motherhood in urban India reveals a much more conflicting picture of capitalism's impact on women and their mothering roles. Overriding consumerist forces encouraged under contemporary economic structures exacerbate, rather than counter, the traditional patriarchal commodification of women's bodies, and in so doing, influence the ways in which motherhood roles are played out. This chapter examines the relationship between capitalism, consumerism and urban mothering in order to expose the deceptive complacence promoted by contemporary social structures—that a move towards western notions of globalization and neo-liberalism will necessarily improve women's roles as mothers.

It looks at the 'motherhood pact' and its performative aspects under patriarchy, and suggests an ongoing challenging of the contractual aspects of mothering. Surrogacy is employed here as a metaphor and cultural trope for the 'empty-womb' identity impressed upon women. We thus examine surrogacy as a signifier, a cultural imprint of the sign of mothering, and look at its implications for women's lived realities, especially in the context of an ongoing commercialization of women's bodies. Influenced by market forces, the manufactured notion of the surrogate mother normalizes the idea of the maternal body as a resource under patriarchy. This chapter explores, among other things, the repercussions of this particular intersection between surrogacy and capitalism.

In keeping with the critique of the image of woman as a vessel, taken up here and in previous chapters, we pursue the basis of the desexualization of the maternal body under capitalist patriarchy. Patriarchal idealizations of the maternal are hinged on a process by which the maternal body is evacuated of sexuality, or sexual agency, at the very least. Whether seen through the lens of religion, psychoanalysis, literature, cinema, or history (as in the historical mapping of the mother's body onto that of the mother nation in Indian nationalist discourse), the maternal body is positioned as the passive receptacle for the projection of the male citizen's erotic desire. Patriarchal, nationalist forces already in place collude with more recent capitalist structures to perpetuate the oppression of women both within the devalued private, domestic sphere and in the public sphere of employment. The work of mothering in this given societal framework thus falls primarily on women whose unpaid, invisible labour upholds the goals of capitalism, which in turn profits from an oppression of women afforded by gender inequity. Further, such structures feed into prevalent constructions of notions of nation, race, class and caste as defined by patriarchy. Thus, capitalism and consumerism partner with patriarchy to ensure that the oppression of women as mothers remains undisturbed. The maternal body, made invisible by a super-structure of capitalist forces, is pushed into becoming one of the central pillars to prop up women's oppression in urban India. Our attempt here is to unfold the narrative through which such recognition of the place of the maternal body in capitalism becomes unavoidable, and suggest remedies in the transformational capacities of education, financial independence, and more equitable sharing of parental roles.

Introduction   XXV

Chapter 6: Of 'Unfit' Mothers: Disability, stereotypes and contestations

This chapter adds a new dimension to the earlier discussions on sexuality and motherhood by bringing the non-normative disabled body into the discourse at a socio-political juncture in which sexuality has moved out of the privacy of the bedroom and made a space for itself in the public domain of politics. The conflicting pulls of assertion and choice on the one hand, and control and policing of sexuality on the other, create a potentially volatile situation. The escalation of sexual violence in the recent past and the equally vigorous public protests against it (as witnessed in the national capital in December 2012 after the gang rape and murder of 'Nirbhaya') exemplify these contradictory trends. Under these circumstances, discussions on sexuality and reproductive rights of women with disability tend to be relegated to the back-burner. The women's movement, which has lobbied for women's right to challenge or reject their roles as sexual partners in compulsory heteronormative relationships and as receptacles to bear children under patriarchal social structures has overlooked the needs of disabled women for inclusion in the domains of sexuality, parenthood, intimate relationships and family life. The desexualization of disabled women and their exclusion from the 'normal' signposts in the life-cycle becomes even more problematic in a context where marriage is the only socially-sanctioned avenue for the expression of sexuality. The chapter draws upon a range of cross-cultural studies in an attempt to contextualize how disabled women are incorporated and excluded. Another cultural stereotype is that of the 'hypersexual' disabled woman. The devaluation and stigmatization of the disabled identity results in societal responses that police and contain disabled sexuality through a variety of techniques, including sterilization and incarceration, which are designed to eliminate the taint of disability from being transferred to the next generation. Disabled women who want to become mothers face immense pressure at the thought that they might produce disabled babies. Their motherhood practices come under surveillance and censure; they face the judgemental attitudes of family, doctors and society at large as they struggle to adjust to the demands of parenting. Intriguingly, it is by attempting to live up to the hegemonic construct of the 'ideal mother' that they challenge the stigma of disability, and reclaim a competent adult identity as women and mothers—as givers and not just recipients of care. Thus we see that the feminist challenge to 'ideal motherhood' as an unrealizable goal that traps and constrains women, in fact, functions as a *resource* that enables some mothers to contest their devalued identity as disabled women. We round off the chapter by drawing upon case studies from the Indian context which became important landmarks in social policy and in feminist theorizing about sexuality, motherhood and reproductive rights of women with disability, namely, the Pune Hysterectomies Case in 1994 and the Chandigarh Nari Niketan Case in 2009. These cases raise the key issues of bodily integrity, rights to sexuality and motherhood, agency and personhood, and the politics of care. The role of the state in safeguarding these rights also comes into sharp focus.

Chapter 7: Mapping the Mother in France and India: Discursive revolutions

The various preceding chapters of this book traverse, if somewhat cautiously, the distance between motherhood ideology in representational discourse, and as lived reality, alternating between the discourse of the social sciences, with its emphasis on praxis and case study, and the interpretive slant of the humanities.

Indian feminist discourse, for various reasons as set out in this final chapter, has leaned, until recently, more heavily on empirical discourse. Here, we argue against the marginalization of interpretive approaches which can be deployed in equally engaging ways to influence and transform our understanding as well as performance of maternal identities in urban India. Given the significant work that has been done in this regard within the realm of French feminist theory, this chapter attempts to locate prevalent Indian discourses about motherhood in the context of this theory, bringing in questions of cross-cultural relevance as well as applicability. Specifically, inferences drawn from the work of Monique Wittig, Judith Butler and Julia Kristeva are examined in the context of the discourse about Indian motherhood. The latter is delineated within dominant Hindu socio-cultural registers at the levels of the celestial, the national, and the familial.

Rather than relegating interpretive discourse to the realm of the 'apolitical', we ferret out its political implications to argue that the discursive strategies employed by French postmodern constructionism could influence ways of imagining the transformation of motherhood ideology and lived reality in India. We do so by addressing predominant questions raised by French feminism's emphasis on the uneasy relationship between language, the maternal, and cultural transformation. These include the much-debated question of the materiality of language and its relationship with culture, and the transformative capabilities of language in influencing the real performance of motherhood, beyond discursive and parodic subversions. In this regard, the question of the materiality of language is linked to that of the body, seeing how the latter is decoded through a prism of discursive representations, to show how a critique of cultural discourse may unleash new ways of conceiving and living motherhood. French feminist theory's dependence on discursive representations of the feminine has raised questions about the potential risks posed by essentialist elements of feminist theory to feminist goals. Significant work has been done in this area by many, such as Judith Butler whose redeployment of sexual and gender identities, and shifting notions of heterosexual and homosexual paradigms, complicates normative understandings of these categories and the power structures which create them. This transforms the decided notion of lesbianism as an unequivocal rejection of a 'pure' heterosexuality, and impels us to re-think normative constructions of heterosexual motherhood as well, which may equally be invaded by homosexual or homosocial elements.

In an attempt to bridge the cultural gap between French and Indian psychoanalytic discourse, we re-visit the work done by Indian psychoanalytic theorists, such as Sudhir Kakar and Ashis Nandy, taken up in a different context in Chapter 2. In their work, we find a dominant trend of exploring the Indian woman's culturally-assigned role as the mother of sons and an almost single-minded focus on the mother-son relationship. The fluid identities of Butler's work, helped by homosocial cultural conventions within India, may offer a cue in the attempt to carve a way out of the solidification of women's roles in Indian cultural and psychoanalytic discourse, and a manner of subverting heterosexual dominance through an evolved notion of sisterhood. Additionally, Julia Kristeva's positing of notions such as the 'maternal chora' takes further the possibility of the subversion of the phallic law at the symbolic plane, by the repressed aspects of femininity available at the level of the semiotic, an area previously underplayed in Freudian and Lacanian theories. The notions of maternal pleasure and maternal aesthetic raised in Chapter 2 re-emerge through our cross-cultural reading of Kristeva's theories of the feminine, her emphasis on Christian religious iconographies, and potential links to images of Hindu goddesses. While this pleasureful repressed feminine has been remarked upon in the work of post-Freudian/Eriksonian psychoanalysts in India, a feminist perspective on maternal pleasure can lead to a very different envisioning of more affirmative maternal subjectivities.

Of course, intersectional gender-caste-class matrices, which are fundamental frameworks in any narration of maternal identities in India, must be kept in full view while inscribing novel maternal subjectivities at the level of theory. We ask, however, for parallel, concomitant emphases on analyses of oppression and movements towards pleasure so that the latter, previously neglected in masculinized subjectivities and constructions, is brought into the ambit of feminist revisionings of maternal subjectivities. Similarly, the chapter underlines the importance of the complementary and mutually-advancing roles that need to be written out for empirical research and interpretive theory in the work yet to be done by feminists in radicalizing cultural constructions of the maternal in India, and in opening up the possibility of cross-cultural alliances through vigilant, contextualized readings of international feminist theory.

As may be evident from the above, the various chapters come together to paint a partial picture of the embodied maternal in India. We have tried to envisage happier visualizations towards a completion of the puzzle of the disembodied maternal body. We invite the reader to participate in such a dream.

Reference

Suleiman, Susan. 'Feminist Intertextuality and the Laugh of the Mother'. In *Subversive Intent: Gender, Politics and the Avant-Garde*. Cambridge: Harvard University Press, 1990, pp. 141–180.

1
Disembodied Mothers: Re-writing the maternal metaphor through goddess iconography

From names to attributes. There is no Devi here.

—Spivak 2001, 133

Introduction

Despite having undergone various modifications through time, the influence of mother-goddess iconography continues to prevail in dominant religious, cultural and nationalist discourses.[1] It is perhaps because of the surprising contemporaneousness of the cultural influence of the ancient mother-goddess that feminist academic interest is repeatedly drawn to this realm. Various embodiments of the ancient mother-goddess have been examined, either as a means of recuperating and re-imaging the feminine in empowering, affirmative ways, or as evidence of oppressive cultural traditions that continue to burden Indian women. Contradictory aspects of the goddess lend themselves to both of these impulses, since the ancient goddess is equal proof of benign, gentle and creative forces as well as malevolent, terrifying and destructive aspects, all of which have been looked at through different disciplinary lenses in the areas of literature, sociology, cultural anthropology and psychology. This chapter seeks out the moorings of the contemporary maternal metaphor in its roots in ancient mother goddess iconography. With the help of a feminist perspective, I attempt to isolate certain propositions that undergird the circulation of representations of the maternal in urban Indian cultural discourse in the 21st century. Finally, I suggest the possibility of productive links between the ancient and the modern through a contemporary re-imagination of the maternal with particular emphasis on the association of the mother goddess to language.

The striking links between modern and ancient representations of the maternal have been noted by various scholars. Mandakranta Bose, for instance, observes that in contemporary India, 'the idea of the goddess functions as a philosophical and social archetype. From that archetype, models of conduct have emerged to dominate women's lives irrespective of caste, social class and sometimes, even religion.' She goes on to note that 'because of their influence, goddesses are potent and ready sources of images and labels for women in their social relations'. (Bose 2010, 13) Although representations of the divine mother are often touted as a source of feminist inspiration (especially in her invincible forms such as that of Kali or Durga), there is an equally widespread and deep-rooted suspicion of such an unequivocal idealization of cultural archetypes. The recognition of a huge chasm between the abstract glorification of the mother goddess within confined places of worship, and the day-to-day material realities within which Indian women grapple with patriarchally-entrenched definitions of womanhood and motherhood is the most obvious cause of such discomfort. The privileging of specific caste- and class-based values stemming from a dominant Brahmanical tradition equally ensure the circumscribed appeal of ancient Hindu deities.

On the one hand, the mother goddess can embody power and promise empowerment, and on the other, she serves to disembody women by robbing them of a direct relationship with their own bodies. Given the tangled web of these contradictory associations, is it possible to seek out a fruitful relationship with the cultural legacies of the mother goddess from a feminist perspective? This chapter will explore the above issues in two sections. The first section will delineate the maternal metaphor through available representations of ancient mother goddesses in dominant strands of Hindu myth and religion, and subsequent reoccupations of the maternal metaphor in projections of the nation as mother. Using a feminist perspective, I attempt to relate the inferences arrived at in the first section to the lived realities of contemporary urban mothers, in the second. I argue that one possible way of linking ancient representations of the maternal in constructive ways with contemporary definitions of mothering is through discursive experimentations, which enable a *re-imagining* of the maternal beyond a mere re-imaging of the goddess. Drawing upon the metaphor of the mother's tongue, as predominantly and literally visualized in images of Vac and Kali, I look for contiguities between the goddess' tongue and subversive possibilities of language. Some aspects of this argument which draw specifically upon feminist psychoanalytic theory are subsequently taken up in the final chapter of this book.

Ancient Mother Goddesses and the Maternal Metaphor

Based on archaeological evidence, various scholars have noted that the earliest icons of fertility goddesses (including snake goddesses) date back to pre-Vedic times in the Harappa and Mohenjodaro civilizations (see, Mandakranta Bose 2010; Sukumari Bhattacharjee 2010; Kamala Ganesh 2010; Wendy Doniger 1975; Liddle and Joshi 1986). Liddle and Joshi surmise that 'the religion of the Indus Valley was based on fertility, and the people worshipped the mother goddess together with other fertility symbols, all of which are found in Hinduism today. Terracotta figurines of the mother goddess, like those excavated at Mohenjo-daro in the Indus Valley, were also found at Buxar in Bihar, which suggests the extension of the Indus Valley culture, with its goddess religion, into the Ganges valley in the Northeast. Kali the destructive goddess was also known in the Indus Valley, and the Shakti cult (female power) may be traced back to this time.' (Liddle and Joshi 1986, 54) Similarly, Wendy Doniger points out that 'strong evidence of a cult of the Mother has been unearthed at the pre-Vedic civilization of the Indus Valley (c. 2000 B.C.).' (Doniger 1975, 238) Ganesh describes the female figures found in the Harappan sites as 'nude, wearing elaborate jewellery and a distinct headdress.' (Ganesh 2010, 78). An exhibition held in 2014 at the National Museum in New Delhi amply brought to the fore the singular importance of fertility goddesses during this period, as well as their diversity and divergence from stereotypical notions of motherhood.[2]

As observed by Naman P. Ahuja, curator of the exhibition, 'Matrakas [mothers] do not conform to the stereotype of nurturing or benign mother. Some have a dangerous and protective aspect that belies the compassion typically associated with the idea of "mother".' (Ahuja 2014, 67)

4   Embodying Motherhood

The 'Saptamatrika' or 'Seven Mother Goddesses' (see Image 1.1) attest to an early recognition of the combined, creative aspect of the female body. These seven goddesses later become the consorts of seven different gods and are always worshipped in a group.

Ancient fertility idols depicting a squatting woman in the act of giving birth, dating back to the 6th century, and later named 'Lajja Gauri' (post-Gupta period, Madhya Pradesh), brings into perspective the forthright recognition of the power and energy associated with birthing as symbolic of the larger process of creation. In many of her images, Lajja Gauri's head is replaced by a lotus, a flower associated with the life-giving aspects of water, and later also with the river-goddess Saraswati. The shift in the status of fertility goddesses and the concomitant denigration of the sexualized female body in subsequent periods are reflected in the association of reproductive functions of the female body with aspects such as shame. Lajja Gauri's attitude of being-without-shame is euphemistically

Image 1.1
Saptamatrika

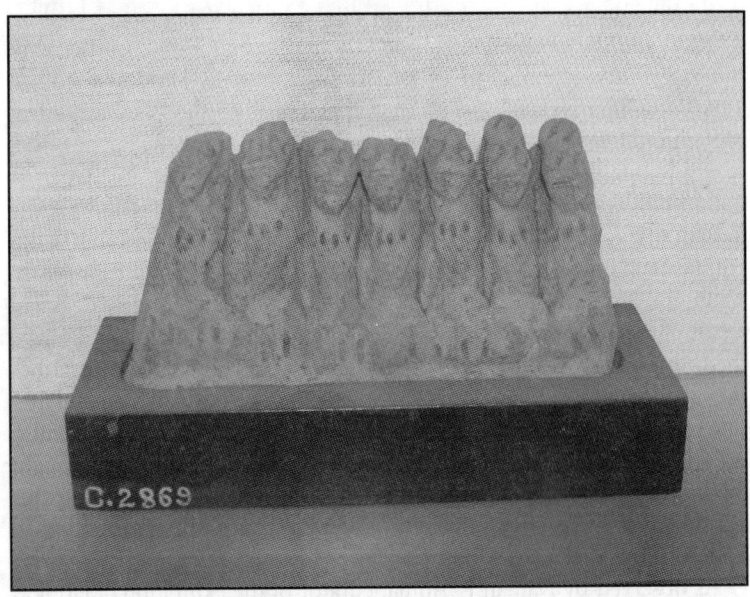

Source: Terracotta, 2nd–3rd century A.D., Probably Kushan, Belwa, Bihar, 7 × 15 cm, Patna Museum.

encompassed in the name attributed to her subsequently ('Lajja' or 'shame'). In either case, it is a manifest reminder of the goddess's direct ownership of her sexual identity and bounty in pre-historic times. Later representations of mother-goddesses embodying procreative powers, such as the 18th-century image from South India of a squatting woman in the act of giving birth (see Image 1.2), reveal the endurance of an ongoing and trans-historical association between fecundity and power in various parts of the country.

The gradual usurpation of the dominant role of the fertility goddess by male gods, and their transformation into consorts of the latter is a process which appears to have begun in the Vedic ages. Bose notes that in Vedic times, 'a goddess is always linked to a male figure as his mother or wife or daughter or sister, which suggests that her very identity rests on her relationships with males, with rare exceptions.' (Bose 2010, 14) However, this trend seems to be characteristic of Brahminical Hinduism with its emphasis on caste hierarchies. Liddle and Joshi view the gradual decline in the status of the mother goddess as the result of a gradual Brahminization of Hindu culture which resulted in greater control over women through a control over female sexuality: 'in the "brahminical" form, the goddess has both aspects [dominant and subordinate], but is more commonly subordinate. In the non-brahminical form, however, the goddess is never represented as married, and is always dominant.... The religious myths of the Brahmins may tell the story of women's destructive power, and how it was constrained by men through control of the women's sexuality, but the religion of the common people tells the story of women's continuing power and their resistance to male control.' (Liddle and Joshi 1986, 55)

The complex history of the dominant/subordinate roles of the mother goddess from pre-Vedic to Vedic times, and her contradictory representations in Brahminical and non-Brahminical cultures, point to both historical and cultural (especially patriarchal, caste-based) factors as some of the principle causes of the apparently contrasting roles she appears in throughout the ages. Moreover, this trend is not restricted to India since scholars of ancient myth and religion, such as Samuel Kramer, Diane Wolkstein, S. H. Hooke and Robert Graves, have noted similar assimilations of ancient, chthonic mother goddesses into male-dominated religious pantheons in Greece, the Middle East and Egypt, with powerful goddesses such as Gaea, Aphrodite, Inanna/Ishtar and Isis being reduced from earth-mother deities to partners of male gods with specific, limited functions and roles.[3] Iconographic resemblances

6　Embodying Motherhood

Image 1.2
Carving of a Squatting Woman Giving Birth Supported by Two Attendants (Wooden figure of Mahamai [The great Mother] South India, 18th century; 28×9×32 cm).

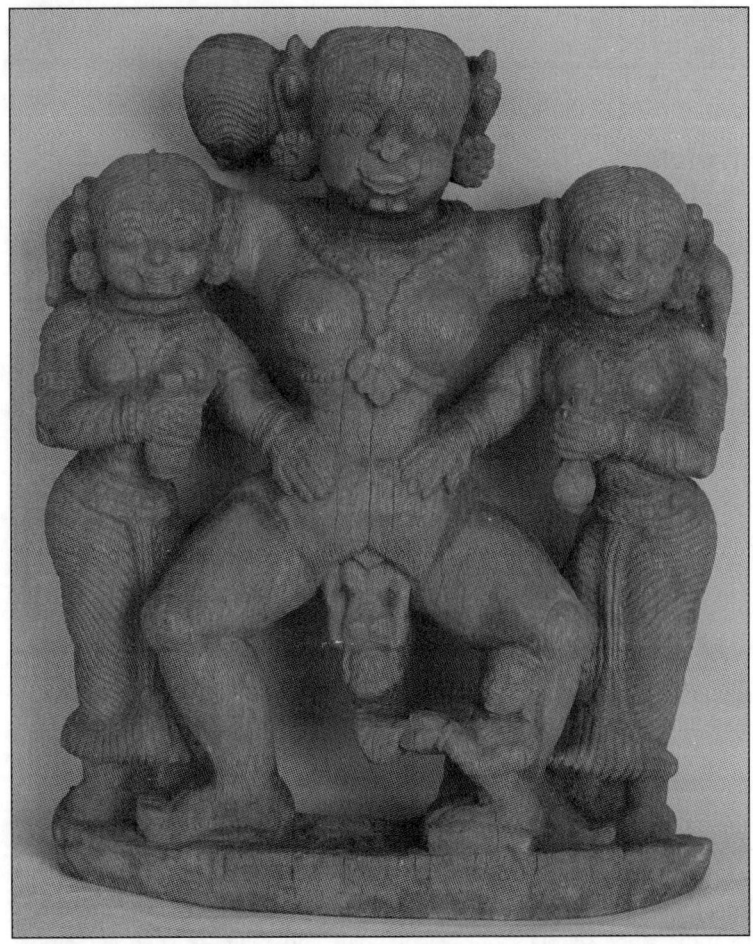

Source: National Museum; Ajit Mookerjee Collection, New Delhi.
Acc no: 82.274

between cults of ancient fertility goddesses across cultures, especially of Mesopotamia and the Indian subcontinent have also been noted, as for instance in the particular case of goddess icons of Lajja Gauri found in ancient Mesopotamia and the Indus Valley civilization: 'It is surprising to note the strong artistic link between the early Hindu art and the enduring design of the early Mesopotamian art passed in India through the Indus valley civilization.' (Le Martin 2012, 6)

Evolution of the Goddess from Vedic to Post-Vedic Times

In India, it is in the Vedic age that mother-goddess imagery achieves its most concrete apotheosis, driven by an increasingly stratified, patriarchal and caste-based society. In her study of the gendered nature of ancient deities, Mandakranta Bose distinguishes between the evolving forms of the mother-goddess from Vedic times. Briefly, these involve the older, independent goddesses such as Vac/Saraswati and Devi, and their later Vedic forms.

From Vedic to post-Vedic times, we see a proliferation of goddesses so that the more abstract concept of an all powerful Devi or Shakti finds concrete and specifically delineated contours in the shape of a variety of goddesses. Among these are Usha (dawn), Vac (speech), Saraswati (knowledge, learning, arts), Lakshmi (wealth and prosperity), Parvati (wife of Shiva, and re-incarnation of Sati), Durga (warrior and mother goddess), and Kali (destruction). In the epics, the *Ramayana* and the *Mahabharata*, incarnations of Lakshmi (Sita, the chaste and subservient wife of Rama, and Radha, the beloved follower of Krishna) continue to dominate the cultural imaginary. Others such as Kunti, Ahalya, Amba and Draupadi in the *Mahabharata* also figure as important models of exemplary conduct for women. The Tantric tradition, with its worship of the goddess Tara, provides an alternate tradition of mother-goddess worship centring on a powerful, eroticized female deity.

Similarly, village deities and goddesses worshipped by indigenous, aboriginal communities present a divergent worldview not always consonant with dominant trends in mainstream Hinduism.[4] Of the latter, one such widely revered goddess, touted for her independence and her abstract, intellectual appeal is the goddess Saraswati. Notwithstanding her popularization as the mother of knowledge and the arts, and her consequent openness to feminist reclamations, it is equally important to note that the relative popularity of Saraswati amongst upper castes and classes has been in consonance with their greater accessibility to documented forms of knowledge. In general, the influence and appeal of dominant Hindu mother-goddesses may not necessarily extend to marginalized sections of the population. Citing the critique of the majoritarian influence of Hindu mother-goddesses by scholars such as Kancha Ilaiah and Flavia Agnes, Rajeswari Sunder Rajan raises similar concerns about the problematic nature of 'goddess-inspired Hindu feminism', and adds that such a question 'is subject to a different orientation in light of this disavowal'. (Sunder Rajan, 1998, WS 37) Evidently then, the deification of the Hindu mother-goddess and its conflicted relationship to women's empowerment within patriarchy is thus problematic both from a majoritarian and from a minority perspective. While for the former, certain aspects of mother-goddess iconography may lead to women's exclusion from patriarchal power relationships, for the latter, cultural and ideological exclusion may be a fait accompli given their location at the margins of majoritarian social structures.

While it is beyond the scope of this chapter to go into a detailed study of the various representations of the mother-goddess worshipped amongst different regions, classes and castes, it may suffice to say that each one of them presents a complex and fascinating array of aspects.[5] One may note, moreover, that the dominant Hindu mother-goddess iconographies have been assimilated over time by patriarchy, and their influence has continued to be reflected in Hindu culture in varying degrees and forms through the ages, thus providing a chain of clues linking the ancient to contemporary representations of the maternal metaphor in urban India.

Dominant Strands: Incarnations of Lakshmi and Devi

Dominant strands of the mother-goddess include the various consorts of Vishnu and Shiva, in their various manifestations, such as Devi/Sati, Sita and Radha, among the more popular ones. Playing a prime role in the domain of mother-goddess veneration, the Devi/Sati/Parvati compendium of goddesses who appear in the Shiva cycle, symbolize erotic desire as well as meditative abilities, extreme kindness and deep fury. In their north-eastern forms as Durga or Kali in Bengal, the dangerous, violent and life-threatening aspects of the destructive goddess are foregrounded.

Sita, who figures in the *Ramayana*, embodies purity, fidelity, the familial life, subservience and self-sacrifice. Her trial by fire, which proves her chastity and her faithfulness to her husband, Rama, even after years of captivity in the hands of Ravana, is seen as evidence of her purity. As a later mother-goddess of post-Vedic, Brahminical culture, she comes to exemplify the model wife and mother, willing to give up everything, including her life, in order to live up to an ideal that she is destined to represent. Her origins in mother-earth ('Sita', meaning 'furrow', is born of the earth), and her final descent into her mother's womb upon being forced to undergo a second test of chastity, however, are played down in the more popular versions of the narrative.

On the other hand, Radha, who figures primarily in the *Mahabharata*, presents the perfect foil to Sita since unlike the latter she forsakes marital relations and familial life in her complete devotion to Krishna and epitomizes the ideal devotee of a *bhakti* cult, which positions love for god above all earthly desires or duties. The legitimacy of her blind and adulterous love for Krishna is beyond social interrogation, as is her erotic display of desire for her divine spouse, since it is to be primarily interpreted as a physical reflection of a supreme love of god. It is interesting to note, however, that the ultimate pleasure available to Radha (comparable to contemporary formulations of *jouissance*), in her erotic and sublime union with her lord, is cast within the narrative of the non-mother/erotic beloved. The figure of Radha serves to bring the cult of *Bhakti* and its future followers, such as the 14th century Mira, into an ambit of social acceptability (Mira, in her utter devotion to Lord Krishna, re-imagines herself as Radha, rejects marital relations and domestic constraints to take up a nomadic existence as a *vairaagini*).

Notably, however, the plot of the Krishna narrative also sets up an alter-ego to the sexually available non-maternal beloved, Radha, in the shape of the idealized foster-mother, Yashoda. Yashoda's tales of unbounded love for her infant son, whom she nurses and nurtures at her breast, form part of the common cultural fabric of the '*mamata*' (unbounded maternal love) upheld for and associated with mothers in a country defined by a predominant Hindu culture. Thus, while eroticism is located in the body of the nubile beloved, non-erotic maternal love finds a separate and distinct space in the maternal body, robbing it of both desire and desirability. Together, they comprise the complex figure of the desexualized maternal and the sexually available mother object, an aspect to which we will return in the next chapter. Although both the beloved and the mother aspire to a 'pure' realm where love is defined ultimately only in its spiritual, ecstatic dimensions, it is clear that the pathways to the divine realm have written out very different scripts to be enacted by these contrasting figures, as evidenced in the clear allocation of roles assigned to women in contemporary times.

From the Ancient Divine to the Modern Prosaic

One particular modern formulation of the compendium of ideals represented by ancient mother-goddesses may be witnessed in the crystallization of the idea of the nation-as-mother during colonial times, an idea which became especially relevant during the nationalist struggle for independence.[6] The coalescing of the contours of the modern Indian nation with the body of the mother allowed the independence movement to garner the support and the energy of its young and able sons, specifically by rallying them in a call for arms against the defiling threat posed by the pillaging colonizer to the pure land of the nation-as-mother. While the metaphorical use of the maternal body in the discourse of battle undoubtedly aided the success of the independence movement, it also ensured the congealing of certain patriarchal values within the maternal metaphor. Popular art, as for instance images used in calendar art, comic book covers, and even stamps, dating from the pre-colonial era to post-independence, reflected the patriarchal coalescence of the nation's contours with the mother's body, literally mapping out one on top of the other and erasing the emotive distinctions between mother, goddess and country. In so doing, the nation is elevated to a realm of spirituality, to be protected and worshipped like a goddess by her soldier sons, while women must see themselves as bound by tradition, aiming towards an ideal future as mothers of the nation's progeny (see Image 1.3).

Just as woman's body becomes one with the nation-mother, the nation's patriotic sons are called upon to defend her honour and offer themselves up in an ultimate sacrifice. It was thus not uncommon to find images of the most well-known freedom fighters, such as Mahatma Gandhi, Subhash Chandra Bose and Bhagat Singh, literally offering up their bodies and their lives for the mother, who swathes her sons in her arms in a glorious moment of ultimate surrender (see Images 1.4 and 1.5).

To counter the perception of a subservient mother-nation, many popular images identified India as the lion-seated, assertive and energetic goddess-mother, as found for instance on the covers of the popular children's comic book series *Amar Chitra Katha*. With the help of images of the goddess Durga or Kali, here the mother is transformed from someone seeking protection to one who inspires terror and will resort to any degree of violence to achieve victory against the colonizers (see Image 1.6).

In this regard, it is significant to note the appearance of altered forms of the mother-goddess in different parts of the country. Sumathi Ramaswamy, for instance, offers a revealing discussion of the Tamil

Disembodied Mothers 11

Image 1.3
Hind Devi (Mother India, Packaging label for the Ahmedabad New Textile Mills, Ahmedabad, circa early to mid 20th century)

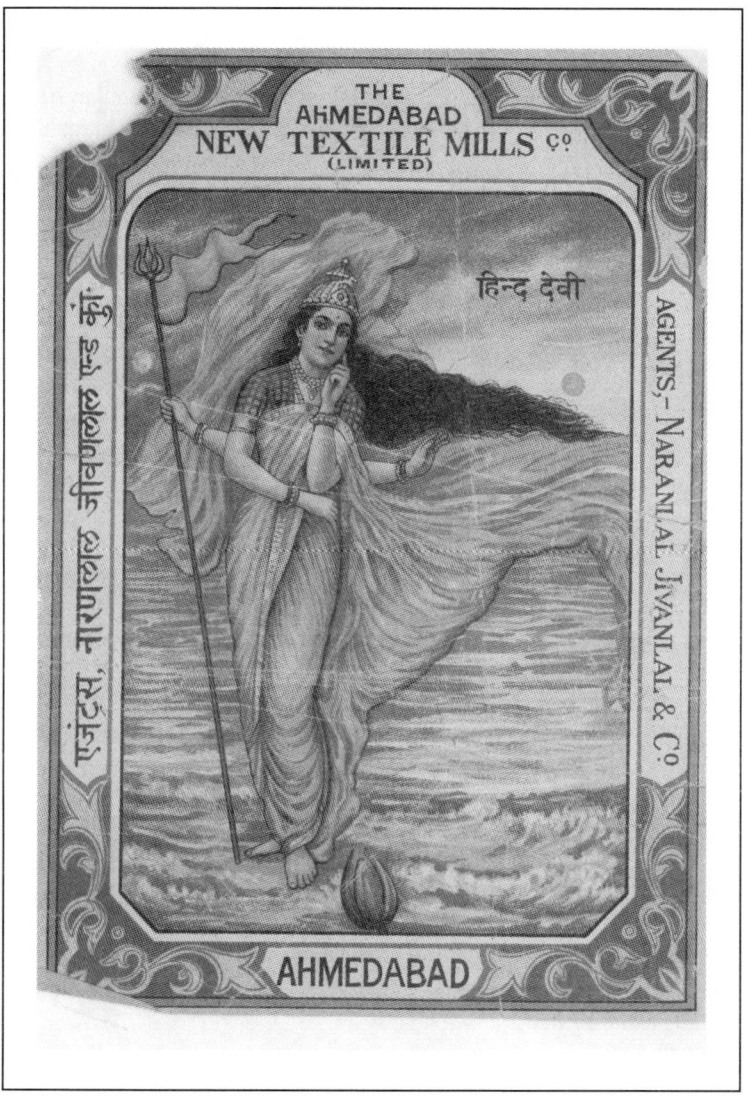

Source: Collection Abhishek Poddar, Bangalore.

Image courtesy: CIViC: Centre for Indian Visual Culture, New Delhi.

Image 1.4
Yama/Bharat Uddhaar

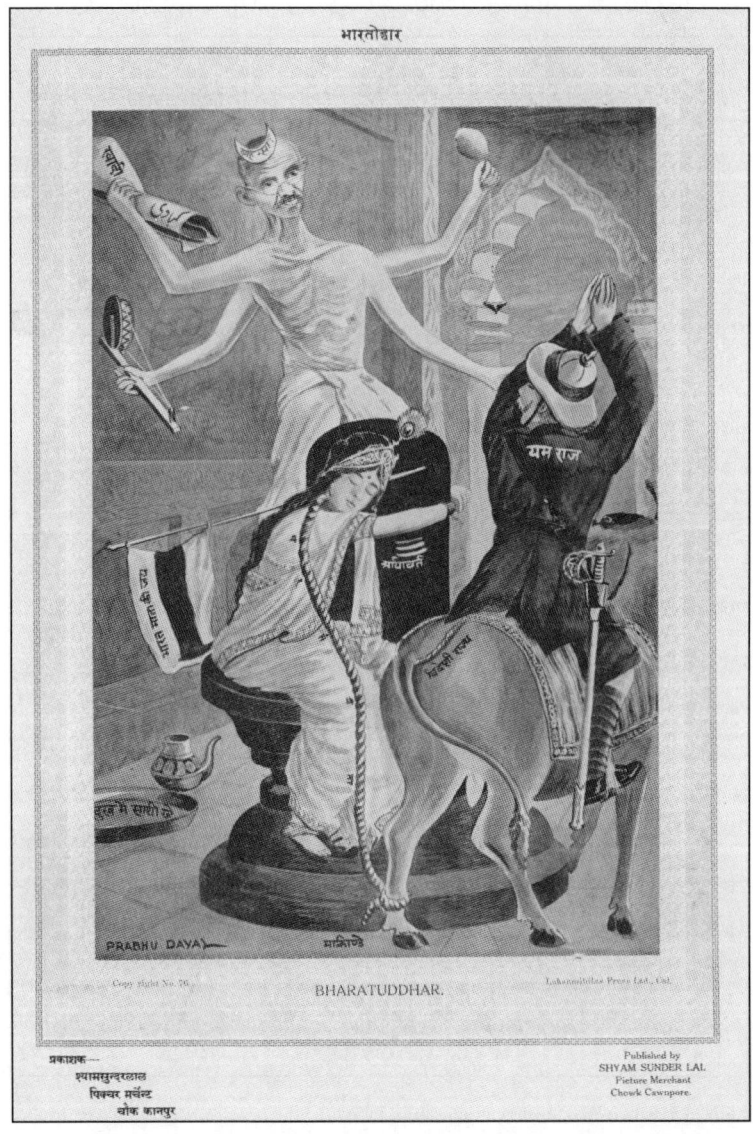

Source: Priya Paul Personal Collection, http://30nuv4405g4fn8jt1dtkzfdc.wpengine.netdna-cdn.com/wp-content/uploads/2014/04/6.314-Brit-Yama-Priya-Paul1.jpg

Disembodied Mothers 13

Image 1.5
Shaheed Bhagat Singh

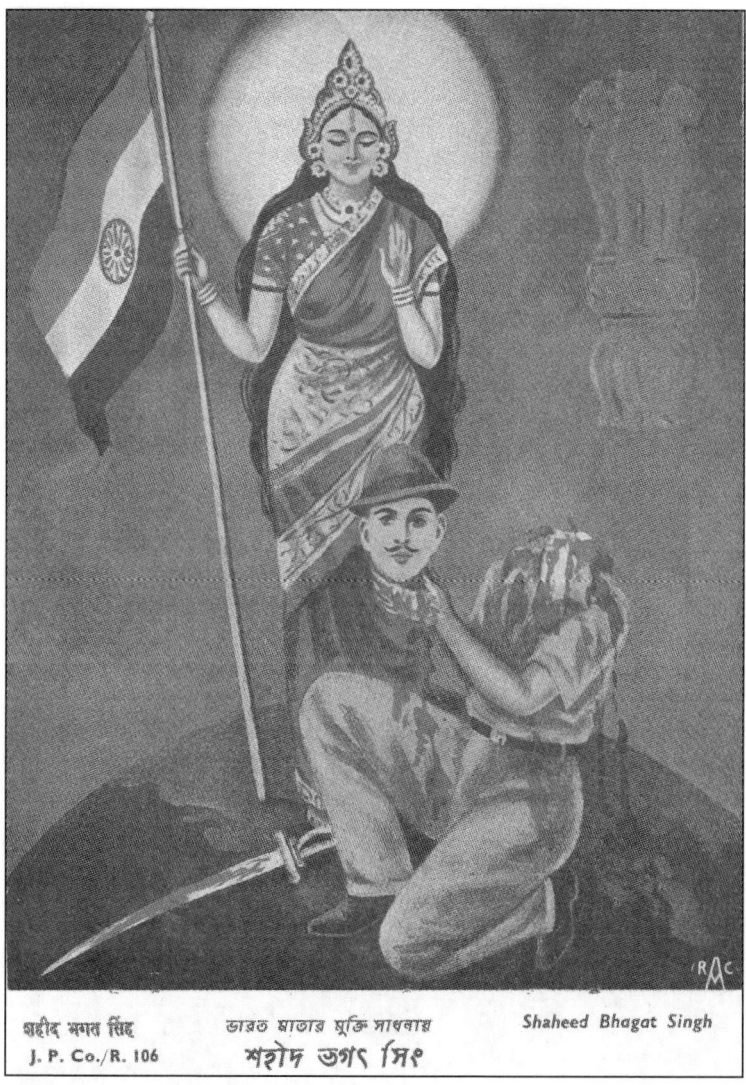

Source: Christopher Pinney Collection, https://reflectionsofindia.files.wordpress.com/2014/08/bhagat-singh.jpg

Image 1.6
Mother India

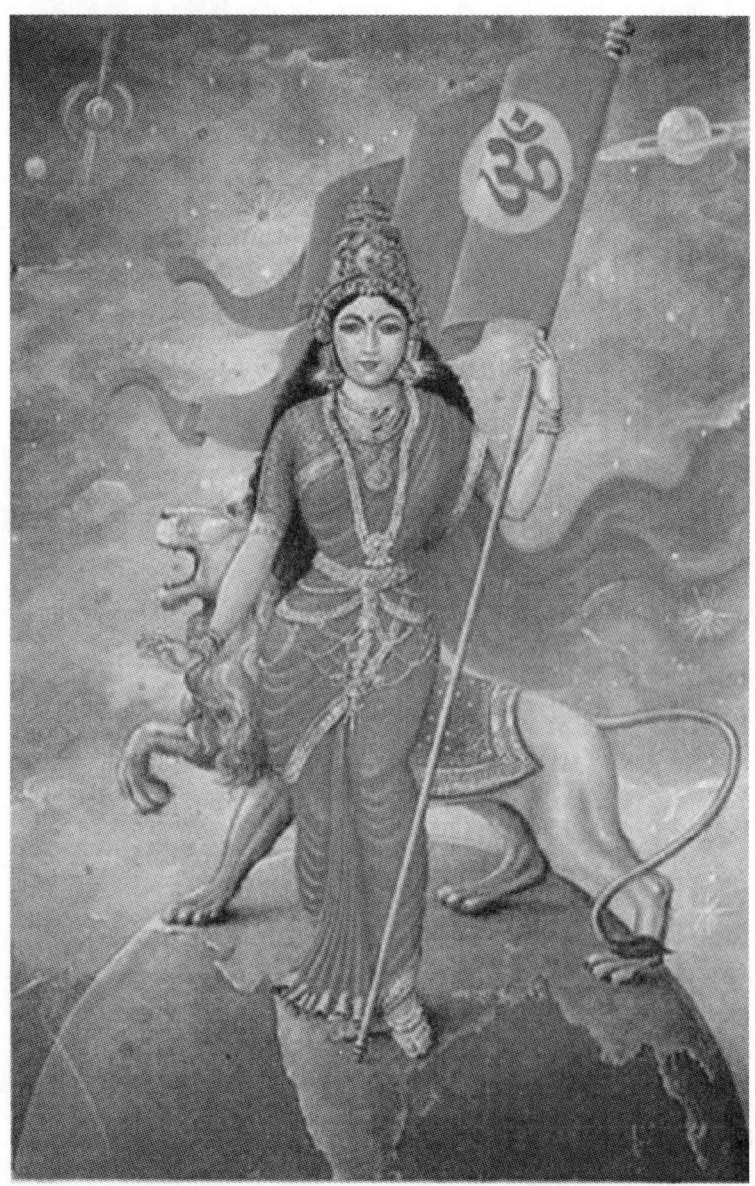

Source: Christiane Brossius Private Collection.

'virgin mother' Tamilttaay, imagined as the mother of the nation. (Ramaswamy 2001, 26) Embodying both virginity and motherhood, Tamilttaay appears on the South Indian national imaginary as the fount of Tamilian culture and language. Reminiscent of the ancient goddess Saraswati, the absence of active sexual desire on the part of goddess Tamilttaay may offer rich comparisons to 'virgin' mothers in other religions, an aspect to which we will return in the subsequent section of this chapter.

Thus, kind and ferocious, self-effacing and assertive, chaste, asexual or violent, Hindu mother-goddesses offer a variety of roles to be emulated by Indian women, promising a sense of unlimited freedom of choice in their very diversity. However, reigning ideologies deriving from caste and class hierarchies, in turn determined by patriarchal mindsets, run contrary to this deceptively democratic and pluralistic impulse, and bolster certain models of conduct over others. Consequently, the amalgamated form of the obedient, self-abnegating Sati-Savitri-Sita model exemplifies one of the most popular and enduring archetypes for urban and rural women.

Thus, the maternal metaphor, with its origins in chthonic fecundity and limitless power, is gradually harnessed through a dual process—on the one hand we see a *proliferation* of lesser goddesses with specific attributes, and on the other, a systematic *prioritization* of these attributes in socio-cultural terms with increasingly clear indications to women about their degree of social acceptability. Exceptions in the form of older, independent goddesses such as Saraswati, or in the form of the *'vairaagini'* or *'bhakt'* as embodied by saintly figures such as Mira, while available, are located at the margins of the mainstream social order and therefore augur ventures beyond the safety of the domestic, familial world.

Feminist Perspectives on the Mother-Goddess

As may be evident from the above discussion, feminist interrogations based on our knowledge about ancient mother-goddesses can lead to significant insights about the conceptualization of motherhood in India. In this section, I focus on three salient observations, which may arise from a feminist reading of the role of ancient mother-goddesses. They are briefly listed below:

- In dominant Hindu iconography, apart from a handful of goddesses such as Vac/Saraswati and Kali, the majority of ancient mother-goddesses fail to appear as singular, independent, empowered entities and remain attached to male gods in the form of their consorts, mothers or daughters.
- Rather than *being*, mother-goddesses are more concerned with *doing*, and with *representing*.
- As a corollary to the above, the inherent loftiness of the mother-goddesses determines the absolute lowliness to which real women are destined, thus ensuring their ongoing denigration.

The above propositions can lead us to explore some interesting ramifications in terms of the cultural influence of goddesses on the construction of maternal identities in India, which I examine below.

Dependence, Independence and Discursive Escapes

The evolution of independent chthonic fertility mothers and their gradual dependence on ascendant male gods in an increasingly patriarchal culture has been variously noted. Even Kali (an alternate form of Devi or Parvati, the goddesses associated with the ithyphallic Shiva), who, in her form as Durga, fights ferociously and kills Mahisha, her arch-rival, is often linked in a spousal relation with her enemy. As remarked by Kamala Ganesh, 'though Kali is often an independent goddess, she is equally often portrayed with a spouse.... Durga is perhaps the only important goddess who is portrayed alone. Though created from the combined energies of the gods, she wields weapons and battles alone with no male support, and slays the buffalo-demon Mahisha. However, even here, there is a strong underlying suggestion of a sexual/marital relationship between Durga and Mahisha,...' (Krishnaraj 2010, 80–81) On the other hand, independent, sovereign goddesses such as Saraswati reign over an asexual, sublimated world of scriptures, knowledge, art and music, which recognizes desire only beyond the physical. The maternal idea, through them, is rarefied to a spiritual level so that rather than childbirth, they hold sway over the world of aesthetic and intellectual creation.

Noted scholar Wendy Doniger, in her book *Hindu Myths* introduces a chapter on 'Devi' by commenting on the changing status of the mother-goddess in ancient times. According to her, the assimilation of the goddess 'into the Hindu pantheon took place... in two distinct phases: first, the Indo-Aryan male gods were given wives, and then, under the influence of Tantric and Saktic movements which had been gaining momentum outside orthodox Hinduism for many centuries, these shadowy female figures emerged as supreme powers in their own right, and merged into the great Goddess.' (Doniger 1975, 238)

Liddle and Joshi note a similar denouement in the position of women from ancient, pre-Vedic culture to Vedic culture, and attribute the trend quite categorically to the culture introduced into the subcontinent by the Aryan migrations. Providing a summary of this historical process, they view the Aryanization of India in terms of a cultural deterioration, especially from the perspective of how it impacted women's status: 'When the Aryans migrated to India around 1500 B.C., they brought with them the patrilineal form of family organization.... The Aryans are believed to have destroyed the superior civilization which they encountered in the Indus Valley, in the northwest of the subcontinent, and gradually to have established dominance over the Dravidians who were the indigenous inhabitants of the main peninsula.' (Liddle and Joshi 1986, 52) Similarly, Kamala Ganesh, tracing the origins of the mother-goddess to a history of over 5,000 years, observes that 'the very goddess who is the domesticated spouse is demonstrably independent in earlier forms.' (Krishnaraj 2010, 82) She further remarks on the curtailment of the sexual powers of the goddess over the ages, which leads to a division between the erotic and the abstract—'in the older stream of the mother goddess, the sexual and reproductive aspects are so starkly explicit as to go beyond eroticism. By completely depersonalizing the context, the icon moves from details into abstraction, and transforms the specific into the universal.' (86)

On the other hand, Sukumari Bhattacharjee explains the shift in the role of the goddess in terms of the economic shift from a nomadic to an agrarian economy brought about by the migrant Aryans: 'When the Aryans arrived in India, circa twelfth century B.C., they themselves were a pastoral nomadic people who watched procreation among their herds and were acquainted with the rudimentary knowledge of biological reproduction.... By the seventh century BC, the Aryans had become an agricultural people and theirs was an agriculturalist's way of looking at life. This led to a positively male chauvinistic view of parenthood: the woman was the field, and the man sowed the seed in her.' (Bhattacharjee 2010 56–57)

Regardless of the explanations offered for the phenomenon, it is evident that the gradual waning of the stature of the mother-goddess is most intriguing from a historical and cultural perspective, and has led to a detailed scrutiny of the dependent relationships of female deities on their male counterparts in feminist scholarship (Bhattacharjee, Ganesh, Ramaswamy and others). Rather than dwelling further on this aspect, I would like to look more closely at its corollary and *converse* aspect—the endurance and nature of those goddesses who, despite the shifts obtained by a dominant, male culture, manage to survive as powerful, independent deities through the ages.

What can the persistence of such ideals of mothering imply in terms of our contemporary understandings of urban mothering? One way of pursuing such a path through Hindu mythology is to explore a myth which predates the dominant Vedic world view. As mentioned earlier, prior to her sanctification as Saraswati, the unnamed goddess who figures in an incest myth is an earlier form of the speech goddess, Vac. (It may be worth noting here that across world-mythologies, 'incest myths' have been interpreted in symbolic terms since they often represent the intermingling of natural forces—such as sky and earth—in the interest of creation, and given their focus on causality, classified as 'creation' or 'aetiological' myths.) In the ancient creation myth of Brahma and Saraswati-Vac, Vac defies both conventional ideational aspects of motherhood, normally understood in terms of procreation and fecundity, and also stands apart from male gods, unattached and solitary in her universe of knowledge and wisdom.

Motherhood and the Creation Myth

The earliest creation myth described in the *Rig Veda* is one of primeval incest, where an unnamed heavenly father sheds his seed upon his earthly daughter, leading to the birth of sacred speech:

> When the father shed his seed in his own daughter, he spilt his seed on the earth as he united with her. The benevolent gods created sacred speech and fashioned Rudra Vastospati, the protector of sacred rites.... Heaven is my father, the engenderer, the navel here. My mother is this wide earth, my close kin. Between these two outstretched bowls is the womb; in it the father placed his daughter's embryo.' (Doniger 1975, 26)

An examination of ancient Hindu myths reveals the existence of similar creation-incest myths in the *Upanishads*, the *Brahmanas* and the *Mahabharata*. In these later myths, the unnamed father is named as Prajapati or Brahma, and the daughter identified as Saraswati or Vac. (Doniger 1975, 25–36; Bose 2010, 17)

Etymologically, Vac (Sanskrit 'vac' or 'vakti'—'word' or 'speech') is linked with Latin 'vocem'/'vox' and to modern Romance languages through 'voice', 'voix' and 'voce'.[7] As the embodiment of originary sound, Vac Devi is the opposite of silence (death) and the source of all life. Not surprisingly, in Naman Ahuja's 'Body in Indian Art' exhibition (2014) and the related publication by the National Museum, Delhi, the iconography of Vac forms a part of a section on 'Light, Sound, Desire Creation'. In the description accompanying the image (see Image 1.7), Ahuja states, 'Vac, the cosmogenic vedic goddess creates speech, or sound. She brings the gift of language and poetry, comprehension and thus cognition.' Further, he adds, 'Speech/sound is primordial, and among Saraswati's many appellations is Vak or Vagdevi, a name that goes back to the Rigveda where she is seen as the very embodiment of the principle of energy. Vak is the deity of erudition and primordial sound, who contains all other gods, and from whose yoni, at the base of the deep seas, springs the ocean of consciousness and intelligence. Sound (nada), and its relationship to vibration, mantra and "the word" is also regarded as the fundamental element of consciousness, or related to the idea of coming into being in several myths and philosophies, including Indian and Semitic.' (Ahuja 2014, 58)

In this early 19th-century image of Vac Devi, from Rajasthan (currently part of the National Museum collections), the body of the goddess contains within it all other gods who appear to spring from her womb, while her tongue is prominently displayed as the primordial organ of sound.

Vac's identification with speech or utterance in early myths is reminiscent of logocentric creation stories in western cultures where the idea of creation coalesces with the utterance of the spoken word. Vac is later identified with the river goddess Saraswati whose principle attributes are speech, knowledge, learning and the arts. As Vac/Saraswati, the goddess of the original word or 'Om', she is fathered by the Creator himself, and features in creation myths as the originary sound as well as the origin of the Vedas. Interestingly, while being part of an incestuous familial relationship, Saraswati is located outside domestic relations. Mandakranta Bose points out that 'in early literature, she is thought to be the daughter of Brahma and in an incestuous relationship with him.... In later Hindu thought, Saraswati loses her early association with a river and is equated with Vac or speech.' (Bose 2010, 27) 'Unlike most goddesses, she is associated with wisdom rather than fertility, and is seen as an independent and *sattvika* (pure) goddess. In current belief domesticity is not associated with Saraswati.' (Bose 2010, 28)

20 Embodying Motherhood

Image 1.7
Vac Devi (Gouache on Paper; Early 19th century, Rajasthan; 22.5 × 13.5 cm)

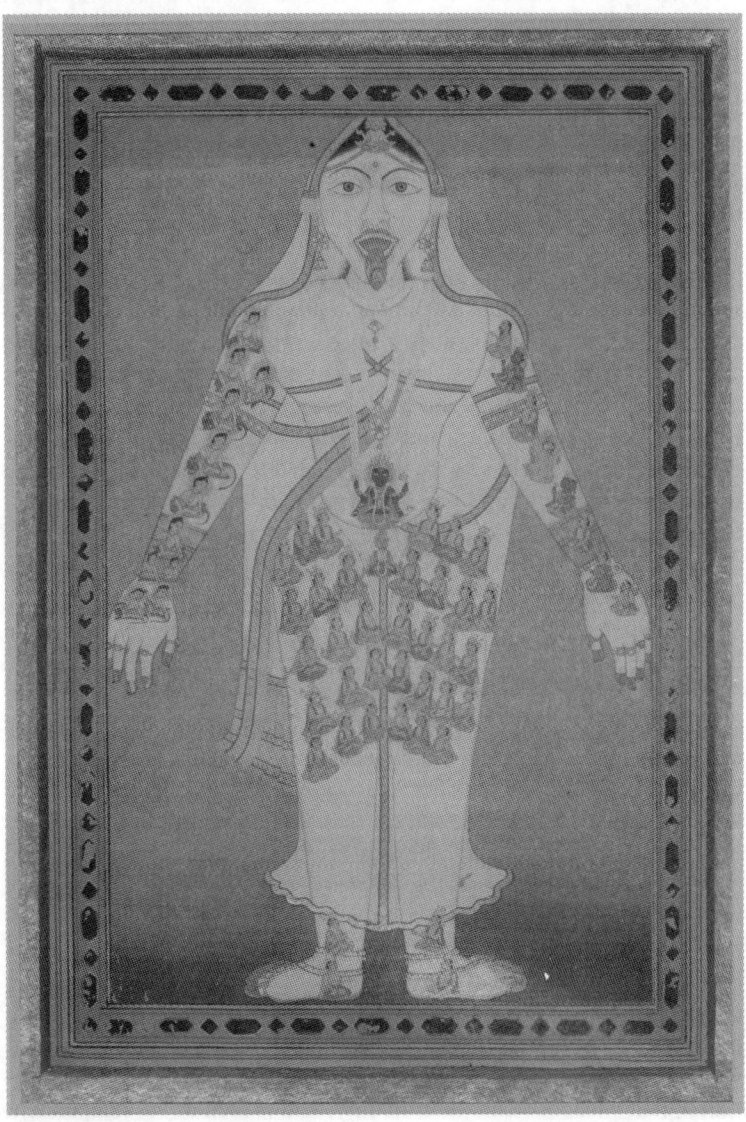

Source: National Museum; Ajit Mookerjee Collection, New Delhi.
Acc. no: 82.489

In her embodiment of speech and sound, Vac appears as the mother of the three Vedas—the origin of all language, speech and knowledge, although her incestuous dependence on Brahma circumscribes her independence under patrilineal ownership. In the Rig Veda creation story, after the completion of the sexual act, Brahma is reprimanded for desiring his daughter, already revealing both the social unacceptability of incestuous desire as well as a societal forbearance towards the act, in the interest of the larger good of the creation of the universe. Indeed, if Saraswati is the mother beyond mothering, it is possible to read the chiding of Brahma by the other gods as a warning that discourse (which is here inherently feminine) cannot be brought under absolute (male) control and is likely to escape patriarchal domination. A feminist reading of the story may thus lead us to view Vac as signifying that quality of discourse which always escapes, a mother's tongue which slips beyond into the illusory realm of maya/fiction. Indeed, in the Rig Veda, speech is said to have four components, of which three remain concealed except to the most exceptional of sages: '*Vac* has been divided into four parts. Those Brahmins with insight know them. Three parts that are hidden in the cave, the mortals do not activate. They speak only the fourth part.' (Asyavamiya hymn, verse 45, Rig Veda, as cited in *Encyclopedia of Indian Philosophies*, 101–102). Of the three concealed parts of speech, it is said that these lie in the silence of the heart, suggesting a transcendental aspect of sound and speech, although grammarians have also indicated syntactical explanations of the segmentation.[8] Concealing more than she reveals, the owner of words and sentences ('akshara' and 'vakya'), the goddess mothers herself, and the universe, into being through her utterances, and is here easily comparable to the western idea of 'logos', albeit via a feminized personification.

While emphasizing the association of the maternal with discourse, it is worthwhile noting, however, that languages are equally susceptible to gendered hierarchization within patriarchal cultures (a theme to which we will return in the final chapter). As pointed out by Susan Wadley, the early differentiation between the Prakriti/Purusha (nature/culture; matter/spirit) dichotomy in Hindu culture gets mirrored in the uneven positions occupied by Prakrit/Sanskrit where the 'masculinized' Sanskrit language is accorded cultural superiority in relation to its 'feminine' counterpart, Prakrit (see Wadley 1986, 116–17). The ongoing association of the female body as fount of 'high' languages is consequently sustained within patriarchy on the basis of an abstracted, inviolable maternal body, devoid of its profane aspects. Any reclaiming of discursive space by a re-constructed, re-sexualized maternal might thus also signal the revalorization of neglected 'mother tongues'.

As mentioned earlier, an interesting comparison from the southern part of India, to such an association of the feminine with language is presented in the form of the late 19th-century Tamil 'virgin mother', Tamilttaay. Sumathi Ramaswamy notes that 'Tamilttaay's bodily intactness underscored the inviolability of the language she embodied, its purity and autonomy, as well as its self-sufficiency, even its divine wholeness.' (Ramaswamy 2001, 26) Further, in the case of Tamilttaay, 'virginity becomes the site where this complex contradiction between absence of sexuality and fruitful motherhood is negotiated.' (27) Finding her place in the gamut of mother goddesses who conjoin inviolable virginity with a higher creative impulse, such as Diana, the Virgin Mary and Saraswati, the Tamil goddess becomes the repository of patriarchal language and culture, and thus beyond the reach of any particular male. Discourse is thus embodied in the feminine principle; abstracted, it remains beyond the profane world of sexuality. The mother goddess of language and learning is thus a sort of meta-goddess, embodying creation but not participating in its 'profane' corollary, procreation.

Based on this cleavage between the realms of creation and procreation, Saraswati, despite being called the 'best of mothers' is not a mother. (Bose 2010, 17) A virgin goddess, she mothers wisdom, knowledge, art and music as her progeny. Her fecundity is abstracted beyond physical fertility so that she alludes to a different perspective on the maternal as creativity, as aesthetic impulse. 'She began as a river with the power of cleansing impurity and of bringing fertility. She is associated with speech, poetry, music, culture and learning.' (26). The four objects held by her in her four hands—the book, the *vina*, the rosary and the water pot, along with the white lotus on which she is seated and the swan that she rides, make her into a metaphysical mother, one who will germinate speech and irrigate wisdom, art and philosophy. In recognition of the fact that such endeavours need to be free of domestic bounds, Saraswati remains independent and outside of domestic concerns and relationships. Thus, Saraswati is suggestive of a submerged definition of mothering as creative impulse rather than mothering as reproduction. In this respect, she is the epitome of the abstracted and universalized mother-goddess who, in Kamala Ganesh's words, is the 'Mother who is not a mother'. (Krishnaraj 2010, 97) Although Ganesh, re-visiting her original paper several years later, finds that she can no longer 'separate

Disembodied Mothers 23

physical birthing from its abstraction in the way the mother has been conceptualized' (Krishnaraj 2010, 97) and that the 'metaphor is rooted in the materiality of birth and yet transcends it' (97–98), the emphasis on mothering as sublimated creative impulse rather than as procreation suggests alternate possibilities in re-defining the circumference bounded by motherhood and mothering.

In contrast to many of the later Puranic goddesses who are domesticated, Saraswati remains independent, as pointed out by Bose: 'Unlike many other goddesses, Saraswati never acts as an intermediary, for she is an independent goddess who constantly breaks out of occasional linkages with other divine beings, in which she is cast in roles controlled by male figures.' (Bose 2010, 27) Thus, for women who seek an alternate lifestyle outside the realm of the domestic, Bose sees in Saraswati 'a viable model within the order of conventional society.' (44) She further remarks that such alternative models point to 'a particularly sophisticated aspect of Hindu thought on femininity, for it acknowledges that there is a part of female nature that resists conventional social roles without subverting them. This acknowledgement centers on Saraswati, the one goddess who refuses to be bound to the service of male figures.' (44)

Kali, another goddess, especially popular in West Bengal, is like Saraswati, fiercely independent, and unconventional in both appearance and action. Kali also initially appears as a solitary, independent and unattached figure. However, unlike the benevolent Saraswati, Kali is known more for her dark, terrifying aspects, associated with blood and death, and often visualized as a black, lion-seated goddess, a trident in her hand, her bloody tongue swaying in lust of violence. 'In the beginning, Kali, this dark goddess of menacing aspect, appears as an unattached figure and is a perplexing being in her terrifying potential for annihilating creation.' (Bose 2010, 26) In her absolute destructive powers, she is thus, in many ways, the antithesis of Saraswati, and epitomizes the male fear of the mother at the other extreme of the spectrum—the mother who annihilates and must therefore be continuously propitiated.

In a persistent trend of the marginalization of matriarchal aspects of pre-historic fertility goddesses, such as Lajja Gauri, who were later relegated to the status of 'outcaste' goddesses, solitary mother-goddesses like Saraswati/Vac and Kali/Durga, embody a feminine that escapes the familial, the domestic and the conventional. In alluding to a joy of creation-destruction beyond the physical, maternal body, they intimate the possibility of pleasures elsewhere—in the realm of writing, music, art and even violence. Bose notes that the 'outsider' status of Kali implies that 'she is a constant threat to social order and so, in her early myth, she is located outside human habitation, residing in cremation sites in the company of spirits.' (Bose 2010, 33) Worshipped as the Mother above all mothers, Kali knits together within her strikingly un-maternal body aspects of the punitive, non-nurturing, death-defying mother.

The Goddess as Attribute

> However the great goddess is made to occupy the place of power, it is always as fiction, not as 'truth'. It is not a question of the multiplicity of manifestation; gods and goddesses share it, it is a *dvaita* world. It is not even a question of doing—both do. But she does through fiction and they... through method.
>
> ...
>
> The name of that fiction or *Ma-ya-* is the apparent magic of fertility— animate and inanimate.... And indeed, women cannot feel fertility as the uncanny in quite the same way. For reverence for fiction (*Ma-ya-*) as female to be unleashed, the *dvaita* trick must happen, and the female subject exit sociality. (Spivak 2001, 133–35)

Evidently, the prevailing and widely influential Hindu mother-goddesses embody ethereal ideals and sacrificial qualities virtually impossible to achieve at the human level, such as *sati* or complete acquiescence of one's life. As a result, they are securely placed at an emotional distance from the lives of real women, for whom they become ideals to be emulated, but ideals that are ultimately unattainable (except perhaps in rare life-abnegating attempts such as self-immolation). Dominant mother-goddesses thus inspire striving and activity aimed at greater social acceptability, ideating for women functions of *doing* rather than those of *being*.

Similar observations have been offered by feminist scholars about the relative significance of doing and being in the context of feminist theology. Following Mary Daly's injunction (1985) that 'goddessing' is an 'active and dynamic concept', which is 'better expressed as a verb than a noun' (Krishnaraj 2010, 92), Kamala Ganesh borrows from Daly to explain the verb to mean 'goddess culture, goddess way of life, goddess practice, and individual experiences and interpretations of the goddess' (Ganesh quoted in Krishnaraj 2010, 92). While Daly's idealization of 'goddessing' as an empowering verb for women is cast wholly within a positive, if non-critical, framework, it is not clear if such an unequivocal affirmative stance can be applied to the majority of mother-goddess deities of ancient India. Rather than acting for themselves, they often appear to act on behalf of the male gods to whom they are wedded or attached, personifying their 'Shakti' or energy. Thus, mother-goddesses merge into the abstract idea of a divine Shakti who is the feminine principle per se, just as Purusha embodies the inert masculine which awakens to act only once partnered with his female Shakti.

The efforts by certain western feminist theologians[9] to locate in Hindu goddesses a 'resource' for contemporary feminist discourse are in line with Mary Daly's attempts to identify the goddess metaphor as a source of strength and agency for women. However, given the ambiguous status of Hindu goddesses, such efforts justifiably create wariness on the part of Indian feminist scholars. For instance, in a critical commentary on such attempts, Rajeshwari Sunder Rajan observes that 'the temptation to idealize non-western societies as a "resource" to meet the inadequacies of western philosophies and lifestyles, is also visible in some of the interpretations: the goddess clearly meets one such lack, especially among feminist theologians.' (Sunder Rajan 1998, WS 35)

As the power of the male god to act and escape permanent inertness and inaction, the goddess may be morphologically visualized as the verb part of a mythological, patriarchal syntax—the god's aspect of doing, rather than being. Alternately, as attributes of male gods, personifying qualities ascribed to the latter, they can also function in the same morphology as abstractions: 'Abstract nouns, grammatically feminine, had occasionally been personified and "wedded" to the great gods; thus Sri (Prosperity) "belonged" to Visnu, and Siva had his Sakti or Power, but these personifications merely expressed the qualities of the god to whom they were attached.' (Doniger 1975, 238) Thus, figuratively, and outside of the few exceptions discussed above, the goddess is more a noun-attribute than a noun-subject in her own right, in an ironic regression from her status as Vac Devi, owner of words and names, and creator of life.

Signifying an attribute (quality of something) she sets herself up as a series of adjectives to be emulated by millions of Indian women aspiring to be good mothers—chaste, devoted, loving, charitable, nourishing, tolerant, malleable, self-denying, self-sacrificing, finding solace in familial and maternal roles. Signifying an act (doing something for someone), and functioning in the patriarchal morphology as verb, she creates, destroys, rewards, punishes, nurtures and castrates, thus embodying the dichotomies of the birthing/castrating mother. In both of these embodiments, the terrifying aspects can easily be arranged to reside safely in her idols, while qualities which magnify patriarchal entitlement are repeatedly endorsed as values to be emulated by real women. It is not surprising, therefore, that the most glorified images in dominant Hindu culture are those of the self-abnegating, husband-worshipping Sita or Lakshmi.

At the level of tautology, the naming of the mother-goddess can be endlessly multiplied since in Hindu myth, all mother-goddesses merge into one another, and ultimately into the concept of Devi or Shakti (for instance, Saraswati/Vac; Kali/Durga/Parvati/Devi; Lakshmi/Sita/Radha and so on). The plurality of names by which she is known ensures that the mother goddess proliferates beyond any one unitary, set definition, abstracted into infinite qualities—benevolent, divine, terrible, violent, splendid, benign, kind, rewarding, self-sacrificing, loving, and erotic. That she is never at any one (nominal) place contrarily also implies that she is denied a stable subject position in patriarchal grammar, and refused a concrete subjectivity. When women as mothers are raised to the power of infinite x, their x factor is diluted to the point of dissolution.

Maternal Incongruence: Abstract deities and real women

Quite obviously, then, there is a stark incongruence between the worship of the female deity as mother, and the scant respect suffered by real women. The idealization of abstract powers of mothering appear in stark contrast against the concrete, material disempowerment of real women; and even more ironically, the fear evinced towards the mother-goddess is in absolute contradiction to the social fears that beset real women.

As observed pointedly by Kamala Ganesh, 'both in the erotic and universal forms, the mother goddess iconography is at variance with the ideology of motherhood as applied to real life mothers.' (Ganesh in Krishnaraj 2010, 86) Contending that 'the mother goddess does not correlate with high secular status for women in India', Ganesh claims that 'it is possible to argue for an inverse relationship.' (88) In a very similar vein, Sukumari Bhattacharjee describes the glorification of the mother-goddess in terms of 'an emotional and ideational compensation for the reality which in most cases was imposed upon her' and adds that 'in India, it was extolled in an inverse ratio to the demotion of woman's position in society.' (Bhattacharjee 2010, 58)

For women living in contemporary urban India, it would be almost impossible to miss the inverted relationship between the stature of the mother-goddess and their own lives. Cases of violence against women, such as the horrendous gang rape of 'Nirbhaya' on 16 December 2012 in New Delhi, which captured the imagination of a horror-struck nation and world, but which was not the only case of its kind, provide ample proof that the violence to which urban women are subjected persists in an absolute contradictory relationship to the deification of mother-goddesses in temples and places of worship. Whether it is in the horrific persecution of girls and women by khap panchayats, violent violations of the female body, the innumerable cases of female foeticide, or the callous remarks of chauvinistic political leaders who fail to see what the fuss is about when confronted by thousands of protesters, rural as well as urban women continue to straddle the contradictions in their daily lives. It is thus not uncommon to see those faced by the protest against the denigration, harassment and violence experienced by women running for cover under the familiar hackneyed defence: 'but in our country, we honour our women as *devis*' (mother-goddesses).

As we have seen, patriarchal conceptions of woman and motherhood necessitate that the creative (castrating) powers of the maternal body be distanced through abstraction and fictionalization. The threat posed by the castrating mother is countered by means of atonement by her male progeny who elevate her idol on pedestals, worship at her feet, and thereby permit their own justification of the denigration of the female body. Such a dichotomization between the perfect, non-available mother and the profane, flawed, earthly woman ensures that the latter must constantly be reminded of her station and her variance from the over-idealized, abstracted mother-goddess, so that she remains forever striving, deficient in comparison.

Remarkable reflections of the contemporary persistence of such contradictions present themselves beyond the landscape of contemporary India, and especially in postmodern discourse on difference and the feminine. In *Spurs*, Jacques Derrida's stylistically playful study of Nietzsche's philosophical commentary on the 'untruth' of woman, Derrida pushes Nietzsche's interruptions of truth to a logical inference by playing with the idea of truth, and woman, as matters of style: 'A woman seduces from a distance. In fact, distance is the very element of her power. Yet one must beware to keep one's own distance from her beguiling song of enchantment. A distance from distance must be maintained.' (Derrida 1978, 49) In the Nietzschean insistence on women's distance, Derrida seems to locate man's need to keep the idea of woman at a distance, veiled, so that the threat of castration may be averted, so that the illusion of male dominance and power remains undisturbed, unruffled. A reification of the feminine as the maternal, and the assigning of the 'name' of 'woman' thus ensures a secure distance from the threat of real women, who are then projected as mere flawed simulacra of the (idealized) feminine, stylized beyond recognition of their subjectivity. In Derrida's re-enactment of the spurs of Nietzsche's philosophy, woman, like writing, denies essence. There is no essence of women for patriarchy since woman has been bifurcated into an idea of the feminine, and a remnant person who merely dissimulates herself to appear as the feminine that she cannot achieve. The mother-goddess as a distant idea of the feminine, we might then conclude, promises to either nurture or kill man. Meanwhile, real (false) women who successively fail to live up to the ideal, can be exposed, violated and eliminated for not being themselves (women).

Re-imagining the Maternal

Given the inherent contradictions in the iconography of the mother-goddess, and its often burdensome influence on the ideology of motherhood, are subservience and subordination the only destiny available to women as mothers? Accommodation to pain and suffering, idealized by mother-goddess deities such as Sati and Sita, appear to circumscribe the choices before the majority of Hindu women. However, as we have seen in the previous section, alternate solitary goddesses, especially those who bear an enigmatic relationship to the metaphor of birthing through language, may indicate other possibilities inspiring us to ask about the possibility of ferreting out another, different subjectivity of the goddess-mother that may be imagined outside the framework of such a depressing scenario. Rather than re-imaging the goddess, such contradictory aspects of the goddess urge us to re-imagine women and mothering with the help of evocative metaphors such as the mother's tongue.

A clue to such an exploration may be located in the suppressed association between the maternal metaphor, and access to language and speech. Rather than an unexamined glorification of the implied powers transferred from mother goddesses to real women, a more nuanced availing of the discursive abilities embodied in autonomous mother-goddesses may serve to open up a re-imagination of the maternal metaphor. Telling signs of the mother's desire for empowerment through access to discourse are available within and beyond the contours of known stories. A re-imagining of the maternal may draw upon our imagined 'no' of Vac to the incestuous desire of her father, and the muted 'yes' of Radha to pleasure, and lead to alternate definitions of mothering through an empowerment of women as mothers. The rich metaphor of Kali's bloody tongue may similarly inspire us to recognize the ferocity of women's ongoing struggle for ownership of words, as well as the desire to relish speech and re-invent the self. Saraswati's sovereignty over the domain of language emphasizes the maternal as intellectual creative impulse rather than as physical procreation.

Vac is the primordial originator of speech, Saraswati reigns over knowledge and discourse from an ethereal place, and Kali's violent utterances are quite aptly located in her bloody 'tongue'. In Kali's figure, the word is literally made flesh since the mother's tongue utters terrible destruction, tastes blood, and consumes flesh in an insatiable appetite for violence. In her form as Durga, whose effigies are immersed annually into the replenishing waters of the river, she offers us the symbolic possibility of cyclical death and rebirth through immersion. Such a symbolism allows us to comprehend mother goddess iconography beyond rigid patriarchal parameters and to interpret 'tradition' as permeable to revitalization, re-interpretations, and renewal. If cultural narratives about the maternal conceal as much as they reveal about the oppression and submerged desires of women (as in the sunken aspects of Vac's speech), retellings of such narratives by women in their own voices may be productive ways of envisaging the maternal in contemporary terms. Like the ancient river-goddesses sunk annually into rivers, they invite us to re-invent emergent maternal narratives in increasingly relevant ways. This would, of course, entail a freeing up of the space occupied by mother goddess iconography within cultural narratives. As helpfully suggested by Jasbir Jain, 'Daughters of mother India... need to reinterpret the body and expand the notion of space to include history and identity. The self-in-the-world has to outgrow inherited constraints of traditional moulds in order to reinvent itself.' (Jain 2006, 1659)

Conclusion

Myth and religion have scripted a definite cultural space in which motherhood stories can be read and inscribed. Although abounding in variety through the representations of multiple, powerful goddesses, they present limited possibilities to women in a material sense since the scripts are written primarily from and within an upper-caste, patriarchal

30 Embodying Motherhood

framework. However, a re-imagining of mothering envisaged in the escape routes, such as the one suggested by discursive deities, such as Saraswati-Vac, may be promising. If it is in and through discourse that imagination functions, then a re-imagination of the maternal metaphor must take into account the significance of discourse in cultural transformations.

If the only mother-goddess to escape patriarchal infringement is a discursive goddess, then it is work on language which is the key needed to open doors to liberating subjectivities; it is in and through a work on speech and language that women can re-cast the feminine, and the maternal. Zeroing in on Gayatri Chakravorty Spivak's declaration that 'there is no Devi here', it is perhaps time to recognize the implication of such an absence, and wrest alternate definitions of the maternal from suppressed and untold fragments of mother-goddess narratives.

Notes

1. A more detailed discussion of the mapping of motherhood across these discourses is provided in Chapter 7, 'Mapping the Mother in France & India'.
2. See http://www.nationalmuseumindia.gov.in/pdfs/English-Announcement.pdf
3. See, for example, Wolkstein and Kramer 1983, 189; Hooke 1963, pp. 20–23 and 39–41; Graves 2001, 71.
4. See the discussion by Mandakranta Bose in her chapter 'Gendered Divinity'.
5. A survey of various facets of each goddess can be found in works by scholars such as Doniger, Bose, Ganesh and others, all of whom have provided detailed examinations of these aspects.
6. This idea has been re-visited and discussed in detail in the chapter on 'Mapping Motherhood'.
7. For an etymology of 'Vac', see for instance, Online Etymology Dictionary, http://etymonline.com/index.php?l=v&p=12&allowed_in_frame=0 which provides the following cognates: late 13c., 'sound made by the human mouth', from Old French *voiz* 'voice, speech; word, saying, rumor, report' (Modern French *voix*), from Latin *vocem* (nominative *vox*) 'voice, sound, utterance, cry, call, speech, sentence, language, word' (source also of Italian *voce*, Spanish *voz*), related to *vocare* 'to call', from PIE root **wekw* 'give vocal utterance, speak' (cognates: Sanskrit *vakti* 'speaks, says', *vacas* 'word'; Avestan *vac* 'speak, say'; Greek *eipon* (aorist) 'spoke, said', *epos* 'word'; Old Prussian *wackis* 'cry'; German *er-wähnen* 'to mention'.

8. For a detailed speculation on the translation and the supposed meanings of the four parts of speech, see http://brahmanisone.blogspot.in/2007/12/translation-of-sayanacharyas-commentary.html as also, http://www.exoticindiaart.com/book/details/aspects-of-speech-in-vedic-ritual-rare-book-IDK927/.
9. See, for instance, Gross 1978, 269–91.

References

Ahuja, Naman P. *Rupa-Pratirupa: The Body in Indian Art*. New Delhi: National Museum, 2014.

Bhattacharjee, Sukumari. 'Motherhood in Ancient India'. In *Motherhood in India*, edited by Maitreyee Krishnaraj. New Delhi: Routledge, 2010, pp. 44–72.

Bose, Mandakranta. 'Gendered Divinity'. In *Women in the Hindu Tradition*. New York: Routledge, 2010, pp. 12–57.

Brown, Robert. 'A Lajja Gauri in a Buddhist Context at Aurangabad', *The Journal of the International Association of Buddhist Studies*. Vol. 13, No. 2, 1990, pp. 1–16.

Derrida, Jacques. *Spurs: Nietzsche's Styles/Eperons: Les Styles de Nietzsche*. (Bilingual edition) Chicago: University. of Chicago Press, 1978.

Devi, Mahasweta. 'The Breastgiver' In *In Other Worlds*, edited by Gayatri Chakravorty Spivak. New York: Methuen, 1987.

Doniger, Wendy. *Hindu Myths*. New York: Penguin, 1975.

Encyclopedia of Indian Philosophies, pp. 101–102, Google Books. Accessed 16 June 2015. http://elibrary.ibc.ac.th/files/private/Encyclopedia%20Of%20Indian%20Philosophy%208%20(Mahayana)%20Buddhism%

Ganesh, Kamala. 'In Search of the Great Indian Goddess: Motherhood Unbound'. in *Motherhood in India*, edited by Maitreyee Krishnaraj. New Delhi: Routledge, 2010, pp. 73–105.

Graves, Robert. *The Greek Myths*, edited by Michel Pharand. Manchester: Carcanet, 2001.

Gross, Rita. 'Hindu Female Deities as a Resource for the Contemporary Rediscovery of the Goddess,' *Journal of the American Academy of Religion*, Vol. 46, No. 3 (September., 1978), pp. 269–91.

Hooke, S. H. *Middle Eastern Mythology*. New York: Penguin, 1963.

Jain, Jasbir. 'Daughters of Mother India in Search of a Nation: Women's Narratives about the Nation', *Economic and Political Weekly*, Vol. 41, No. 17 (29 April–5May 2006), pp. 1654–660.

Kramer, Samuel N. *Mythologies of the Ancient World*. New York: Anchor Books, 1961.

Krishnaraj, Maitreyee (ed.). *Motherhood in India*. New Delhi: Routledge, 2010.

Le Martin, Max. 'Lajja Gauri, the goddess of sexuality, from Mesopotamia to India' https://www.academia.edu/5246382/Lajja_Gauri_the_goddess_of_sexuality_from_Mesopotamia_to_India. Accessed 15 June 2015. Originally published in *The Goddess Lajja Gauri: On the Footsteps of the Universal Goddess of Sexuality*. Createspace, 2012.

Liddle, Joanna and Rama Joshi. *Daughters of Independence*. London: Zed Books, 1986.

Ramaswamy, Sumathi. 'Virgin Mother'. In *Signposts*, edited by Rajeswari Sunder Rajan. New Jersey: Rutgers, 2001, pp. 17–56.

Sunder Rajan, Rajeswari. 'Is the Hindu Goddess a Feminist?' *Economic and Political Weekly*, Vol. 33, No. 44 (31 October–6 November 1998), pp. WS34–WS38.

Spivak, Gayatri C. 'Moving Devi', *Project Muse: Cultural Critique*, 47, Winter 2001, pp. 120–63.

Wadley, Susan. 'Women and the Hindu Tradition'. In *Women in India: Two Perspectives,* edited by Doranne Jacobson and Susan Wadley. New Delhi: Manohar, 1986, pp. 113–39.

Wolkstein, Diane and Samuel N. Kramer, *Inanna: Queen of Heaven and Earth*, New York: Harper & Row, 1983.

2
Anticipating the Mother's Dream: Maternal subjectivity in psychoanalysis, literature and cinema

Il est urgent d'anticiper

—Cixous 1975, 39

As we have seen in the previous chapter, religious iconography, in both India and the west, is testament to the dominance of patriarchal world views, which reduce images of powerful ancient goddesses to castrating witches. Whether imagined as the laughing Medusa, 'petrifying and shattering constraint' (Cixous 1986 a, 32), formidable in her spree of irrational decapitations, or as the furious Kali, wilful upon death and destruction, the manic glee of mother-goddesses emerges from a brutal pleasure in violence, and triggers the overwhelming fear of a devouring, castrating mother. Across the world, the fear of feminine power and dominance has been embodied by formidable iconic goddesses such as Durga, Inanna, Ishtar and Isis. Freudian and post-Freudian psychoanalytic theory looks for answers to the puzzles of castration anxieties in gendered relationships represented in western mythopoetic narratives, especially those which match the assumptions it is out to prove. In the various efforts to unravel such complexities, the maternal metaphor has been posited in relation to the (male) Freudian subject so that the Oedipal dream of the mother becomes one of the major inroads in the interpretation of dreams, 'the royal road to the unconscious' (Freud 1900). The Oedipal myth thus assumes an unprecedented centrality, and becomes, from here onwards, 'the specimen story of psychoanalysis' (Felman 1987, 101). Consequently, the mother is imagined as a figment of someone's dreams, rather than the one who dreams, and figures in the subject's unconscious, but does not really 'figure' in and of itself. One may wonder then whether it is possible to define maternal subjectivities in India in relation to available psychoanalytic models. Further, given the close connection between the 'symbolic' work of psychoanalytic theory, and that of representational discourse such as literature and cinema, what can such works tell us about the links between discursive representations of the maternal and motherhood ideology in India? This chapter will attempt to respond to these issues through an examination of works which speak to the various inter-linkages.

The feminine, as delineated in psychoanalytic theory from Freud to Lacan, occupies a position of the desired object as well as of absence or 'lack', since the (implied male subject's) desire for the mother gets enmeshed with the threat of castration. Feminist attempts at retrieving other, absence-defying maternal narratives have led to the focus on alternative dimensions of the primal mother-child dyad, such as the 'emotional' quotient as described in Object Relations theory. In early feminist work, although relational aspects of the mother-child dyad within patriarchal social environments became important areas of concern, the subjectivity and sexuality of women-as-mothers beyond the mothering paradigm remained yet to be fully explored. Describing some of the work on mothering in the 1940s, Nancy Chodorow remarks that, 'most of the studies were not concerned with the lives of the mothers, but only with how their children were affected.' (Chodorow 1978, 212) Moreover, the focus of these studies was primarily on the role played by the mother in the early phase of child development, a tendency which dominated much of the preliminary work undertaken by feminists within psychoanalytic theory, as well as in literary and cultural discourse. For instance, Juliet MacCannell points out that other than a few exceptions (such as Jane Flax, Melanie Klein and Nancy Chodorow), in the work of many other feminists, '"the mother" ceases to exist as any sort of presence after the pre-oedipal phase (mothers die off), she returns in her impact on a son's and daughter's chosen substitute objects.' (MacCannell 1991, 628)

French feminism, particularly, in a concerted critique of Lacanian positions, set out to resolve this imbalance to some extent. In the 1970s, two of Hélène Cixous' popular essays, 'The Laugh of the Medusa' and 'Castration or Decapitation' were aimed at upsetting the conventional association of the feminine and the maternal with castration and madness, and at exploring the image of the mother as artist, creator, and dreamer. Various other attempts have since then been made to address the consequences of the lacuna afforded by an inadequate analysis of the mother's subjectivity in literary, cultural and psychoanalytical discourse. Alison Stone, for instance, speaks to the question of the cultural positioning of the mother as the background from which one has to separate in order to individuate:

> in Western civilization there has been a widespread tendency to understand the maternal body and the self in opposition to one another.... The mother has been interpreted as the background, environment, first home and container, which everyone must leave behind to become a self.... The modern version of these assumptions is instead that one must leave the maternal body behind to become an autonomous individual subject, a self-conscious and autonomous agent who is the source of normative authority and meaning. (Stone 2014, 326)

Similarly, Hadara Katsav hints at a clearing up of representational space for the male subject and a vanishing of the maternal in observing that 'the maternal subject has been pushed aside and curtained off behind the symbolic system. As a consequence, the mother... has become absorbed at the symbolic level into society, law and order. She has been shaped as a category, that is, as a patriarchal signifier, and not as a subject.' (Katsav, 2014, 299)

In efforts to extricate the suppressed maternal, 'new directions in motherhood studies' as initiated by Adrienne Rich, Susan Suleiman, Nancy Miller and others have led in recent years to explorations of maternal subjectivity beyond the narrow walls of patriarchally informed ideologies.[1] Leading work in this context has been undertaken by Bracha Ettinger, Alison Stone, Julie Rodgers and others.[2] Ettinger, in referring to Freud's bewilderment around the loss of the mother and the absence of attention to maternal subjectivity in Freud's work wonders that 'he is surely aware of the profoundness of some lacuna in his theory' and goes on to add that 'this lacuna is related to archaic maternality and to pre-birth'. (Ettinger 2014, 124–25) The impulse that drives these recent explorations urges us towards what Rodgers calls a new 'positive maternal subjectivity', which does not 'inevitably entail the annihilation of the self,' (Rodgers 2014) an assumption which had previously caused deep concern to feminists such as Simone de Beauvoir (Beauvoir 1949, 377), and whose detrimental effects are far from over.

The Mother, in Theory...

The Desexualized Mother

One of the notable consequences of the prioritization of the focus on the mother as patriarchally embedded maternal metaphor, rather than the embodied mother-as-subject, has been the a priori idealization of motherhood and an accompanying erasure of maternal subjectivity and sexuality, duly reflected in representations of the maternal in both myth and in psychoanalysis. The singular magnitude of (patriarchal) fantasy and the focus on the (male) subject's dreams conjures up a world of reductive representations in which the mother is imaged as the captive reflection in the mirror, to be gazed upon in adoration or in horror. As the mirrored reflection, the maternal object re-generates and clones itself into perpetual existence as spectacle: 'The object can, indeed, must repeat itself exactly as it has been thought. It must even claim to establish, maintain, and justify its objectification. Its sole "activity" is reproductive: the reiteration and reinforcement of itself as picture.' (Allen 1983, 319)

In its prescribed function of responding perfectly to the other's desire, the maternal must be evacuated of any desire for itself, leading to the erasure of sexuality and sexual desire. The cultural demands of motherhood necessitate the submersion of feminine subjectivity in favour of what Sara Ruddick called 'maternal thinking', which 'emerged out of maternal practices that are oppressive to women and children' (Rudick 1983, 224) Although Ruddick has been criticized for what some see as an unexamined narration of maternal thought,[3] she is not alone in her call for the inclusion of fathers in western parenting practices as, for instance, emphasized by Nancy Chodorow.[4]

In a work which may have particular resonances with the situation of Indian women, Jessica Benjamin, in her work *Bonds of Love* had remarked upon 'the desexualized mother whose hallmark is not desire but nurturance.' (Benjamin 1988, 91) She adds that 'the idealization of motherhood' is consummated 'by idealizing woman's desexualization and lack of agency. This attitude toward sexuality preserves the old gender system, so that freedom and desire remain an unchallenged male domain....' (92) Similarly, in the Indian context, Sudhir Kakar has remarked upon the role of the desexualized maternal as a partial fulfilment of male fantasy, given that [male] 'desire needs the woman to be sexually dead for its fulfillment.' (Kakar 1989, 134). Further, Kakar emphasizes the detrimental effects of idealization on Indian women: 'Besides desexing the woman, another step in the denial of her desire is her idealization (especially of the Indian woman) as nearer to a purer divine state and thus an object of worship and adoration.' (125) 'Primarily seeing the mother in the woman and idealizing motherhood is yet another way of denying female eroticism.' (126) However, he modifies this statement later by signalling that the association of the mother with sexuality is not completely obliterated in the process of idealization, and may subsist as a remnant in the unconscious: 'Hindus, too, share this widespread orientation wherein the image of woman as mother is sought to be superimposed upon and thereby to obliterate the picture of woman as a sexual being. Yet, during this superimposition, and this is the most salient feature of male fantasy in India, what emerges is a composite image of the *sexual mother*.' (143)

The Dark Continent

The counterpart to the desexualized mother is thus the castrating mother, since together they constitute the 'composite image' necessary for the attainment of male fantasy. This may at least partially explain the singular importance of castrating mother-goddesses such as Medusa and Devi across the mythologies of patriarchal cultures, and the overarching image of the phallic mother in psychoanalytic discourse, which draws heavily upon the Freudian and Jungian contiguity between myths and dreams (where myths are seen as a projection of the waking person's unconscious).[5] Not surprisingly, Sudhir Kakar, in his analysis of myths of Devi, Ganesha and Skanda, describes 'the sword- and spear-wielding Devi' in her relationship to her enemy and sexual pursuer, Mahisasura (whose trunk she cuts off), as a 'phallic mother.' (Kakar 1989, 138) Striking cross-cultural correspondences may be uncovered here with more recent comments by feminist critics such as Hadara Katzav who observes that 'every fantastic perception of the maternal body serves as a veil to conceal the castration. Moreover, the solution of fantasy in order to erase the lack creates a total structure of the body: the omnipotent mother constitutes a perfect paradise or a predatory monster.' (Katzav 2014, 313)

In the fascinating conflict between the unconscious attribution of sexuality to the mother, and a deliberate attempt at erasing maternal sexual desires, the maternal feminine has consequently been the 'dark continent' of male imagination, much as the unexplored land of the other during the colonial enterprise. This 'veiling' of castration and a consequent projection of an enigmatic maternal feminine in Freudian psychology, has, of course, been adequately critiqued in the works of post-Freudian feminists across cultures. Reading the Freudian notion of the inscrutability of women in the context of the colonial gaze, Hélène Cixous famously declared that woman and Africa have been projected as the two dark continents—'... because you are Africa, you are black. Your continent is dark. Dark is dangerous'—and challenged this imagery with 'The "Dark Continent" is neither dark nor unexplorable'. (Cixous 1986 b, 68) The simile has been taken up by others such as Ranjana Khanna who states that psychoanalysis has 'situated itself, with fascination, in opposition to its repressed, concealed, and mysterious "dark continents": colonial Africa, women, and the primitive.' (Khanna 2003, 6)

Sudhir Kakar, however, weighs in against comparisons which paint various oppressed groups in the same colour and emphasizes the unique position of women: 'Although oppressed in many societies, women still cannot be likened to any other exploited group, such as the blacks in South Africa or the "untouchable" castes in India.' (Kakar 1989, 142) According to him, the singular exploitation of women, especially Indian women, impacts gender relations in very specific ways. One of the effects of oppression on Indian women, according to Kakar, is that while the desexualized mother inspires terror in men, the erasure of female sexuality may leave women with a sense of despondency: 'in contrast to the fear and dread pervading men's fantasies of women, anger and disappointment are a large part of the women's feelings in relationship to men.' (Ibid., 145)

Despite its universal significance, then, the western Oedipal narrative of attraction and castration may not completely suffice to explain gender relations in India, and more specifically, the oppression of Indian women as mothers, in whose case explorations of alternate psychological schemas become necessary. Interestingly, the inadequacy of the Oedipal model has also been noted beyond India, as for instance by Israeli artist and psychoanalyst, Bracha Ettinger:

> Women suffered and still suffer from interpretations concerning penis lack and penis envy and the foreclosure of the maternal (archaic motherhood) in the process of subjectivization in our culture. Axes offered for meaning by the Oedipus as myth, as well as the Anti-Oedipus fragmentation, are insufficient for giving meaning to the woman-to-woman (and, more generally, same sex) difference and for the difference (of males and females) from

the mother. We have to ask what kind of human subject and society was shaped in view of man's lack of womb not as organ but in terms of lack of a whole symbolic universe of meaning and value stemming from the matrixial sphere where the containing of and the proximating to the Other occur on a subsubjective and pre-subjective level, and the passage from non-life to life and sometimes from non-life to death, as well as birth and birthing, enter the unconscious in the feminine. (Ettinger 2014, 124)

Elsewhere, Ettinger emphasizes 'connectivity' as an alternate prism for approaching maternal subjectivity: 'Maternal subjectivity, which contains pre-Oedipal and post-Oedipal positions, is also a carrier and transmitter of feminine-matrixial connectivity that is charged by—and charges—specific modalities of affected encounter-eventing and makes their effects specific.' (Ettinger 2010, 1)

Stanley Kurtz, on the other hand, identifies a specifically 'Hindu counterpart' to the western Oedipus complex and offers in its stead the 'Durga complex.' (Kurtz 1992, 133) Taking Spiro's question 'How could the Oedipus complex possibly *not* be universal?' as his reference point, Kurtz refutes such an inherently universalizing contention to confidently claim that his work 'on the Hindu psyche provides an answer to this question.' (235) However, Kurtz's analysis of the 'Hindu' psyche (as if there were only one!), in its relationship to what he calls the 'Durga complex', employs an inherently patriarchal lens in which the male child, surrounded by various mother figures ('in-law mothers') resolves his Oedipal conflicts by turning away from the biological mother to a guided maternal consolation offered by the group of mothers. Thus, in Kurtz's reading, the group of mothers blend into a more or less blurry, indistinct maternal space making it nearly impossible to discuss the mother as individual, desiring subject, and leaving intact the symbolic space occupied by the maternal object in the (male) child's unconscious. Obviously then, one may wonder about the possibility of alternate readings in which maternal subjectivity is not quite so inescapably drowned in an obscure maternal collective.

The Dominant Narrative of Devi

A point on which Kurtz and Kakar seem to be in agreement, however, is the cultural significance of mother-goddess myths in India. Sudhir Kakar contends that myths continue to exert an ongoing and powerful influence on cultural relations and individual imaginations in India: 'Myths in India are not part of a bygone era.... Vibrantly alive, their symbolic power intact, Indian myths constitute a cultural idiom that aids the individual in the construction and integration of his inner world.' (Kakar 1989, 135) However, in his analysis of the role played by the figure of Devi in male fantasy, Kakar refutes the purported link between male fantasy and social structures, most notably, the 'system of patriarchy.' Rather, in a divergence from the Jungian notion of the 'collective unconscious', he foregrounds the 'individual' source of the fantasy. (141) Yet, Kakar underscores the dominance of Devi as a 'hegemonic narrative' within Indian culture: 'It is the ubiquity and multiformity of the "primitive idea of being a woman" and the embeddedness of this fantasy in the maternal configurations of the family and the culture of India, which I would like to discuss.... My main argument is that the "hegemonic narrative" of Hindu culture as far as male development is concerned, is neither that of Freud's Oedipus nor of Christianity's Adam. One of the more dominant narratives of this culture is that of Devi, the Great Goddess, especially as mother in the inner world of the Hindu son.' (131–32)

The archetype of the great mother goddess, of course, is not exclusive to Indian myth and religious tradition. A distinctive aspect of the latter, however, is the primary focus on the mother-son dyad in the Indian 'hegemonic' tradition. Feminist scholar Marianne Hirsch, in fact, makes a case for the predominance of the mother-daughter bond in her discussion of familiar models of the 'archetype of the Great Mother' in western cultures: 'All stress the continuity between mother and daughter. Demeter and Kore are merely two sides of woman, the mother and the maiden.' (208–9) Similarly, Bracha Ettinger employs the Demeter-Persephone myth of mother-daughter love as the screen through which a gaze, other than the phallic one of the Oedipal myth, becomes possible: 'The Oedipal complex will be informed and relativized by the Demeter-Persephone complex infused by fleeting feelings of compassion.' (Ettinger 2014, 126) She also offers an alternative lens to enable the emergence of a previously denied subjectivity: 'The Demeter and Persephone myth offers ways to subjectivize oneself as mother, "monster" or not, and woman, crazy or not....' (129)

One could argue that such readings of selective western archetypes obviously glance away from other equally famous Greek examples such as the male-identified Athena who addresses patriarchy's concerns before any others: 'Athena springs fully armed from the head of Zeus; a child springs from the head of its father, fully adorned with the markings of patriarchy.' (Allen 1983, 319) But Ettinger's Demeter is a deliberate and concerted effort to write against the 'phallic phantasy' of the Athena narrative. (Ettinger 2014, 132)

Turning back to India, there is no denying that the paucity of mother-daughter narratives in Indian myth and theology leave very little room outside of male-centric readings of the corpus of stories of Devi. Of course, the centrality of the representations of Devi in Indian cultural discourse sets this Hindu goddess apart, making it hard to ignore or escape her all-encompassing presence as the mother who is the source and the ultimate destination of all life. The wide-ranging and all-inclusive representations of Devi lead Kakar to comment that 'certain forms of the maternal-feminine may be more central in Indian myths and psyche than in their western counterparts.' (Kakar 1989 131–32) In contrast to Kakar's 'individualistic' explanation for the dominance of the fantasy constituted by mother-goddess narratives, Kurtz offers a rationale which links goddess primacy to a more or less homogenized 'world of women' phase of early Indian childhood: 'Why, on the other hand, is Goddess worship so important a part of Hinduism? The notion of the Durga complex suggests a possible answer. The Hindu child's sojourn in the world of women lasts longer than it does in the West.... In worshipping the Goddess, Hindus recapitulate and reinforce their successful developmental journey through the world of women.' (Kurtz 1992, 174) The ubiquity of mother-goddesses in Kakar's telling, and the 'world of women' in Kurtz's narrative are, however, no indicators that motherhood in India is any less constrained by patriarchal considerations. 'Why take it for granted', Spivak rightly asks, 'that the invocation of goddesses in a historically masculinist polytheist sphere is more feminist than Nietzsche or Derrida claiming woman as model?' (Spivak 1993, 185) It appears then that psychoanalytic theory regarding the role of the maternal in India leaves us struggling to peer through the murky clouds of the male child's dreams to obtain a clear sense of who the mother is, what she feels, and what her desires may be, outside of those constructed for her by such patriarchal readings. In the next section, let us attempt to see whether representational discourse, with its access to the free play of imagination, provides a clearer vista within which responses to such questions may be elicited.

Anticipating the Mother's Dreams through Literature and Cinema

The close affinity between psychoanalysis, and literary and cinematic discourse, points to a possible approach to the exploration of maternal subjectivities through the world of representation. In a relationship which parallels the one between psychoanalysis and its scrutiny of myth, Hindi cinema offers to psychoanalysis what Kakar has called a 'sure-footed grasp of the topography of desire' and promotes 'the conscious social understanding of various human relationships in the culture.' (Kakar 1989, 30) Myth and cinema, fed by the world of fantasy and fertile imaginations, are allied in a mimetic impulse valuable for a study of the human psyche. Perhaps due to this natural alliance, cinematic and other works of art very often draw upon mythological representations as embodied in religious and cultural discourse. Gayatri Spivak's suggestion that the division between history and literature may not be entirely self-evident—'That history deals with real events and literature with imagined ones may now be seen as a difference in degree rather than in kind' (Spivak 1987, 243)—may be especially useful in this regard. Where literature and cinema borrow from the extant maternal iconography of mythological traditions, they offer important insights into the links between complex maternal metaphors in current circulation and the social subjugation of women and mothers. Metaphor, as Kakar tells us, is an integral part of both the theory and practice of psychoanalysis: 'La métaphore et l'analogie ne font pas seulement partie intégrante de la théorie psychanalytique, elles appartiennent aussi à sa pratique.' (Kakar 1993, 271) (Metaphor and analogy are not only an integral part of psychoanalytic theory, but belong as well to its practice.) The analysis of a few works from India offered below is thus a partial attempt at puzzling out such nuances within such a larger enterprise. In the light of the preceding discussion, the choice of works considered here is based on representations of the maternal which alternate between the desexualized mother, and an emerging acknowledgement of maternal subjectivity as well as sexuality, as a way of anticipating the mother's dreams through literary and cinematic imagination in India. A feminist investigation of the linkages between mother-goddess iconography, and literature and cinema is undertaken in the hope that it may deepen our understanding of the burden of deification on Indian women-as-mothers, as well as enable us to conceive of future possibilities where the mother is not just dreamt about, but where she becomes the dreamer—in other words, to anticipate the mother's dreams.

The thematic exploration of the maternal has been one of the most popularly explored themes in Indian literature, cinema and art. Replete with representations of the maternal drawn both from theological iconography and from culturally determined codifications of motherhood, they offer rich terrains for critiquing maternal stereotypes and exploring the complexities of the maternal metaphor. From the classic film, *Mother India*, to nationalist images of Bharat Mata as popularized by famous artists like Raja Ravi Verma, to renaissance and contemporary cinema, representations of the maternal are ubiquitous. Bombay cinema of the 1960s and 1970s abounded in images of the hapless, incessantly coughing, sick, poverty-stricken, and dying mother played to perfection by tragedy queens like Nirupama Roy. (The good mother/bad mother dichotomy was often achieved by creating the alter-ego of the self-abnegating, suffering mother; such roles of the conniving and cruel mother-in-law, were very often deftly played by 'villainous' actresses such as Lalita Pawar.) Similarly, literary works offer a plethora of diverse explorations of the maternal.

Nowhere is this more conspicuous than in West Bengal, where the extant predominance of the goddess in religion and culture ensures multifarious representations of the maternal in literature and film, and critical engagements with the cultural idealization of the maternal. These include the famous short story 'The Goddess' by Prabhat Kumar Mukherjee (originally published as 'Devi' in Bengali), a Satyajit Ray film by the same name inspired by the former, and Mahasweta Devi's short story 'The Breast-Giver'. These narratives, although divided by time, offer startlingly similar examples of women protagonists destroyed by the extreme consequences of a mythical, oppressive maternal idea imposed upon them by a patriarchal society that fails to see women other than as procreative bodies. Two major goddess cults—that of Devi/Kali and of Yashoda—are employed in these works to create a sense of ironic tension in the light of established religious and cultural idealizations of the maternal.[6]

Dreaming the Mother

<u>'The Goddess': The short story</u>

Prabhat Kumar Mukhopadhyay's Bengali short story 'Devi' (translated as 'The Goddess'), whose idea was allegedly gifted to the author by Rabindranath Tagore,[7] is known to have inspired the much better-known film of the same name by Satyajit Ray. Despite the similarities in the storyline, Ray's film presents a significant departure from the plot of the original story. Below, I will look at both the versions of the storyline from the perspective of their varying impact on representations of the maternal.

44   Embodying Motherhood

Mukhopadhyay's 'The Goddess' interrogates what Jashodara Bagchi calls 'the investiture of motherhood' (Bagchi 2010, 163), a representation of motherhood ideology in which 'motherhood is made to stand for the sacrosanct space, not sullied by any petty influence.' (163) The short story narrates the events that take place in an upper-class Bengali household. In the story, Umaprasad, the younger son of a wealthy landlord, recently married to his sixteen-year-old bride, Dayamoyee, has just discovered the pleasures of wedded life. His father, Kalikinkar, an educated man, is a devotee of the goddess Kali (the prevalent form in which Devi is worshipped in Bengal). He is equally besotted by his daughter-in-law, the compassionate and beautiful Daya, whom he refers to as 'Little Mother'. One morning, Umaprasad is rudely awakened to be informed that his father has categorically arrived upon the idea that the young bride is a physical personification of the goddess Kali herself. Kalikinkar's unshakeable faith in his daughter-in-law's incarnated form is based on a vivid dream of the previous night: 'The holy mother, Kali, the goddess herself, has descended to my household in the mortal form of my daughter-in-law. Last night, the Mother herself sent me a message in my dream.' (Mukhopadhyay 2014, 8) The story takes a quick and decisive turn when, 'in a matter of moments, the flesh-and-blood Dayamoyee was branded as the goddess.' (8) The author makes it evident that Kalikinkar's fantasy is symbolic of a collective will to envision women as divine mothers at whose feet the male devotee can atone, since the speedy transmogrification of Dayamoyee into Kali is supported by the blind faith of hundreds of devotees who travel great distances to worship the goddess, to plead for her mercy and an end to their sufferings. So complete is the transformation that it soon becomes impossible, even for Daya, to distinguish between her real identity and the theatre in which she has been assigned a specific role. Shocked by the turn of events, Daya initially consents to the clandestine arrangements made by her distraught husband for a quiet escape. However, at the last moment, the weight of her fabricated life and an alternate, imaginary performance that she has become accustomed to, prove so burdensome that she becomes incapable of escape: 'Don't touch me as you'd touch your wife. Am I your wife? Or am I really the goddess? I'm not sure anymore.' (13) When Umaprasad wonders if she has gone mad, her response throws into question the sanity of all those who have led her into this madness: 'He said, "Daya, have you gone crazy too?"... Daya said, "How do you explain so many people getting cured? Hundreds of devotees come to catch a glimpse of me every day. Is everyone insane?" (13) Gradually, Daya the daughter-in-law becomes indistinguishable from her form as Devi, the goddess. Put to the test several times, Daya's otherworldly powers appear to work as one by one, sick and dying children are brought to her for miraculous cures. However, the collective fantasy soon comes to a crashing halt when her beloved nephew, Khoka, falls incurably ill. At the end of a long, miserable night during which the child is left to the mercy and ministrations of the 'goddess', Khoka dies in the goddess's lap. The confrontation with the failure of her godly powers proves insurmountable for Daya; she is no longer able to hold on to the imaginary narrative of her deification, or to distinguish between reality and fiction, the sane and the crazy. The story concludes when Daya abruptly puts an end to the unbearable double life: 'the next morning, when Kalikinkar opened the door of the prayer room, he found the goddess hanging by the neck from the ceiling.' (16)

'Devi': The film

The plotline of Satyajit Ray's film *Devi* (1960) largely follows the one in the short story described above. In the film, Ray emphasizes the 'maternal' aspects of Daya (played by the famous actress Sharmila Tagore), from the very outset. The first frame of the film focuses on a large effigy of goddess Kali, and a prayer song devoted to the goddess in which the devotee sings, 'I won't call you mother anymore.... You've become my eye... the light of my path'. Throughout, the erudite but extremely pious father-in-law repeatedly refers to Daya as 'mother'. Indeed, the young bride seems to have taken to the idea of her maternal role and is completely submerged in it, administering timely medicines to her father-in-law, and playing the mother to her loving nephew, Khoka, who is inseparable from her. When Khoka asks his beloved aunt to tell him the story of the demoness who devours the flesh of little children, we are offered a subtle forewarning about a twist in the goddess's tale. In the crucial dream sequence, Kalikinkar imagines the third eye of the goddess (usually associated with 'higher knowledge' as well as with destruction) suggestively merging into the 'bindi' on Daya's forehead, with Daya's face blurring into that of the goddess. When Kalikinkar decides to 'live' his patriarchal fantasy by declaring it irrefutable, the patriarch's unconscious desires embedded in the dream are given immediate manifestation and gratification. Meanwhile, the child bride Daya remains a mute spectator to her metamorphosis and deification, which robs her of all human pleasures. In Ray's film, the young husband Umaprasad is represented as perhaps equally victimized by the insanity of patriarchal control. Although he hurriedly returns from his travels when he hears of his wife's predicament through a letter, he seems to be almost as paralysed by the events and unable to assert his rights as lover or husband.

As in the short story, when Khoka dies in his aunt's embrace, we witness the swift transformation of Daya from goddess to witch, a demoness capable of devouring her own children. The shock of Khoka's death, and the realization that the drama of her deification was indeed the stuff of someone else's fantasy leaves Daya incapacitated, unable to deal with the shifting boundaries between the real and the unreal. While in the short story, the young protagonist commits suicide, Ray chooses a different ending for the film—a scene perhaps less tragic, but equally disturbing. The final frame leaves us witness to a deranged Daya disappearing into the horizon, trailed by the desperate cries of her husband. Ray's protagonist finally 'escapes' the insanity of an oppressive maternal idea imposed upon her by a collective patriarchal fantasy by fleeing the patriarchal narrative. However, her 'escape' is an equally 'insane' response, since the viewer realizes that she is running away into a perhaps equally dangerous and unaccepting world. The open ending of the film leaves the spectator wondering what will become of Daya in a world which places women's lives at such dire peril.

Visualized as an embodiment of the goddess, Ray's heroine, though alive at the end of the film, is left utterly disembodied by the idealized goddess image that has robbed her of all connections to her physical body and its desires. Kali, the terrifying goddess who is often upheld as a symbol of feminine power is unveiled, here, as the manifest form of the patriarchal 'bad mother' who purges real women of any hope they may have of free will, and crushes the individual woman under the weight of divinity. Gayatri Spivak's view—'I think it is a Western and male-gendered suggestion that powerful women in the Sakta (Sakti or Kali-worshipping) tradition *necessarily* take Kali as a role model' (Spivak 1993, 185)—is particularly on the mark, just as is Ettinger's rejection of Athena, for whom the latter reinforces the idea that 'matricide is a phallic solution to symbiosis.' (Ettinger 2014, 132) As Ray's film clearly shows, Kali, far from being a role model for women, becomes a tool in the hands of men to sustain the sexist dichotomy between divine mother and dead (or mad) wife.

Despite its interrogation of the tragic effects of blind goddess worship, one may argue that Ray's choice of an alternate ending to the story minimally 'anticipates' a different future for its female protagonist. Daya's final act of madness is a disruption of the oppressive ideology of the maternal imposed upon women. A 'hysterical' choice, it maps out a disorderly route, which in its escape from patriarchal norms, unflinchingly denies male control over women's bodies and desires. In doing so, it signals the possibility of an escape from an oppressive maternal—the stuff of male fantasy—to a recognition of the sexual, desiring subject, moving beyond the ending provided by the short story, which had 'strangulated' any such possibility. As such, it is indicative of the energy of resistance and madness, a foretelling of different times to come, and, in the words of Gilbert and Gubar, prefers engaging with, rather than 'castigating... the incoherence or destructiveness of female language'. (Gilbert and Gubar 1988, 236) In a similar feminist reading, to which we will return shortly, for Ettinger, 'hysteria is one of the ways a subject unconsciously rebels against the phallic-Oedipal cultural foreclosure of the matrixial links to the (m)Other in the family, in the society, and in the transference; it is a mode of subversion and resistance.' (Ettinger 2014, 135)

The madness exhibited by Daya as divine mother in 'The Goddess' may well be located in the context of the relationship between divine mysticism and madness, which has been studied at length within psychoanalytic theory, as for instance, in Catherine Clément and Sudhir Kakar's *La Folle et Le Saint* (1993). Here, the authors take up the question of the mysticism of Ramakrishna and of Madeleine in a section tellingly entitled 'Fou ou mystique? Mystique ou folle?'. (Kakar 1993, 185) In her conversation with Kakar, Clément claims that one can go as far as to name the mystic as someone who wants the loss of consciousness at all costs: 'On peut meme aller plus loin, et appeler mystique celui ou celle qui veut la perte de conscience à tout prix.' (174) Seen from a feminist perspective, and given the suppression of maternal subjectivity in favour of the mother-icon, as narrated from the perspective of Satyajit Ray, it is not surprising to see Daya moving from divine mysticism to an act that appears clearly insane from the perspective of the society she lives in. Insanity, a measure of the extent to which one does not belong to the 'normal' is, to that extent, also culturally determined. In his book *Inner World*, Sudhir Kakar observes, 'culture is so pervasive that even when an individual seems to break away from it, as in states of insanity, the "madness" is still influenced by its norms and rituals.' (Kakar 1981, 9) In case of Daya, one could say that her act of madness is both driven and defined by patriarchy, and to the extent that it escapes its oppressive circumstances despite such control, it is a denial of the patriarchal hold over the female body.

In its element of 'escape' then, it offers a third alternative to the two kinds of madness Kurtz identifies, which according to him, are recognized in Bengal—the ordinary and the divine:

> Ordinary Bengali madness is said to be rooted in desire, greed, frustration, and disappointment. Such madness is characterized by an instability of mental state. Divine madness, on the other hand, transcends these angry, grasping impulses, achieving thereby a stable, continuous vision of the multi-formed Goddess.... The distinction between ordinary and divine madness is said by Bengalis to parallel the transition from *kam* to *prem* (from selfish love to spiritual, generous love) and as such can be linked to the child's movement... from the natural mother to the larger group of mothers.... On the ther hand, if the immature tie to the mother is broken, a divine madness of merger can be experienced on the stable and mature level of connection with the collective mothers, i.e., the multiformed Goddess. (Kurtz 1992, 185)

Whereas in Kurtz's analysis, the male child's merger with the group of mother-substitutes is experienced as a madness at a 'stable and mature level of connection' and a merger with the 'multiformed Goddess' (safely accomplishing the burial of the 'mad mother' at the stage of early childhood), the maternal idea of the divine mother in Ray's film acts as an oppressive force, and results in the hysteria of the mother gone mad. Both, however, conform to the association of madness with the mother, a linkage that adheres to conventional psychoanalytic concepts in which maternal madness, castration and engulfment are woven into the web of the male subject's fantasies and anxieties.

Referring back to Marguerite Duras, Ettinger points to this primal image that dominates psychoanalytic discourse:

> 'I believe that always, or almost always, in all childhood and in all the lives that follow them, the mother represents madness. Our mothers always remain the strangest, craziest people we've ever met', said Marguerite Duras. Therapeutic interpretations that pathologize this experience shape the ways in which our mothers remain the craziest people we've ever met. Interpretations made by the analyst/therapist that are empathic with the 'ready-made mother-monster' (without compassion to the maternal figure) and which locate a 'cause' of our sufferings (the 'unconsciously poisonous mother', the 'intoxicating mother', the never 'good-enough mother', the always 'over-controlling' mother, the always 'constantly abandoning' mother) turn this important, painful and vital conscious and unconscious real-phantasmatic experience into a symbolic 'truth-cause' and turns the intimate mother to whom we are transconnected (whether we like it or not) into the craziest of all figures. (Ettinger 2010, 4)

In India, additionally, when the short story and the film are 'read' in the context of the impact of colonial rule in Bengal, an interpretation of the site where the positing of male fantasy in psychoanalytic discourse intersects with the collective reaction to western imperialism becomes possible, so that it is not just the mother who is mad, but an entire nation is driven to insanity by the violence of hegemony. Noting the significance of the dominant role of the goddess in colonial Bengal, Jashodara Bagchi comments that 'the prevalence of goddess worship in Bengal certainly facilitated the empowering of the mother image in the state so that it becomes the most dominant myth of colonial Bengal.' (Bagchi 2010, 163) Bagchi further shows how motherhood is now used to serve a dual purpose—its original purpose being the gratification of a certain patriarchal fantasy, and its coalescence with the idea of the pure nation as a way of resisting the cultural adulteration seen as a perceived threat in the form of western imperialism: 'With the emphasis on the fact that one's selfhood and identity were opposed to that of western rulers, motherhood emerged as the domain which the colonized could claim as their own.... Motherhood was seen as the 'ultimate' identity of Bengali women. It was an excellent ploy to keep women out of privileges, like education and profession that were being wrested by men, and to glorify womanhood only through her reproductive powers.' (161) Later she adds, 'motherhood becomes the site of struggle in colonial Bengal as the notion of unadulterated motherhood is constructed as the marker of the superiority of the culture in the dominated east.' (169)

Seen in the context of the freedom struggle, Ray's film *Devi* denies the male nationalist the satisfaction of fighting imperialism on the back of women's bodies, which they have deified as divine goddess. In the narrative of *Devi*, the mother 'escapes' the burden of her idealization, even if through a choice marked by hysteria. More urgently, both the story and the film draw attention to the violence wreaked upon Indian women's lives and maternal subjectivities in the process of transforming the body into the deity.

While 'The Goddess'/*Devi* deals with the disembodiment of the upper-class, upper-caste woman by exposing the process which drains her of her subjectivity, Mahasweta Devi's short story 'The Breast-Giver' (originally published as 'Stanadayini') focuses on the burden of motherhood on the subaltern woman. Interestingly, both stories hinge on dreams that interrupt reality and transform it. Notably, the dream sequence has been a popular tool in mainstream Indian (Bollywood) cinema over the decades, where it has offered a convenient way of introducing alternate desires, locales, song and dance routines, and any other variations to the plot, which do not otherwise 'fit' into the main storyline. As an acceptable 'interruption', the illusions offered up by dream sequences enable film directors to introduce a childlike element of play in a cinema that quite often constructs an implicit pact of the infantalization of its audience. In his *Intimate Relations*, Sudhir Kakar attributes the 'ubiquity of fantasy' in Indian cinema to specific cultural practices because of which the 'Indian ego is flexible enough to regress temporarily to childhood modes without feeling threatened or engulfed' with Hindi films providing such a 'regressive haven' (Kakar 1989, 28) for its audience. Kakar's approach to popular cinema is to 'think of film as a collective fantasy, a group daydream' (26) where 'Hindi films, perhaps more than cinema of many other countries, are fantasy in this special sense.' (27) The importance of the dream can consequently not be understated in a cinema which makes no bones about offering mass escapism through collective cinematic fantasies in an implied 'leave your brains behind at home' kind of covenant. The employment of the dream as literary tool thus draws its ironic depths from this context, with Mahasweta Devi's 'The Breast-Giver' mocking the conventional uses of fantasy in cultural narrative, and displaying an exaggerated caustic irony to achieve its literary effects.

Can the Mother Dream?
'Stanadayini' or 'The Breast-Giver'

Mahasweta Devi's short story, 'Stanadayini', written originally in Bengali, was greatly popularized by Gayatri Spivak's English translation 'The Breast-Giver', which appeared in 1987. 'Stanadayini' tells the story of the protagonist Jashoda (whose name has obvious linkages with the mythic Yashoda, the adoptive mother of the baby Krishna), who is forced by her circumstances to become a 'professional mother'. Following an accident in which her husband, Kangalicharan, loses his legs after being run over by one of the son's of the wealthy Haldar household, the orthodox patriarch of the family attempts to atone for his son's carelessness by offering Kangalicharan a job. As luck would have it, the master dies an untimely death, before being able to come through on his commitment. Jashoda, whose lactating abilities have been astutely noticed by the mistress of the house, is then employed as a wet nurse for the regularly procreating daughters-in-law of the Haldar household, who are subsequently able to reproduce without losing their figures. Over a period of thirty years, Jashoda gives birth to twenty offspring in order to keep milk flowing through her breasts. Soon, her reputation as a universal mother leads to her identification with Durga, the lion-seated goddess, in whose temple her husband is employed. Despite having successfully nursed various infants of the Haldar household, Jashoda meets a tragic end when the milk-providing breasts, to which she owes her livelihood and her stature, are attacked by cancer, and she ends up dying alone and uncared for in a hospital bed.

Mahasweta Devi's Jashoda is pushed towards her destiny by events both real and sacred: 'Finally, the Lionseated came to her in a dream as a midwife carrying a bag and said, "Don't worry. Your man will return."' (Devi 1987, 224) Elevated to the level of fantasy by her 'Cow of Fulfillment' prowess (227), her lactating capacity creates a blur between her identity and that of the lion-seated goddess: 'For a few days, whenever Nabin tries to think of the Lionseated, the heavy-breasted, languid-hipped body of Jashoda floats in his mind's eye. A slow rise spreads in his body at the thought that perhaps she is appearing in his dream as Jashoda just as she appeared in Jashoda's as a midwife.' (225) The dream is taken to be a fortuitous omen, as Jashoda soon finds herself gainfully employed, and well taken care of by the Haldar mistress and its other inhabitants whose respect for her position as the mother of the household goes up considerably once they witness the milk gushing endlessly from her breasts for all the babies of the household.

Provided boarding and lodging in the Haldar household, whose inhabitants appear to live by the cultural codes of the 16th century, Jashoda's stature in the house 'is now above the Mother Cows' (228)—milch cows raised in some respect by the Haldar family. The tragedy that befalls Jashoda is so poignant that the protagonist can be imagined as at once both real and metaphorical, the subaltern subject as well as a caricature of extreme oppression. Using irony and sarcasm as stylistic tools, Mahasweta Devi astutely digs at the patriarchal-, class- and caste-structured society, which constructs the maternal idea in such a way that it imprisons both women and men with its captivating seduction: 'Jashoda is fully an Indian woman, whose unreasonable, unreasoning, and unintelligent devotion to her husband and love for her children, whose unnatural renunciation and forgiveness have been kept alive in the popular consciousness by all Indian women from Sati-Savitri-Sita through Nirupa Roy and Chand Osmani. The creeps of the world understand by seeing such women that the old Indian tradition is still flowing free....' (225) In her astounding ability to nurse innumerable infants at her breasts, Jashoda recaptures the mythic Yashoda, idealized as the sacrificing mother. Elevated to the status of the mother-goddess, the protagonist is also compared to the lion-seated goddess herself. However, Mahasweta Devi cleverly exposes the myth and the miracle of the goddess. When the effigy of the lion-seated goddess in the temple is found to have turned its back on worshippers blindly devoted to her powers, the narrative reveals that the miracle was actually a clever ploy by the temple keeper Nabin, who remorselessly uses his cunning to manipulate the crowds for his personal gain: 'Nabin is the proof of all the miracles that can happen if, even in this decade, one stays under the temple's power. He had turned the goddess's head himself and had himself believed that the Mother was averse because the pilgrim-guides were not organizing like all the want-votes groups.' (232)

Located in between the iconic Durga and the motherly Yashoda, the Jashoda of the story appears to embody both, temporarily, but inevitably fails to live up to both ends of the spectrum defined by the miracle of patriarchal motherhood. Her final confused thoughts burst upon the reader's consciousness with their sharp interrogation of the cultural norms which have inscribed for her such a tragic destiny: 'Jashoda thought, after all, she had suckled the world, could she then die alone?... One must become Jashoda if one suckles the world. One has to die friendless, with no one left to put a bit of water in the mouth. Yet someone was supposed to be there at the end. Who was it? It was who? Who was it?' (240) The repeated question of the search for the 'someone' who is supposed to be there for Jashoda, but does not materialize, is asked equally of the reader, who cannot help but participate in the collusive history written out for Indian women. 'Who was it?' is a question raised pointedly about responsibility, about where one can lay the blame for the ending of this story. It asks if the rotting maternal body will ever be rescued from the plot endlessly repeated in an India where 'someone' fails to arrive in time to cure the cancer. Finally, 'Jashoda's death was also the death of God. When a mortal masquerades as God here below, she is forsaken by all and she must always die alone.' (240) Mahasweta Devi thus unveils the hypocrisy of a culture in which women who succumb to an emulation of imposed patriarchal ideals, will ultimately find themselves forsaken once their use-value has been exhausted. In obvious uses of Marxist feminist literary strategies to critique both patriarchal and imperialist hegemonies, the sub-texts of Mahasweta Devi's story work at multiple levels simultaneously.

Not surprisingly, the story induces Gayatri Spivak to comment that 'Mahasweta's Jashoda tells me more about the relationship between goddesses and strong, ordinary women than the psychoanalyst.' (Spivak 1993, 185) As Spivak points out elsewhere, Jashoda's narrative is an allegory for the postcolonial nation, and she goes on to interpret it as such:

By Mahasweta Devi's own account, 'Stanadayini' is a parable of India after decolonization. Like the protagonist Jashoda, India is a mother-by-hire.... I suppose if one extended this parable the end of the story might come to 'mean' something like this: the ideological construct 'India' is too deeply informed by the goddess-infested reverse sexism of the Hindu majority. As long as there is this hegemonic cultural self-representation of India as a goddess-mother (dissimulating the possibility that this mother is a slave), she will collapse under the burden of the immense expectations that such a self-representation permits. (1987, 244)

However, Spivak adds, 'this interesting reading is not very useful from the perspective of a study of the subaltern' since it metaphorizes the subaltern so that the 'effect of the real must necessarily be underplayed.' (244) The metaphor, for Spivak, obstructs a true reading of maternal subjectivity experienced at the level of the real. It does allow us, however, to get a sense of the measure of the subaltern's experiences by laying out a graph of extremes on an allegorical map.

Although Jashoda belongs to an upper-caste (Brahmin) family, stripped of all economic and social status, she comes to represent the subaltern woman destroyed by the idea of motherhood, in stark and ironic contrast to the mythic Yashoda. The latter, mother of Krishna, who embodies and revels in her motherliness or *mamta*, and who, according to Sudhir Kakar, is ample proof of the belief that her son's godly identity 'is vital to the consolidation and confirmation of a Hindu woman's identity around the core of motherliness.' (Kakar 1981, 153) Jashoda, quite contrarily, debunks the 'core of motherliness' as a cancer-ridden myth in provocative defiance of the health-giving *mamta* that flows through the breasts of Krishna's mother.

The lion-seated goddess appears in Jashoda's dream in the form of a 'midwife', promising the return of her husband, rather than an end to her own miserable existence. Jashoda's dream marks the internalized oppression of the subaltern woman in revealing the unconscious depths at which male fantasy intrudes upon maternal subjectivity—Jashoda dreams what all men would dream for her, and has no dreams of her own. In the words of Hélène Cixous, '...l'horreur du noir, nous l'avons intériorisée.' (...we have internalized the horror of darkness.) (Cixous 1975/1976, 41) In such pitch darkness, the suppression of maternal subjectivity is almost complete, and only the overarching mother-goddess of male fantasy reigns supreme.

Interestingly, then, an analysis of literary works from the perspective of maternal subjectivity thus links us back to the world of ancient myth and exhorts us to lament the disappearance of goddesses, such as Vac, who, one sanguinely imagines, may have been able to speak their mind. Such a stirring up of cultural memory brings to the fore the declining role of ancient mother-goddesses after Vedic times in India, much like the historical shift in mother-goddess imagery from the Minoan to the Mycenaean civilization in classical Greece. If, as suggested by Jashodara Bagchi, '*Shakti* worship' in India was 'fed by pre-Aryan, often tribal cults of mother goddess, sometimes going back to matriarchal forms of society' and, if the Vedic '*vacha* (speech) ecstatically expresses her complete union with the great One (Brahman, Logos)' (Bagchi 2010, 166), one can only feel regret at our collective history, given the awareness that Vac's utterances are soon to be muted.

As we have seen, the irony inherent in the silencing of the goddess of speech and her denigration into a muted, helpless temple idol unable to carve her way out of her stony silence is nowhere sharper than in Mahasweta Devi's 'The Breast-Giver'. But what happens, one may wonder, when the mother does decide to speak/dream/write differently. How does one traverse the distance between the patriarchal dream of the maternal and the mother who dares to dream? 'Imagine the mother playing', suggests Susan Suleiman audaciously, and adds with some intrepidity, 'imagine the mother laughing.' (Suleiman 1990, 179) The plucky invitation is immediately followed up with 'But why? Why should we imagine the mother playing and laughing? And why are the stakes political (in the broadest sense) as well as aesthetic?' (179) By way of a response, Suleiman proposes that 'to imagine the mother playing is to recognize her most fully as a subject—as autonomous and free…' (179), thus signaling the link between laughter and subjectivity. But of course, in order for the mother's 'play' and 'laughter' to become feasible, especially in contexts where the maternal has been submerged under prescribed models of normativity, which brook no defiance, it is crucial that the mother be able to begin by *dreaming* of herself as that carefree creature. In solidarity with Suleiman's brave invitation, I see in the possibility of the dreaming mother someone who can imagine herself as the unrestrained, laughing, playing mother, and so, in imagination, the potential to bridge the gap between the real and the desired. The energy of imagination is of course nowhere more palpable than in creative work, leading us to look for examples of fiction and film where representations of the maternal leave behind the desexualized, castrated mother of male fantasy, and are drawn towards other, more pleasureful subjectivities.

The Mother Dreams

Deepa Mehta's film *Fire* burst upon the international and Indian screen (1996/1998) by courting controversy, with several cinema houses in India set ablaze by right-wing protesters. The film defies religious and cultural norms, and subverts established patriarchal mores through a feminist sensibility. To an Indian audience, the names of the two protagonists, Radha and Sita, would not only be immediately recognizable, but would also summon the ideological values associated with their namesake Hindu goddesses. In a deliberate upsetting of normative expectations, the characters played by the two protagonists interrogate the oppressive heterosexual structures of marriage and motherhood prevalent in the middle classes. Moreover, the naming of the protagonists inverts the conventional characterizations of the passionate Radha and the subservient Sita of Hindu mythology. In the film, Radha is the name of the older, traditional wife struggling to make her peace with familial and social demands, while the younger, passionate and rebellious daughter-in-law is named Sita. Neither of the two protagonists is a true 'mother' in the literal sense of the word, and neither one is enticed by the notion of 'playing the mother' to her husband. Married to two brothers in the same household, their mutual relationship is defined at the outset by the patriarchal setup in which they find themselves. Yet, the cinematic perspective brings into play a kind of maternal relationality found missing in all the other relationships portrayed in the film.

In *Fire*, the older woman, played by Shabana Azmi, is a good wife but a 'failed' mother, unable to conceive and live up to the idealized role of the good Hindu wife. The maternal body's failure to reproduce suggests the place of an absence, drawing attention towards the frustration of conventional expectations of triumph through birthing. Consequently, when she is seduced by the younger and passionate, Sita, the heterosexual 'maternal failure' that Radha experiences is overshadowed by their mutually discovered erotic pleasure, upsetting conventional understandings of 'maternal fulfilment'. In a climactic kitchen scene where Radha's sari catches fire, the mythological Sita's self-consecrating ordeal by fire in the *Ramayana* is used as a cross-reference to highlight its contemporary opposite—Radha's passage to a combustion of everything that holds her back from finding herself. Ironically, when Radha's husband sees her struggling to douse the flames, he immediately rushes past her, lifts up and rescues his mother instead, and leaves his shocked wife to literally fend for herself. Deepa Mehta's film thus lays bare the uninterrogated acceptance of the denigrated wife/idolized mother dichotomy arising out of stereotypical, culturally upheld notions of womanhood and motherhood. Mehta also goes beyond by offering a radical departure in terms of the middle-class woman's transgressive search for pleasure outside the boundaries of an oppressive, patriarchal culture. Rejecting the confining of the maternal within the prison house of privileged male fantasies, the two female protagonists opt to enter a lesbian relationship in which female sexuality is undergirded by care, and romantic love supported by a maternal succor that stands in stark contrast to the disdain and hazardous survival that otherwise marks their life. Through its portrayal of a lesbian bond between two otherwise unlikely partners, the film thus invites the spectator to imagine femininity and the maternal beyond the reproductive relationships acceptable to the patriarchal family unit, and outside the frame of the heterosexual gaze. In doing so, it enables a viewing that brings about a separation between our understanding of the maternal as biological function, and the maternal as an *other* relationality, with the coupling between the two as *not necessarily* natural. Curiously, while a subversive lesbian relationship defined by mutual care enables the film to move against the grain of a privileged heterosexual paradigm, it is the latter—the middle-class patriarchal joint-family structure—that brings the two women together and makes the subversion possible in the first place. Thus, in the film at least, the oppressive, extended patriarchal family unwittingly slices open a space for a mutual female relationality, which can be upended by women and re-deployed in a revised understanding of the maternal.

The relational aspect of motherhood has, of course, been brought to the fore to varying degrees by various psychoanalytic theorists. In her landmark study of mothering, Nancy Chodorow constructs her argument regarding the 'reproduction of mothering' by foregrounding the role of culture in determining the relational and empathetic abilities of women. In the Indian context, both Sudhir Kakar and Stanley Kurtz have noted the significance of the cultural emphasis on relationality in mothering. For instance, Kakar notes that 'in addition to the "virtues" of self-effacement and self-sacrifice, the feminine role in India also crystallizes a woman's connections to others, her embeddedness in a multitude of familial relationships.' (Kakar 1981, 62) Stanley Kurtz's interest seems to be in the phenomenon of group mothering in India (in-law mothers) in reference to his 'model of the Hindu psyche as an ideal type drawn from the characteristic setting of the joint family in traditional, rural India', a focus which he finds to be 'far more productive of insight even in the urban and modern setting than has heretofore been recognized.' (Kurtz 1992, 188) Given this blurring of the rural and urban, 'ideal' and peculiar, and irrespective of regional or class distinctions, the text rushes towards a homogenization of the 'Hindu' child or family. Kurtz focuses primarily on the impact of the group on the child's early development and individuation, as a way of achieving separation from the mother through a learnt 'renunciation'. For instance, he concludes that 'both the child and the mother must realize that the real mother is not, in fact, separate from the in-law mothers. The realization that 'all the mothers are one' permits the mother to share the child, and also permits the child to allow himself to be shared among his various mothers.' (147) Thus, for Kurtz, 'the Hindu pattern is to break the incestuous attachment to the mother by interposing not a rival of the child for the mother but a group of rivals of the mother for the child. This in turn entails a different resolution altogether from that found in the Oedipus complex.' (236) Relationality, here, is a set of shifting lines that centre on the child, and bring into 'his' ambit the mother or other mothers in dyadic alliances, but is hardly ever presented as bringing women into mutually affirming relations with each other. Kurtz's tunnel vision zeroes in on the group in the Indian setting at the cost of all other facets of psychological development. His use of a western model as a comparative yardstick brings him to the conclusion that there is a 'lack of individualized empathy between mother and child in these cultures, the absence of smiling response, or even a feeding experience carefully calibrated to the child's precise emotional state.' (256) In an obviously conciliatory tone, Kurtz apologizes for what may appear to some as a culturally insensitive reading: 'Perhaps the reader wonders whether I argue here that mothers in non-Western cultures do not love their own children. After all, however harsh or radical such a statement would appear, it does seem to be an implication of the position I have taken. Well, I certainly am not asserting that mothers outside the west lack strong positive feelings for their children. On the other hand, I do think we open ourselves to many difficulties if we simply translate these feelings by the use of *our word* and *our concept* of love.' (emphasis added) (259–60) Taking as his 'Indian' model, the very specific Tamilian word '*anpu*', which, because it connotes a love that is hidden, he reads as 'a troubling or damaged kind of love' (260), he adds, 'this collective child rearing works precisely because it is *not* based on the one-to-one empathic link we call love' but rather is a 'culturally distinctive process'. (263–64) Conveniently, Kurtz gives this process a culturally acceptable word, one that would resonate with the history of Hindu tradition—'renunciation' (264)—and contrasts it against an American model so that it becomes clear what it is *not*: 'in the American case,... our basic principle of child rearing is love, and this depends for its function on an intimate, long-term, individualized empathic relationship.' (264) Thus, if we were to follow Kurtz's line of reasoning, it would appear that the typical 'Hindu' child renounces the mother in favour of a group of mothers to resolve 'his' Oedipus complex, while the 'Hindu' mother does not 'love' her child but rather conceals her 'strong positive feelings' to help the child achieve this goal. A careful reading of the 'hidden' aspects of love in the Indian context reveal that what also gets concealed, in the process, is the mother's subjective position in a narrative that foregrounds the child's access to the mother's love.

The insistence on dichotomies such as 'individual' vs. 'group' and 'love' vs. 'renunciation', which lend a culturally essentialist stance to Kurtz's work, has not gone unnoticed by his critics. As observed by Thomas Ellis, 'If Freudians are seduced by the siren of individualism, it would appear that many authors working with non-Western material are similarly seduced by the siren of the group.... Needless to say, this smacks as much of Orientalism as the assignation of pathology to the un-individuated Hindu.' (Ellis 2009, 14) This is not to say, of course, that the joint or extended family does not determine the shape of motherhood in India. However, Kurtz's rush towards identifying the 'difference' of India makes him breeze past his own blind spots, so that he ends up ignoring both individual dynamics and maternal subjectivity in the process. Despite Ellis's and our reservations about Kurtz's Orientalist readings, it must be acknowledged that the traditional Hindu family, as Kakar and others have pointed out, does privilege relationships between the group. The problem in psychoanalytic readings such as Kurtz's is then not so much in the fact that they focus on the role of group dynamics in child psychological development, but rather in the way the group is brought into focus while allowing the individuals (especially women) who constitute the group to fade out into a hazy background. Additionally, while others such as Sudhir Kakar do give considerable space to an account of the relational aspects of Indian women, both Kurtz and Kakar are interested in the child's unconscious rather than the mother's, and thus keep intact the dyadic emphasis of the child-mother pairing. Kakar, in his 'recognition of the crucial role of this original relationship' (Kakar 1981, 52) between mother and child, concludes that 'this mutuality is by far the most important factor in enabling an infant to create a coherent inner image of a basically reassuring world and to lay the foundation for a "true self"'.(55)

Fortunately, feminist scholarship has demonstrated the importance of expanding the notion of relationality beyond the dyadic structure of self and other in which it was bound by conventional psychoanalysis since Freud. Linked with the cultural emphasis on women's relational capacities, it allows us to venture beyond the 'original' relationship that the mother has with her child. Such forays are, of course, not without risk. As pointed out by Emily Jeremiah, the idealization of women's relationality hazards essentialist pitfalls, even while promising dissident feminist potential: 'an emphasis on women's relationality could be viewed as dangerous from a feminist point of view. It could lead to a re-inscription of ideas of women as unstable, excessively emotional and "naturally" inclined to care of others.... But the idea of relationality may also be understood as subversive.' (Jeremiah 2002, 12)

In the context of India, as pointed out by Kakar, women's mutual relations are set within a 'well-defined community of women' who 'are not only an Indian girl's teachers and models but her allies against the discriminations and inequities of that world and its values' creating what he terms, an '"underground" of female culture.' (Kakar 1981, 61–62) Certainly, in *Fire*, any reading of the subversive elements of the lesbian relationship between the two women must be placed in perspective against the larger framework of feminist warnings about the risks of essentialism. But what we can take away from a viewing of films such as *Fire* in the light of Kakar's references to an 'underground of female culture' is the subversive possibility of a cultural grouping which may, at any time, morph itself into a resistive political group.

An expanded notion of relationality is visible in other works as well. Citing recent work by Judith Butler, Steven Botticelli emphasizes Butler's argument that 'relational ties need to be construed more broadly than the dyad'. (Boticelli 2014, 468) Botticelli furthers Butler's view as he interprets it: 'I hear her arguing that relationality needs to be conceived within a larger framework.' (469) Alison Stone also, in her discussion of maternal subjectivity, makes a case for widening the ambit of maternal relationality beyond the conventional mother-child dyad. Stone refers back to Suzanne Juhasz for whom maternal subjectivity consists of multiple relational positions: 'those of mother and child, the mother and her own mother, mother and woman, ideal and real mother.' 'Building on Juhasz', Stone suggests 'that the mother weaves specifically between two relational positions and transposes them upon one another—her past self as child coupled with her own mother, and herself now as the mother of and carer for her child.' (Stone 2014, 334–35) These recent efforts at revisioning maternal relationality in expanding circles, which bring into view the nurturing relationships between women, especially mothers and daughters, offer a stark contrast to earlier paradigms of female jealousy and rivalry in works such as Kurtz's. For Kurtz, 'in traditional Hindu India, the main barrier between the child and his mother at this time is not the father but the in-law mothers. These women, moreover, are not primarily rivals of the child for the love of the mother. Rather, they are rivals of the mother for the love of the child.' (Kurtz 1992, 235) Additionally, Kurtz traces this pattern of rivalry back to Hindu mythology's 'Durga complex': 'A pattern of rivalry among mothers can be identified in the mythology of Durga and related goddesses' (150), which he strangely does not interpret in terms of the patriarchal effects of early Vedic society. In a refreshing contrast, contemporary feminist discourse offers a distinct shift from the pitting of mothers as rivals for the child's attention, moving away from paradigms of jealousy to those of connectivity and mutuality. Contrast Kurtz's 'Durga complex,' for instance, with Bracha Ettinger's 'Demeter-Persephone complex': 'In the Demeter-Persephone complex "hysteria" will receive a relief for meanings of femininities beyond gender. In the Demeter-Persephone configuration, "hysteria" will acquire fruitful new paths to understanding the female-to-female issues of femininity alongside and beyond (the Kleinian) issues of animosity, envy, and jealousy.' (Ettinger 2014, 134)

However, much of the feminist critique of psychoanalysis stops short of exploring affirmative mother-daughter relationships afforded by nuclear family structures to seek out maternal relationality between women beyond the narrow familial. Taking a cue from the 'multiplicity' of maternal relationality brought to the fore by western feminists, and the multiple, fluid identities created within traditional familial and social structures in India as pointed out by Kakar, Kurtz and others, I suggest that feminist insights may be productively deployed in the context of re-visioning maternal relationality in India and beyond. Thus, for example, in a subversive move, we may use our recognition of an unwitting effect of patriarchal kinship structures—that of bringing together victims of heteronormative oppression in close contact—to see how this effect opens up a space for rebellion and transgression through multiple subversions of motherhood ideology, and a revisioning of new maternal relationalities (as seen, for instance, in Deepa Mehta's *Fire*).

Here, Hadara Katzav's suggestion that motherhood and femininity are not completely removed from one another is particularly helpful: 'in regard to the relationship between motherhood and femininity... it can be seen that there are cases in which this relationship does not incur a mutual exclusion, but clearly each is derived from the other. Such a relationship is precisely the way by which to establish sexuation that enables the potential of the "other *jouissance*" that which will express, not the desire to fill the lack but, rather the partial or constant presence of the relationship with the other woman.' (Katzav 2014, 315) The 'relationship with the other woman' referred to here is evocative of an expanding maternality which refuses to be reduced to the phallic dyadic structure of presence and absence set up by post-Freudian theory. In such an expansion, it may bring us closer to naming, without fear, the availing of maternal pleasure by women in relationships with other women at the level of sexuation rather than sexuality, and locating the maternal not only amongst women but within a larger homosocial structure of mutuality. Thus, moving away from a narrative which rests solely on sexuality, one may secure other equally valuable emotional components such as compassion. For Bracha Ettinger, compassion, is not only a dominant marker of the primary relationship between mother and infant, but also enables a therapeutic model for the interface between analyst and patient: 'I view the effect of primary compassion as a primal psychic access to the other.... Compassion signals contact and connection, yet it is not reactive. Contacting yet not being reactive—here is a psychic potential for subjective freedom.' (Ettinger 2010, 1)

A lack of compassion, according to Ettinger, leads to hatred towards the mother, and the construction of 'mother-monsters' which obstruct the perception of a complex maternal subjectivity and keep it restricted to its predetermined constructions: 'Systematic empathy (to the other—the patient) without compassion and respect (to the other's others)—coupled with systematic offering of the ready-made mother-monster (as an automatic cause of suffering) that gives rise to mother-hate—leads to a fixation in a "basic fault" positioning while delegitimizing and dehumanizing maternal subjectivity.' (Ettinger 2010, 4)

Work such as Ettinger's opens up the possibility of experiencing the capacity for relationality beyond the mother-child dyad, and in relation to the pleasures afforded by the community. Thus, the 'failure' of motherhood defined in relation to the purely biological, may be rebutted by the success of pleasures experienced in a revised maternal relationality beyond the anatomical.

In reference to the notion of 'failed' mothers who search for pleasures in their relationships with other women, an interesting contrast to the film *Fire* is presented in Manju Kapur's novel *A Married Woman* (2002).

The novel traces the struggles for personal freedom of its heroine, Astha (whose name means 'faith'), who is trapped in an arranged marriage to an upwardly mobile middle class Indian man, Hemant. With a successful, ambitious husband and two children behind her, Astha seems to live the Indian woman's dream.

> Astha often looked at her family, husband, daughter, son. She had them all. She was fulfilled. Her in-laws frequently commented, 'Woman is earth,' and it is true she felt bounteous, her life one of giving and receiving, surrounded by plenty. Visitors to the house would say, 'A mother's love' and then trail off, words collapsing into significant silence, which in turn washed over Astha and made her feel that she had partaken of the archetypal experiences marked out for the female race. (69)

The superficial nature of this fulfilment, however, soon begins to weigh on the artistically inclined Astha, who begins to question her life, and search for meaning in art and politics. In sharp contrast to the short-lived bountiful existence is a gnawing realization.

> Well, Astha was a woman, and she was sick of sacrifice. She didn't want to be pushed around in the name of family. She was fed up with the ideal of Indian womanhood, used to trap and jail. Excuse me, stop the juggernaut and let me off. (168)

Astha gets off the 'juggernaut' by joining an activist theatre group, taking part in political rallies and protests, much to the chagrin of her conservative husband, and venting her feelings on canvas. Drawn to the unconventional life, she ends up finding love in the arms of a politically and intellectually vibrant woman, Pipee. Although the relationship with Pipee presents a temporary refuge from the sham of normative marital and maternal comforts, Astha is unable to abandon these comforts, and Pipee, realizing the futility of continuing, flies off to an American university for graduate study. Unlike the ending in *Fire*, the relationship between Astha and Pipee easily crumbles under the overwhelming demands as well as lures of heterosexually defined marriage and motherhood. At the end of the novel, Astha remains tied to the vestiges of her marriage, 'stretched thin, thin across the globe'. (307)

Thus, women's search for pleasures beyond the heterosexually defined relationships of adulthood becomes possible only through a hazardous escape from the patriarchal paradigm which sets women up as rivals for the phallus. *Fire* and *A Married Woman* are examples of such possibilities, but they remain the exception rather than the rule. As exceptions, they encourage us to ask if it is possible to relocate the maternal at some other place of pleasure, once it is extricated from all of its oppressive aspects such as its forced, unilateral burden on biological mothers, and their subservient performance of idealized maternal roles. They also urge us to interrogate the locating of maternal pleasures solely within the constricted space of the heterosexual family, and to expand our understanding of maternal *jouissance* beyond its borders, to 'clarify the woman-to-woman non-sexual Eros, a love that enters heterosexuality and homosexuality equally.' (Ettinger 2014, 133)

This said, the literary and cinematic works discussed above are equal evidence that the detrimental effects of patriarchy on women's relationality are hardly mitigated by the occasional maternally informed lesbian bond. Patriarchal kinship structures are also responsible for institutionalizing exogamy, and the forced separation of mothers and adult daughters through marriage in adulthood. It is this culturally widespread practice of the severance of the newly married bride from her childhood home, and its resultant melancholia, which has led to its pervasive metaphorization as a kind of death, in poetry, cinema and music. In a well-known song by Nawab Wajid Ali Shah, the poet's forced exile from his homeland (Lucknow) during the British Raj is imaged as the bride's departure from her *naihar* (the matrixial home of childhood), and simultaneously as death, a leaving behind of everything familiar on a journey into the unknown. On this journey, the bride, departing from her father's house, is carried in a palanquin supported by four bearers, just as a coffin would be:

The four bearers lift my palanquin

I'm leaving those who were my own.

(Song: 'Baabul mora naihar chooto hi jaaye'. Film: *Street Singer*, 1937, lyrics by Wajid Ali Shah. http://en.wikipedia.org/wiki/)

The lament about the forced departure from the parental home, the *naihar* or the *maika* as it is commonly referred to in the north, thus becomes entrenched in women's folklore as a sign of the psychological trauma experienced by the Indian bride. Kakar describes the world of the matrimonial home as 'alien, often threatening, and sometimes humiliating' (Kakar 1981, 72), and a stage during which the psychological development of the young bride is still incomplete. This trauma, which marks the event of an irreversible chasm between mother and daughter, brings with it a parallel recognition, that the widely discussed infantile separation from the mother is primarily a male (son's) narrative. Kakar points out that mother-daughter relationships in India are marked by the 'culturally sanctioned maternal indulgence of daughters' and the mother's attitude to her daughter is 'normally leavened with a good deal of compassion.' (Kakar 1981, 63)

> Before her departure for her husband's family and household, a very special relationship tends to develop between an Indian girl and her mother, who becomes at this time her daughter's confidante and counselor in the bewildering turmoil of adolescence and the newness of the prospect of marriage... the daughter none the less seeks to recreate the emotional closeness to the protective mother of her childhood. (71)

For the Indian daughter, the separation from her mother in adulthood may end up displacing her onto the platform of either melancholy or hysteria. If, as Ranjana Khanna describes it, melancholy is 'an affective state caused by the inability to assimilate a loss, and the consequent nagging return of the thing lost into psychic life' (2003, 16–17), then it is this struggle to resolve by any means possible the irrevocable loss of childhood ties that will haunt the young bride forcibly removed from her parental home. An inability to resolve the trauma, may, as seen in the 'The Goddess', portend the onset of manic reactions. Seen in this light, the hysteric is someone whose nonsensical acts and utterances only mimic the insane world of which she struggles to make sense. Escaping it, she crosses over into a transgressive zone, a place reserved, as Cixous describes it, for the excluded of society: 'Somewhere every culture has an imaginary zone for what it excludes, and it is that zone we must try to remember *today*.' (Cixous 1986a, 6)

Coalitions

The narrative of displacement is not, however, a singular narrative restricted to India. Western feminists have, in fact, viewed displacement as a particularly western concern. According to Sandra Gilbert, homelessness is a feminine narrative in patriarchy, 'but returning, a sorceress and a hysteric—that is a displaced person—everywoman must inevitably find that she has no home, no *where*.' (Meaney 1993, 9) Forced to let go of the mother, and made subservient to the law, the daughter acquiesces to the patriarchal contract. For Cixous, the daughter's giving up of the mother is akin to a submerging of the self, or as Gerardine Meaney interprets it, 'the quest to escape the mother is a denial of self.' (44)

Interestingly, while Kurtz saw renunciation as the non-western counterpart to western love, Alison Stone reads the renouncing of the mother as a particularly western cultural demand and challenges the denial of maternal subjectivity it effects, since for her, 'maternal subjectivity is a specific form of subjectivity that is continuous with the maternal body.' (Stone 2014, 329) Defiantly, she adds that, 'contrary to Western tradition, we do *not* have to renounce our mothers in order to become selves.' (336) Stone's reading, juxtaposed against Kurtz's, may help us to identify the renunciation of the maternal body not in terms of culture, but in terms of a gendered effect, i.e., patriarchy's insistence on the castration of the self from the feminine maternal. Such an understanding would bring us closer to the kind of transnational feminist coalitions spoken of by Ranjana Khanna. Just as Chandra Mohanty has previously argued for a 'feminist solidarity across borders', which is based in 'grounded particularized analyses' (Mohanty 2003, 223), Khanna, while acknowledging the importance of 'difference' in the postcolonial context, argues for a 'transnational feminism' since 'feminist interaction across national borders does not exist simply because of globalization; rather it exists because of the *idea* that women internationally are materially oppressed *because they are women*.' (Khanna 2003, 214)

If a delineation of oppression is common to feminist discourse, so is, in a Foucauldian sense, the archaeology of resistance. It is owing to this ongoing confrontation that a feminist reading of maternal subjectivities and desires across cultures continues to unearth both oppressions and, to use Kristeva's term 'revolutions'. A maternal idea resistant to its own typologies allows us to view it as a disruption of history, so that we can recognize in it something more than what Simone de Beauvoir perceptively identified as an enslavement—the 'servitude of maternity'. (deBeauvoir 1949, 35) Delineating feminism's conflicted relationship with the maternal, Gerardine Meaney has pointed to two 'strands of thought' which have marked the relationship: 'One concentrates on maternity as exile from history, the other on the maternal as a powerful disruption of the linear history from which women have been excluded.' (Meaney 1993, 78) An examination of fictional works from India clearly shows evidence of both impulses—exile and disruption. More importantly, what such works also illuminate is the path that can lead us from one to the other. That it is literature and cinema which bring to light these possibilities points to the significance of the discourse of representation in acting as a disrupter of (his)story, in a search for other pleasures, and a precursor to what has been called, in recent works, the 'maternal aesthetic'. (Jeremiah 2002, 10)

Maternal Aesthetic, Subjectivity, Pleasure

The pleasure signified by the maternal aesthetic presents a departure from phallic pleasure. According to Hadara Katzav,

> In contrast to phallic pleasure, these aspects of maternal subjectivity are not subject to the Oedipal mechanism. Instead, they enable another experience of pleasure, bound up,... by means of art, in the possibility of reconstructing the partial lost relationship that had existed in the womb. (Katzav 2014, 300)

Thus, if the maternal aesthetic alludes to an ability to dive into the memory of the proximity to the matrixial space in order to re-find that pleasure in creativity, or in Katzav's words, to open up 'the possibility for another jouissance resulting from retracing the pre-natal relationship' (308), can we then, like Emily Jeremiah, envision 'the notion of a maternal aesthetic', as 'political strategy'? (Jeremiah 2002, 10) Certainly, works ranging from Kate Chopin's *Awakening*, to Manju Kapur's *A Married Woman* allude to the search for aesthetic satisfactions and a concurrent escape from the stifling life of marriage and motherhood. And while none of them pretends to collapse the pleasures of art with maternal pleasures, they do mark a singular identification between the maternal and art at the place of relationality, that is, as work which incorporates a satisfying rapport with an Other.

Pushing the boundaries of this exploration, Bracha Ettinger's artwork and writing offer the 'matrixial space' as an alternative to the phallocentric analyses of relationality, and a movement towards what Ettinger describes as a 'transubjective dimension', which she posits in the context of the Demeter-Persephone myth: 'Rethinking the feminine in terms of the Demeter-Persephone complex and bringing the shocks of maternality and the Eros of borderlinking into account is part of my project to rethink the human subject as infused by the transubjective dimension.' (Ettinger 2014, 123)

Reading Ettinger's project from the perspective of queer theory, Sudeep Dasgupta sees in her work the possibility of an alliance with the project of delineating queer subjectivity in terms of a relationality mapped out beyond the individualistic model: 'I am tempted to suggest that the focus on relationality in Ettinger's theorization of matrixial subjectivity might help re-direct the focus on deconstructing subjectivity in queer theory, broadening out the latter's emphasis on self-shattering toward a politics based on forging alliances and a being-together between several selves rather than individual dissolution and dissipation.' (Dasgupta 2009) The reference to 'several selves' is reminiscent here of the multiple ways in which feminist theorists have attempted to map out maternal relationality, and speaks at the same time, to works which cast lesbian relationships in the context of a revised maternal.

Bracha Ettinger's work also shows that the relationality inherent in maternal subjectivities resonates with a sublimated relationality with art, inviting mothers to invert the image of the male artist writing on the body of the mother. Writing against the maxim that 'Mothers don't write, they are written' (Suleiman 1985, 356), and contrary to Roland Barthes' declaration that 'the writer is someone who plays with his mother's body' (Barthes 1975, 37), Susan Suleiman reminds us about the infantalization of the artist in psychoanalysis: 'Psychoanalytic theory invariably places the artist, man or woman, in the position of the child. Just as motherhood is ultimately the child's drama, so is artistic creation.' (Suleiman 1985, 357) Suleiman attributes this mother-child drama to the fact that 'psychoanalysis is nothing if not a theory of childhood' (358), leading her to conclude that 'It is time to let mothers have their word.' (360) In continuance with Cixous's famous call for 'writing the body' with the 'white ink' of 'good mother milk' (Cixous 1986b, 94) and the association between mothering and artistic production, Emily Jeremiah observes that 'literary production is also a relational business...' (Jeremiah 2002, 12), while Ettinger embodies this other relationality through her artwork.[8]

What does it take, then, for the mother to write, to express herself through art? What disruptive language is available to her, if any, in the tunnels and recesses of the memory of matrixial space? In Gilbert and Gubar's *No Man's Land*, we find an early inkling to this puzzle: 'It seems clear that women's imaginary languages, unlike men's, are for the most part founded on a celebration of the primacy both of the mother tongue and the tongue of the mother' they say, adding that 'for these artists, the lure of the mother's lore always takes precedence over what Lacan calls the "Law of the Father."' (Gilbert and Gubar 1988, 262) Noticeably, Gilbert's and Gubar's juxtaposition of the 'word' as embodiment of 'female power' is not that far removed from the concept of the pre-Vedic goddess of language, *Vac*: 'But the very fact that one can metaphorize the mouth as a womb, the Word as the child of female power, implies that women need not experience any ontological alienation from the idea of language as we know it.' (265) Supplementing this with our knowledge of contemporary feminist work in this direction, we might add, that neither do they need to experience an ongoing alienation from the maternal body.

It is then a revised maternal subjectivity that promises the possibility of delving into the matrixial space to find the mother within—women who will mother and nurture themselves, and in positive relationships with other women, each other. Moving beyond oppressive histories in the future, one can anticipate that women, who are daughters before they become mothers, will be able to disrupt these histories in order to bring forth a re-telling of maternal narratives. Inscribing new maternal subjectivities in literature, art and film can help to rummage through the recesses of representation, and bring to light an enabling maternal metaphor employed in productive links to the real. The 'feminist insight', as Susan Suleiman has proposed, allows us to see 'that the stories we tell about reality *construe* the real, rather than merely reflect it. Whence the possibility, or the hope, that through the re-writing of old stories and the invention of new forms of language for doing so, it is the world as well as words that will be transformed.' (Suleiman 1990, 143)

However, any route whose goal is the search of pleasure has to pass by, rather than by-pass, oppression. According to Luce Irigaray, 'In order for a woman to arrive at the point where she can enjoy her pleasure as a woman, a long detour through the analysis of the various systems of oppression which affect her is certainly necessary.' (Irigaray 1985, 105) A singular insistence on the search for pleasure which ignores the oppressive ways in which ideologies pertaining to women, such as that of motherhood, are defined, may run 'the risk of missing the reconsideration of a social practice upon which *her* pleasure depends.' (105) Thus, while we work on alleviating the material conditions which oppress women and mothers, the dream of pleasure that germinates in a maternal aesthetic provides, at the minimum, a blueprint for a better future. In such an anticipation, it is helpful to have in place both short-term and long-term plans at the level of the real, as well as at that of the imagination. As far as the material conditions against which Indian women grapple, one reflection of positive transformations is the changes in women's social and economic roles as more women begin to work outside the home, and as these begin to effect changes on the re-shaping of motherhood ideologies. In a conversation with Madhu Sarin, Sudhir Kakar acknowledges the extent to which such changes are impacting the roles of both fathers and mothers, especially amongst the urban Indian middle classes:

> The ideology impinging on traditional fathers in India (in common with other patriarchal societies), which was of a gender based dichotomy in parenting roles and obligations, is now changing. In the older ideology, there were decided notions of things that men do in household and childcare, and others that they don't. Playing with or taking care of their infant and small sons was not what fathers did; their major role lay in the disciplining of the child.... The second major change is the one you mention about the altered self perception and role of the Indian woman. Hers is perhaps the driving force in the changes taking place in the Indian family, an institution that is inherently conservative and changes at a much slower pace than political, economic and other institutions of society. Slowly, but surely, the middle class woman is pushing the family towards a greater acknowledgment, grudging or otherwise, of the importance (if not yet the primacy) of the marital bond. A greater individuation of the child will be an inevitable consequence of this psychological nuclearization within the joint family, as also a boost in the pleasure and sorrows of individuality. (Kakar 2008, 179)

Curiously, although Kakar describes women as 'the driving force' behind the change, he sees the child as the principle beneficiary of the social transformations, leaving it up to others to pursue questions of shifting maternal subjectivities. As we have seen, creative representations of pathways of resistance, and the exploration of re-visioned maternal subjectivities through the revolutionary potential of art provide an essential complement to traditional psychoanalytic delineations of the maternal psyche, especially in India.

Conclusion

Feminist discourse has tracked an evident shift in the way maternal subjectivity is constructed, in response to an urgent need to anticipate maternal identities beyond paradigms of oppression. If dreams are indeed the pathways to our unconscious, as Freud famously declared, then it is time to interpret the mother's dreams alongside the child's. 20th-century works like 'The Goddess' and the 'The Breast-Giver' postulate the hysteric's disruptive act to interrupt imposed maternal ideologies, or to fantasize about an escape from the dichotomy of oppression and idolization. More recent examples like *Fire* and *A Married Woman* indicate the possibility of exploring new maternal subjectivities. Illuminated by feminist insights, the recognition of revised relationalities between women and women's right not to be alienated from the maternal body can be used to explore a maternal aesthetic which impinges upon and disrupts the real. Thus, it may be re-deployed as a political tool, both at the level of the symbolic and as a way of actively constituting a political solidarity against patriarchy through cross-cultural coalitions.

Notes

1. See, for instance, Rich 1976 Suleiman 1990 and Miller 1996.
2. See list of works cited by Bracha Ettinger, Alison Stone and Julie Rodgers.
3. See, for instance, Patrice DeQuinzio's critique of Sara Ruddick's concept of 'Maternal Thinking' in *The Impossibility of Motherhood: Feminism, Individualism and the Problem of Mothering* (Routledge, 1999).
4. Nancy Chodorow argues that 'the elimination of the present organization of parenting in favor of a system of parenting in which both men and women are responsible would be a tremendous social advance.' (pp. 219) For a detailed discussion, see 1978.
5. For one possible source for Freud's discussion of links between dreams and myths, see Freud 1908. See also Edmunds 1990, 424.
6. See the discussion on the role of ancient mother-goddesses in the previous chapter.
7. See Tagore 2014
8. See, for instance, artwork by Bracha Ettinger in her work Ettinger 2014, 146–54.

References

Allen, Jeffner. 'Motherhood: The Annihilation of Women'. In *Mothering: Essays in Feminist Theory*, edited by Joyce Treblicot. Maryland: Rowman & Littlefield, 1983, pp. 315–30.
Bagchi, Jasodhara. 'Representing Nationalism: Ideology of Motherhood in Colonial Bengal'. In *Motherhood in India: Glorification without Empowerment*, edited by Maithreyi Krishnaraj. New Delhi: Routledge, 2010, pp. 158–85.
Barthes, Roland. *The Pleasure of the Text*. New York: Hill and Wang, 1975.
deBeauvoir, Simone. *The Second Sex*. London: Vintage/Random House, 2010. Originally published in French in 1949.
Benjamin, Jessica. *Bonds of Love: Psychoanalysis, Feminism and the Problem of Domination*. New York: Pantheon, 1988.

Botticelli, Steven. 'Globalization, Psychoanalysis, and the Provision of Care'. In *Mothering & Psychoanalysis: Clinical, Sociological and Feminist Perspectives*, edited by Petra Bueskens. Bradford: Demeter Press, 2014, pp. 463–71.
Chodorow, Nancy. *The Reproduction of Mothering*. Berkeley: University of California Press, 1978.
Cixous, Hélène. *'Le rire de la medusa'*. 1975. ('The Laugh of the Medusa', translated by Keith and Paula Cohen. In *Signs* 1 (4). 1976, pp. 875–99.) Reprint *New French Feminisms*, edited by Elaine Marks and Isabelle de Courtivron, 1989.
——. *'Le sexe ou la tete'* in *Les Cahiers du GRIF*, 13. 1976, pp. 5–15. ('Castration or Decapitation', translated by Annette Kuhn. In *Signs* 7. 1981.)
——. 'The Guilty One'. In *The Newly Born Woman*, edited by Hélène Cixous and Catherine Clément, translated by Betsy Wing. Minneapolis: University of Minnesota Press, 1986, pp. 3–57.
——. 'Sorties'. In *The Newly Born Woman*, edited by Hélène Cixous and Catherine Clément, translated by Betsy Wing. Minneapolis: University of Minnesota Press, 1986, pp. 63–132.
Dasgupta, Sudeep. 'Resonances and Disjunctions: Subjectivity and Queer theory', *Studies in the Maternal*, 1 (2), 2009. www.mamsie.bbk.ac.uk
Devi, Mahasweta. 'The Breast-Giver'. In *In Other Worlds*, Gayatri Chakravorty Spivak. New York: Methuen. 1987.
Doniger, Wendy. *Hindu Myths*. New York: Penguin, 1975.
Edmunds, Lowell (Ed.), Approaches to Greek Myths. Baltimore, MD: Johns Hopkins University Press, 1990.
Ellis, Thomas B. 'I Love You, I Hate You: Toward a Psychology of the Hindu "Deus Absconditus"', *International Journal of Hindu Studies*, Vol 13, No. 1. 2009, pp 1–23.
Ettinger, Bracha L. '(M)Other Re-spect: Maternal Subjectivity, the Ready-made Mother-monster and the Ethics of Respecting', *Studies in the Maternal*, 2 (1), 2010. (http://www.mamsie.bbk.ac.uk/documents/ettinger.pdf. Accessed 30 January 2014.)
Ettinger, Bracha L. 'Demeter-Persephone Complex, Entangled Aerials of the Psyche, and Sylvia Plath'. In *English Studies in Canada*, Vol. 40, No. 1. 2014, pp. 123–54 (Project Muse, Accessed 30 January 2015).
Felman, Shoshana. *Jacques Lacan and the Adventure of Insight: Psychoanalysis in Contemporary Culture*. Cambridge: Harvard University Press, 1987.
Freud, Sigmund. *The Interpretation of Dreams*. In *The Standard Edition of the Complete Psychological Works of Sigmund Freud*, translated by James Strachey, 1900.
Giffney, Noreen, Anne Mulhall and Michael O'Rourke. 'Seduction into Reading: Bracha L. Ettinger's *The Matrixial Borderspace*'. In *Studies in the Maternal*, 1 (2). 2009 (www.mamsie.bbk.ac.uk. Accessed 30 January 2014)
Gilbert, Sandra M. and Susan Gubar. *No Man's Land: The Place of the Woman Writer in the Twentieth Century*. Vol. 1. New Haven: Yale University Press, 1988.
Hirsch, Marianne. 'Mothers and Daughters'. In *Signs*, Vol. 7, No. 1. 1981, pp. 200–22.

Irigaray, Luce. *This Sex Which Is Not One,* translated by Catherine Porter. Ithaca: Cornell University Press, 1985.
Jeremiah, Emily. 'Troublesome Practices: Mothering, Literature & Ethics', in *Mothering and Literature.* Journal of the Association for Research on Mothering. Vol. 4, No. 2. Fall/Winter 2002, pp. 7–16.
Kakar, Sudhir. *The Inner World.* New Delhi: Oxford University Press, 1981.
Kakar, Sudhir. *Intimate Relations: Exploring Indian Sexuality.* New Delhi: Penguin, 1989.
Kakar, Sudhir. 'Psychanalyse et Religion: Une Réévaluation' In *La Folle et Le Saint,* edited by Catherine Clément and Sudhir Kakar. Paris: Seuil, 1993.
Kakar, Sudhir and Madhu Sarin. 'A Conversation with Sudhir Kakar' *India International Centre Quarterly,* Vol. 35, No. 2. 2008, pp. 168–82. (http://www.jstor.org/stable/23006365. Accessed 3 December 2014)
Katzav, Hadara Scheflan. 'Artistic Expressions of Maternal *Jouissance* – Beyond the Phallus'. In *Mothering & Psychoanalysis: Clinical, Sociological and Feminist Perspectives,* edited by Petra Bueskens. Bradford: Demeter Press, 2014, pp. 299–321.
Khanna, Ranjana. *Dark Continents: Psychoanalysis and Colonialism.* London: Duke University Press, 2003.
Kurtz, Stanley. *All the Mothers Are One: Hindu India and the Cultural Reshaping of Psychoanalysis.* New York: Columbia University Press, 1992.
MacCannell, Juliet Flower. 'Mothers of Necessity: Psychoanalysis for Feminism', *American Literary History,* Vol. 3, No. 3. 1991, pp. 623–47.
Meaney, Gerardine. *(Un)Like Subjects: Women, Theory, Fiction.* New York: Routledge, 1993.
Mehta, Deepa. *Fire* (Film), 1996.
Miller, Nancy, *Bequest & Betrayal.* Oxford: Oxford University Press, 1996.
Mohanty, Chandra. *Feminism Without Borders.* Durham: Duke University Press, 2003.
Mukhopadhyay, Prabhat Kumar. 'The Goddess'. In *14 Stories That Inspired Satyajit Ray,* edited and translated by Bhaskar Chattopadhyay. New Delhi: Harper Collins India, 2014.
Ray, Satyajit. *Devi* (Film), 1960.
Rich, Adrienne. *Of Woman Born.* Norton, 1976.
Rodgers, Julie. 'Exploring the Possibility of a Positive Maternal Subjectivity: An Introduction to Lisa Baraitser's *Maternal Encounters: The Ethics of Interruption'.* In *Mothering & Psychoanalysis: Clinical, Sociological and Feminist Perspectives,* edited by Petra Bueskens. Bradford: Demeter Press, 2014, pp. 375–90.
Ruddick, Sara. 'Maternal Thinking'. In *Mothering: Essays in Feminist Theory,* edited by Joyce Treblicot. Maryland: Rowman & Littlefield, 1983, pp. 213–30.
Spivak, Gayatri Chakravorty. 'French Feminism in an International Frame'. In *In Other Worlds.* New York: Methuen, 1987.
Spivak, Gayatri Chakravorty. 'The Politics of Translation'. In *Outside in the Teaching Machine.* New York: Routledge, 1993, pp. 179–200.

Stone, Alison. 'Psychoanalysis and Maternal Subjectivity'. In *Mothering & Psychoanalysis: Clinical, Sociological and Feminist Perspectives*, edited by Petra Bueskens. Bradford: Demeter Press, 2014, pp. 325–41.

Suleiman, Susan. 'Writing and Motherhood'. In *The (M)Other Tongue: Essays in Feminist Psychoanalytic Interpretation*, edited by Shirley N. Garner, Claire Kahane and Madelon Sprengnether. Ithaca: Cornell University Press, 1985, pp. 352–77.

———. 'Feminist Intertextuality and the Laugh of the Mother'. In *Subversive Intent: Gender, Politics and the Avant-Garde*. Cambridge: Harvard University Press, 1990, pp. 141–80.

Tagore, Sharmila. 'My Experiences with Devi'. In 'P.S.: Insights, Interviews and More', *14 Stories That Inspired Satyajit Ray*, edited by Bhaskar Chattopadhyay. New Delhi: Harper Collins India, 2014.

Treblicot, Joyce (ed.). *Mothering: Essays in Feminist Theory*. Maryland: Rowman & Littlefield, 1983.

3

'Mere Paas Maa Hai': Reflections on representations of motherhood in Hindi cinema

> Whether her family is poor or wealthy, whatever her caste, class or region, whether she is a fresh young bride or exhausted by many pregnancies and infancies already, an Indian woman knows that motherhood confers upon her a purpose and identity that nothing else in her culture can. Each child born and nurtured by her safely into childhood, especially if the child is a son, is both a certification and redemption.
>
> —Kakar 2008, 56

Introduction

Sudhir Kakar's pithy observation on motherhood in Hindu India encapsulates the social and ideological weight accorded to the maternal role and its centrality in gender ideology. It is as a mother of sons that her existence gains value; '*putravati bhavo*' (may you be the mother of sons) is a blessing routinely given to a new bride by the elders in the family. The representation of the mother figure in myth, folklore, art, literature and popular culture has engaged feminists across disciplinary boundaries and earlier chapters in this volume have dealt with it in detail. This chapter reflects upon the construction of the ideology of motherhood using illustrations from mainstream Hindi cinema. The universe of Indian cinema is a fertile ground for gender theorizing and this chapter revisits the much-travelled terrain and familiar texts that have become an inextricable part of how we imagine ourselves as Indian mothers and citizens of Mother India. It traces the co-option of motherhood into a masculinist world-view that reinforces patriarchal social structures and cultural prescriptions, and simultaneously opens up the possibilities for a reframing of motherhood through an engagement with different subjectivities and ways of being in the world, as new themes and new filmmakers question and complicate the meanings of motherhood in contemporary India.

Cinema is an important cultural resource for generations of Indians, like the author, who has grown up with its images, music and melodramas; it is not just an objective reality 'out there' but an indelible living memory that is internalized and absorbed and constitutive of our collective identity. In the words of Christopher Pinney (2011), 'In a nation as dramatically divided as India, there are some curious places of shared desire: the melodies of Hindi film songs, the curves of Amitabh's or Madhuri's bodies, the vivid materiality of popular visual culture.' (1) This chapter emerges out of an engagement with Indian cinema as an 'insider' whose cultural competence is profoundly shaped by it as well as a feminist social scientist trained to analyze and critique social reality and cultural products with a gendered lens. Following Karen Gabriel (2010), I use the term 'mainstream' rather than 'popular' or 'commercial' to denote a particular kind of film that 'explores and engages, in particular, with issues that it hopes will be well received by popular imagination, sentiment and politics, even as it is also formative of them.'(xxvi) As the primary driver behind such cinema is commercial success, the themes it takes up are necessarily those that find a resonance with a vast and heterogeneous audience, and its narratives tend to conform to dominant social and political ideologies. It attempts to create a 'national' audience by 'sculpting and defining the diverse philosophies and values of a heterogeneous audience into a singular "coherent" national sensibility.' (xxvii) It therefore tends to homogenize and simplify the complexities of Indian society, and provide a formula of what constitutes 'Indianness'. Asha Kasbekar (2001) designates the Hindi film as a 'something for everyone' project; a bricolage that combines 'visual pleasures' from different genres in the same film and providing its socially and ethnically diverse audience the spectacle they seek. (289) In particular, Kasbekar draws attention to the complex situation and position of the female spectator who is both fetishized as a 'commodity' in screen portrayals and is simultaneously a paying 'consumer' who views and participates in her own commodification. (290)

> Every Hindi film in search of commercial success must not only identify the desire for different kinds of pleasures… but it must also accommodate sometimes incompatible desires within the same film and make them concordant with the existing cultural and moral values of the society in which it circulates. Such social and moral pressures force complex negotiations and contestations within any filmic text that wishes to successfully mediate between the state, the industry, and the audience. (290)

The Hindi film industry located in Mumbai has a century-old history, and its resonance and reach is immense and multi-layered. Films are much more than popular entertainment in contemporary India; they construct and redefine identities, provide aspirational agendas, reinforce and challenge cultural values. Described as 'the opium of the Indian masses' by Gokulsing and Dissanayake (1998, 88), 'Bollywood', as the creative and commercial universe of the Mumbai film industry is affectionately called, has a global outreach. The vast and proliferating Indian diaspora has emerged as a key market. It thus provides a rich and complex resource for the social scientist to map continuity and change in the socio-cultural landscape. Bollywood cinema also reflects upon issues of community, gender, family, individualism, social justice, identity and nationhood through its primary function of 'entertainment', characterized by melodramatic plots, song and dance, elaborately staged fights and chases. The Mumbai film industry is an essentially syncretic and secular space that has made room for persons of all caste, class and religious backgrounds, and is often touted as an exemplar of pluralism and multi-culturalism in a society riven by divides based upon primordial identities. A recent telling example is the phenomenal commercial success of Rajkumar Hirani's film *PK* (2014) which had Aamir Khan (one of the Khan triumvirate along with Shahrukh and Salman Khan, who have been the most popular leading men for the past quarter of a century) as the 'hero'. The film was accused by some of making fun of Hindu gods and spiritual leaders; a charge that was magnified by the fact that the lead actor was a Muslim. However, this did not deter the audiences from flocking to theatres.

Creativity and marketability have been the major criteria for success, however the logic of the marketplace ensures that the Hindi film reinforces and validates the world-view of the society within which it is embedded. However, as we shall later see in the chapter, there have been a few recent attempts by a new generation of filmmakers to question and challenge existing cultural stereotypes, which have received startling commercial success and critical acclaim. Unlike 'art-house cinema', which has had a parallel existence along with the mainstream, these new films unabashedly claim commercial space even as they tweak the winning formulae and the condiments in the 'masala'.

The figure of the mother forms the moral epicentre of the cinematic universe, and is in a sense the lynchpin that holds together the diverse and often incoherent pieces of the plot. She is the glue that binds together warring brothers; the inspiration that causes men to perform noble deeds; the epitome of sacrifice and selflessness. Even in the staged fight sequences, which form an essential ingredient of many a potboiler, men invoke the power of mother's milk when they challenge their opponents: 'agar ma ka doodh piya hai to mera saamna karo' (if you are a man who has drunk his mother's milk, then come on and face me). (Riaz 2013, 167) In a socio-cultural setting where motherhood can be described as 'glorification without empowerment' (Krishnaraj 2010) the complex imaginings of the mother provide rich material for discussion, as the previous chapters have underscored. Hindi cinema has universalized and essentialized what an 'Indian' mother ought to look, think and act like. Thus, she is almost inevitably clad in traditional garb—a saree or salwar kameez, the yardage and drape of the saree reflecting an upper-caste and class identity even if the character she portrays is that of a poor woman. If she is a *suhaagan* (one whose husband is alive), the markers of her 'blessed' status, like *sindoor* (vermilion, applied in the parting of the hair) and glass bangles are prominently displayed. If she is a widow, her austere whites and absence of ornamentation are highlighted. Irrespective of the socio-economic class she is shown to occupy, her value system is rooted in a caste-Hindu template, which derives from scriptural sanctions and prescriptions. The notion of the 'ideal Hindu woman' is exemplified in her persona; her trials, tribulations and sacrifices made for the larger good of the extended family are valorized; she is celebrated in songs that have an almost devotional fervour. From S. D. Burman's plaintive *'meri duniya hai maa tere aanchal mein'* (mother, my world is your presence) to the feelings of a vulnerable child in Taare Zameen Par (2007)—*'tujhe sab hai pataa, meri maa'* (mother, you know it all)—the emotional weight of the relationship is reiterated and raised to a mythic plane. The story of the mother can also be read as the story of the nation, as mainstream cinema has also been a key player in constructing the narrative of the nation. (Mishra 2002; Virdi 2003)

Jyotika Virdi (2003) maps the manner in which film narratives configure the nation, providing an account of its social history and cultural politics. This chapter too attempts to capture key moments in the socio-political history of the nation and the manner in which these resonated in the representation of the mother in select films that enjoyed huge popularity and achieved 'cult' status. Hindi cinema has always been a mirror reflecting social realities, and has spun morality tales drawn from a rich repository of myth and cultural symbols.

Films produced during the phase of the national movement and after Independence became a site for the reinvention of the newly emergent nation, breaking free of colonial subjugation and preparing itself to script a great future. The conflation of Mother India with the ideal Indian woman emerging out of servitude and reclaiming her lost glory through the deeds of her dutiful sons emphasized nationalist ideals and the aspirations of the newly emergent nation state which had shed the yoke of two centuries of colonial subjugation. The 'ideal woman'—submissive, chaste and self-sacrificing—was framed within the discourses of popular cinema by indulging in 'hyperbole and tumescent rhetoric on the subject of Virtue and Honour.' (Kasbekar 2011, 293; MacDonald 2009, 6) Her honour was co-extensive with that of her family, community and the nation, and films became a vehicle for celebrating and solidifying nationalist discourse. The figure of the mother was also used to represent the distinctiveness of Indian culture from the West; while emerging as an independent, modern nation, the traditional values that vested the mother(land) with its timeless glory had to be upheld and reiterated. Bagchi (2010, 172) provides this telling quote from Swami Vivekananda:

> ...the ideal woman in India is the mother, the mother first and mother last. The word woman calls up to the mind of the hindu, motherland, and god is called mother.
>
> In the west, the woman is wife. The idea of womanhood is concentrated there as the wife. To the ordinary man in India, the whole force of womanhood is concentrated on motherhood. (Vivekananda 1951, Vol. 8, No. 57)

The socio-cultural constructions that shape and inform representations of womanhood, sexuality and motherhood provide a useful backdrop against which to view and analyse representations in cultural products like films.

Constructs of Gender, Sexuality and Motherhood

As the previous chapters in this book have demonstrated, the construct of the 'ideal woman' as a chaste wife and devoted mother is deeply rooted in Hindu ideology, and actualized through socialization practices. Susan Starr Sered's (2009) formulation of 'Woman' as symbol and 'women' as agents points to the paradoxical situation wherein women continue to be discriminated against by religious systems and ideologies even though they have made progress and secured rights in secular domains. While women as agents can demand rights, enter negotiations, and protest unfair treatment, as women's movements across the world have demonstrated, patriarchal models of the ideal 'Woman' are highly resistant to change.

> Although Woman may have very little grounding in the real experiences of women, in religious interactions these two ontologically distinct categories tend to be conflated. Woman as a symbol is often associated with some of the deepest, most compelling and most tenacious theological and mythological structures as religious traditions, and these structures imprint the lives of women involved in those traditions (Sered 1999; 2009, 10)

In other words, the idealized construct of 'Woman' propagated by religious systems is frequently at variance with the lived realities of ordinary women. Yet, there is a strong pressure exerted by religion upon women, through the processes of socialization and enculturation, to conform to the ideal. In the context of Hindu India for example, idealized notions of womanhood are communicated through myth, stories, songs and proverbs and other cultural forms. Religious ideologies also include the construct of the 'bad' or 'evil' woman—the witch, the she-devil or demoness who does not comply with the cultural mores. These women run the risk of having cultural symbols of 'bad woman' imprinted on their bodies by force; they may be raped, stoned or burned to death. During communal riots, acts of violence are performed on the bodies of women of the 'other' community. They may be raped, their breasts and genitals mutilated, religious symbols of the 'rival' community branded on their bodies to serve as a permanent reminder of their humiliation. Here, women serve as the symbols of their communities; their desecration and defilement targets the community as a whole. Women thus symbolize the honour (*izzat, laaj*) of their family, caste or religion. Recent instances of gender violence, including the so-called 'honour killings', rapes and molestations, are justified by perpetrators and considered necessary by them to punish women who transgress social norms and values. A stark and telling example was the assertion by the lawyers of the accused in the infamous Delhi gang rape case of December 2012, captured in Leslie Udwin's documentary *India's Daughter* (2015), that women were like precious diamonds to be guarded within the four walls of the home and risked violation once they stepped out of the safe space. One lawyer went so far as to say that he would burn his daughter alive if she ventured out with a boyfriend. Similar outrageous utterances by public figures across the political spectrum have been critiqued by feminists. They reflect the salience and deep-rooted identification of these values and constructs in a highly gender-stratified society. In her analysis of the representation of women in the films of Rituparno Ghosh, Alison MacDonald deploys Rajeshwari Sundar Rajan's (1993) theoretical distinction between 'real' and 'imagined' women. The dominant portrayal in the media of the 'female ideal', as MacDonald terms it, is 'more often than not, seamless packaged "imaginary" women that pertain to a socially constructed and deeply mythologized model of idealized feminine identity and behavior, whereas "real" women are marginalized or completely absent. Attempts to portray the 'modern' or 'new' woman are also carefully calibrated to ensure that they do not challenge tradition or question the status quo; the modern woman is expected to be liberated without 'jeopardising national tradition.' (MacDonald, 1)

What then, are the attributes that make up the feminine ideal in Hindu tradition? I draw upon Susan Wadley's well-known (1986) essay 'Women and the Hindu Tradition'. Wadley highlights the 'duality' represented by the woman in Hindu ideology: her benevolent, fertile form associated with good fortune and well-being, as well as her malevolent and destructive form, which brings misfortune and ruin in its wake. Wadley unravels this dualism with reference to the two facets associated with woman, namely, *shakti* (energy, power, the 'energizing principle of the universe') and *prakriti* (nature, the undifferentiated matter of the Universe). *Shakti* is the female creative principle that defines divinity and the powers of creation, the energy that drives the Universe. *Prakriti* is the second facet of femaleness, the counterpart of the *purusha* (the 'Cosmic Person'). While *prakriti* represents the undifferentiated matter of nature, *purusha* is the spirit or the code that structures it. The union of the two (matter and spirit) leads to the creation of the world and all life-forms.

Uniting these two facets of femaleness, women are both energy/power and Nature; and Nature is uncultured.... Uncultured power is dangerous. The equation 'Woman=Power+Nature=Danger' represents the essence of femaleness as it underlies Hindu religious belief and action about women. The equation summarizes a conception of the world order that explains the woman/goddess as the malevolent, aggressive destroyer. (Wadley 1986, 117)

Essentially capricious in nature, her energy can be harnessed through male control for the benefit and prosperity of the world: 'good females—goddess or human are controlled by males, that is, Culture controls Nature.' (117) For instance, in the popular myth of the rampant Kali and her wild dance of destruction, Shiva defuses her destructive potential by lying at her feet. She realizes the impropriety of placing her feet on him and stops her bloody rampage. The earth is saved from destruction because Shiva regains control over her.

The 'benevolent' goddesses in the Hindu pantheon are those who are 'properly married' and have transferred control of their sexuality to their husbands as a woman is a man's 'half-body' whose powers are transferred to the husband for his use. (118) As long as she is in control of her own sexuality, she remains potentially dangerous and destructive; if her sexuality is transferred to her husband, she remains forever benevolent. The dual character of the Hindu woman, according to Wadley, is clearly seen in the roles of wife who is 'good, benevolent, dutiful, controlled', and the mother who is 'fertile, but dangerous' and uncontrolled. (120)

A 'good' woman is necessarily a good wife, and this mythic ideal of wifehood is epitomized by Sita in the *Ramayana*. Kakar (2008) points out that, as a role model, the Sita legend has an immediacy and familiarity to the average Hindu, far surpassing that of similar figures in say Greek or Christian mythology to the average westerner.

> This intimate familiarity does not mean historical knowledge, but rather, a sense of the mythical figure as a benevolent presence, located in the individual's highly personal and always actual space-time. From earliest childhood a Hindu has heard Sita's legend recounted on any number of sacred and secular occasions.... and absorbed the ideal feminine entity she incorporates through the many everyday metaphors and similes that are associated with her name. (Kakar 2008, 64)

The ideal of *pativrata-dharma* (code of conduct for the virtuous wife), which she embodies, is the cornerstone of Hindu wifehood. Shalini

Shah (2012) elaborates upon this ideal, emphasizing the manner in which it robbed women of their individuality and made selfless service of their 'lord' their sole purpose for living. While in the Vedic texts, woman is depicted as *patni*, that is, the mistress of the house and wife of the master, it is in the epics (the *Mahabharata* and *Ramayana*) that her role as *pativrata* is systematically elaborated and glorified. So much so, that Sita could even be banished in a pregnant state because one of King Rama's subjects cast aspersions on her virtue. The epics became the vehicle through which *pativrata dharma* became the only duty enjoined on the wife and, through a 'master-stroke of patriarchy' as Shah terms it, convinced women that protected subordination offered them many advantages and security. (80) This ideology becomes the means through which compliance to patriarchal norms is ensured in households where women had to render service not just to their husbands but also his parents and other wives. The passivity that this dharma produced enabled the householder to carry out his dharma without the 'distraction' that an active questioning wife who exercised her agency was expected to cause. The *'padhi-likhi patni'* (educated wife) diverting her dutiful husband's attention away from his responsibilities to his parents and extended family, and demanding his time and attention is frequently conceptualized as the villain of the piece. She is deemed as a threat to the unity of the joint family. This is a theme that frequently appears in mainstream cinema.

The immense cultural weight of these epics is evidenced in their invocation in mainstream cinema through plot structures revisiting familiar conflicts and moral dilemmas; through the names given to protagonists which provide a key to their characters; and in the enthusiastic, sometimes over-the-top reiteration of the 'virtuous' woman as a repository of culture and tradition. The popularity of the epics was leveraged in their televised avatars on the state-run broadcaster Doordarshan in the 1980s, which enjoyed a huge and dedicated viewership. Prabha Krishnan, in her semiological analysis of episodes of the tele serials *Ramayana*, *Mahabharata* and *Uttar Ramayana*, locates them against the backdrop of the 'congealing of communal ideology' (Krishnan 2010, 107), and a centralizing State dominated by a majoritarian ideology and the dominance of Hindi-speaking, twice-born Hindus who 'define themselves as the norm setters and value givers, the cultural mainstream.' (Oommen 1984, 17, cited by Krishnan 2010, 108) The epics symbolize the primacy of the family; its capacity to articulate an entire symbolic order and confer identity upon its members.

> Every character, major or minor, becomes a semiotic unit. For example, Sita becomes Sita's world-view, women can hope to appropriate a signifier, and ideal womanhood becomes the signified. By appropriating the signified, much like a commercial, for say, instant coffee, whereby using the coffee can confer on the user membership of a privileged class. Sita and all other ideal and non-ideal types become semiotic units, while the narrative as a whole becomes the symbolic order. (Krishnan 2010, 110)

The importance of marriage as the sole rite of passage available to the Hindu woman, and her status as a '*parayi*' (Johri 2013) or a 'counterfeit child' (Das, 1990, cited by Johri, 2013), whose time in the natal home is of limited duration, reflects in cultural practices that socialize a young girl to prepare for a life of subservience and service in her conjugal home. Safeguarding her purity and ensuring that her sexuality is kept under wraps is a source of much anxiety, as her future as a good wife and mother depend upon it. Leela Dube (2001) observes that religious ceremonies like Durga Puja in Bengal and Gauri Puja in Karnataka, Maharashtra and other regions convey the unmistakable message that the natal home is only a temporary residence for the young girl; her ultimate destination is in the home of her husband. The goddesses are welcomed to the natal home with joy, and sent off with tears and a heavy heart. The departure of the young bride to her husband's home is accompanied by a variety of wedding rituals whose poignancy cannot fail to move even the most cold-hearted observer. *Bidaai* scenes and songs in Hindi films are rich with references to the abandonment and loss faced by young women leaving the sanctuary of the home of their *baabul* (father) to an unknown destination and future. Songs like '*Baabul ki Duayein Leti Ja*' (go on with the blessings of your father) (*Neelkamal*, 1968) are played and sung at weddings to this day and evoke much emotion. The story narrated about this particular song is that the singer Mohammad Rafi recorded it on the day of his own daughter's wedding and the tremor in his voice, which renders the song so moving, was not deliberate, but a genuine expression of his feelings.

As mentioned earlier, a girl's purity as a value has great salience. Worshipping and ritual feeding of virgin girls (*kanya puja*) is observed in several parts of the country. The situation changes dramatically once she attains puberty. A menstruating woman is considered ritually impure and the process is associated with a range of taboos and proscriptions ranging from seclusion to activity and dietary restrictions. The girl's changed status as a potential sexual partner, biologically ready to procreate, places her, and by extension her natal family, in an extremely uncomfortable position until the time she is 'safely' married and dispatched to her conjugal home, without tarnishing her virtue and bringing shame or dishonour upon the family. There are a great many injunctions and restrictions on her dress, comportment and demeanour. Girls are scolded for running, jumping, walking with long strides, sitting carelessly with legs apart; they must speak softly, be self-effacing in their posture and movement so as to keep strange male eyes from noticing their sexuality. The commonly held belief in all strata of our society that 'eve teasing' or sexual harassment is the result of a girl's provocative dress or demeanour stems from this. Therefore, a girl who transgresses these boundaries 'gets what she deserves'. Hindi cinema makes the unequivocal distinction between the pure and virginal *sanskari* (traditional) 'heroine' and the westernized, cigarette-smoking, whisky-drinking 'vamp' (who sometimes has a heart of gold, which redeems her in the final reckoning) brought to life by actresses like Nadira, Helen, Bindu and Aruna Irani. In the film *Abhimaan* (1973) for instance, the character played by Amitabh Bachchan of a world-weary successful singer is attracted to the 'purity' and traditional values of the daughter of a classical musician living an austere life far from the hustle-bustle of the city. He abandons his long-time girlfriend, a sophisticated, urban mature woman in favour of the musician's daughter and marries her. Ironically, the relationship becomes strained when his ego is bruised by her growing popularity as a singer in her own right. All through the film, however, she is shown as a woman who hates the limelight and would much prefer a life of anonymous domesticity. Decades later, the theme is repeated in the immensely successful *Aashiqui 2* (2012), where the talented Aarohi (Shraddha Kapoor) is ready to sacrifice her brilliant career to tend to her alcoholic singer boyfriend whose career suffers even as hers flourishes. The character of Anita (Parveen Babi) in *Deewar* (1975) is a departure in that she is a 'liberated' working woman who sleeps with her lover; however, when she becomes pregnant and her gangster boyfriend decides to reform and marry her, she is killed by a rival underworld don. Her chance at redemption through normative domesticity is thwarted. Even in a supposedly unconventional contemporary film like Homi Adajania's *Cocktail* (2012), the free-spirited, sexually liberated 'party girl' Veronica ultimately loses Gautam, the man she loves, to a 'good' Indian girl Meera, whose simplicity and traditional values win him over. Veronica is 'good enough' for sex and enjoyment but Meera is the perfect girl to bring home to mother. Veronica pays the price for the assertion of her sexuality; chastity trumps. A recent, unusually quirky departure was Shoojit Sirkar's *Piku* (2015) in which the eccentric and chronically constipated father Bhaskar, memorably portrayed by Amitabh Bachchan, is unwilling to let go of his adult daughter Piku even though he has no problems with her occasional sexual encounters. Indeed, when Piku's aunt tries to introduce her to an eligible bachelor at a party, the old man loudly informs the prospective suitor that his daughter is not a virgin! Bhaskar's reluctance to let go of his daughter is an interesting reversal of the ideal of *kanyadaan*, where the gift of a virgin daughter is a means of attaining salvation. Bhaskar's 'salvation', when he makes peace with his past, recovers his lost roots, and then dies peacefully in his ancestral home after finally voiding his clogged bowels, takes place alongside Piku's growing involvement in an adult relationship and the possibility of a new beginning.

Dube (2001) also brings out the importance given to training girls in domestic work and the inculcation of the value of service (*sewa*), specifically with regard to the serving and distribution of food. Leftovers are usually eaten by women and girls in the family; the rice that sticks to the bottom of the vessel or the first dosa on the griddle, which is frequently misshapen or not properly cooked, is reserved for women. A young bride is usually the most vulnerable and voiceless person in a patrilocal and patrilineal setting, and the often traumatic adjustment from the natal to the conjugal home is viewed as a test of her character and resilience. Her behaviour is evaluated as a reflection of the training she has received from her mother in her natal home. She is expected to 'win' her place in the new household through her exemplary behaviour, her *sewa*, and most significantly, through procreating male progeny. It is only when she conceives and gives birth to children (preferably male progeny) that the subservient, wifely role becomes transformed. As the giver of life, a woman is both venerated and feared. The mother, transformed into the mother-goddess whose devotees are her children, can be both benevolent and dangerous; she can give and take away. While the wife is expected to be dutiful, subordinate and obedient at all times, it is the mother who loves, gives, sometimes rejects and must be obeyed. (Wadley 1986)

Even though Hindu ideology conceptualizes the reproductive role of the woman as the 'field' on which the man deposits his seed and the father as the source of the child's lineage and identity, her role as the life-giver, and her moral power in nurturing and training her children is acknowledged and celebrated. For instance, Yashoda, the foster mother of Lord Krishna, may not have been his biological mother, as per the legend, but her utter absorption and devotion to the child, and her exasperation and delight in his pranks and naughtiness are lovingly told and retold through song, dance and stories. The mother as the font of values and ideals, which makes a man a worthy one, forms a recurrent theme in literature and cinema. The Marathi text *Shyamchi Ai* (Shyam's Mother) by the freedom fighter and social reformer from Maharashtra, Sane Guruji (first published in 1940 and reprinted several times since), which was subsequently made into a very popular Marathi film, is a good example of the reverential and yet extremely intimate bond that exists between a mother and her favourite son, and the values of honesty, self-respect and dignity that he imbibes from her. Shanta Gokhale's (2010) reading of the text locates it as an important source of middle-class Maharashtrian identity formation and the unquestioning acceptance of gendered roles and values. As a sentimental text invoking the sweetness and self-sacrificing nature of the mother, it locates her feelings, thoughts and behaviour in terms of the consequences these would have on her growing child and firmly places the onus of raising morally superior children on her shoulders. The subtitle to *Shyamchi Ai* is translated as 'a sad and sweet narrative picture of a mother's sublime and loving teaching, and of a simple and beautiful culture'. As Gokhale aptly remarks, 'Not much new thought is possible with the(se) adjectives.... the very same words which have been used so effectively throughout history to keep exploited people firmly in their socially appointed places.' (Gokhale 2010, 251)

Mother's Body and National Identity

As the mother is regarded as the repository of culture and the sanctity and integrity of the collectivity, she is also invoked as the metaphor for the nation. Writing about the representations of motherhood in the context of Tamil culture and politics, C. S. Lakshmi (2010, 188) remarks that in classical Tamil literature, mothers' bodies turn into sites of 'divinity, sanctity and purity' and their wombs into the 'lairs of tigers' that produce brave, majestic sons who can only be found on the battlefield. Their breasts produce the 'milk of valour' that nurtures warriors. It is the quality of their wombs and milk that produces either the hero or the coward; if mother's milk fails and the son turns out to be a coward, her first instinct is to slash her breasts off. The Tamil epic the

Silapadhikaram depicts Kannagi running on the streets of Madurai with her breast cut off after her husband dies, as it has now become a useless impediment in the absence of children. Thus, the woman's body, her womb and breasts exist precisely because of their function in breeding and feeding valorous sons. Daughters unfortunately occupy no such exalted place; rather, the birth of daughters rather than sons is viewed as a deficiency or innate defect in the mother. The publication of the entire *Silapadhikaram* in 1892 coincided with the efforts at the time to establish a 'pure' Tamil identity through the discovery of a 'pure' Tamil language. The ideological peg on which neo-Tamilian ideas of purity, identity and historical continuity were hung was the 'pure' Tamil woman, embodied in the mother.

> In the mother's body is vested the totality of an identity. Once the mother's body is established as a sacred site, all other elements of identity are rendered valid and hence necessary to revive and hold on to. The mother's body then becomes a metaphor for anything considered sacred and pure like land or language. (Lakshmi 2010, 192)

Tamil women have been conceptualized as the mothers of warriors fighting battles for the sanctity of Tamil culture and identity. In the 1920s, during the Self-Respect Movement led by E. V. Ramaswami Naicker, which revolted against the rituals and superstitions of the caste system and Brahminism, mothers became the agency through which Tamil ideology, the greatness of Tamil culture and the need to fight casteism and Brahminical ritualism were instilled into the young. The *Dravida Munnetra Kazhagam* (DMK), which emerged under the leadership of C. N. Annadurai, carried forward the torch of Dravidian identity and the imagery of a humiliated and insulted 'Mother Tamil' who demands that her sons avenge her. The involvement of the DMK in the world of cinema is a fascinating example of the overlapping of the 'reel' and 'real', and the utilization of a potent medium of mass communication by a political party to construct culture. The theme of the mother as goddess and embodiment of Tamil culture is extravagantly visible in the films of M. G. Ramachandran (MGR) who went on to become the Chief Minister of Tamil Nadu. His invocation of the *thai-kulam* (community of mothers), revival of the worship of forgotten goddesses and appointment of women ministers in his government enabled him to project himself as the devoted son and warrior for the upliftment of Tamil womanhood at large.

His popular female co-star and political heiress J. Jayalalitha who had to fight a bitter personal and political battle with MGR's kin and overcome the tag of the 'other woman' has over the years become the supremo, simultaneously commanding a cult following and attracting bitter enmity from within the various factions of the erstwhile Dravidian movement. *'Amma'* addressed by the honorific *Puratchi Thazzaivi* (Supreme Leader), is celebrated as a present-day goddess and a bringer of bounty (the Amma kitchens which serve decent meals at very low prices are an example of her largesse) before whom grown men bow. The recent images of men and women beating their breasts and tearing their hair when Jayalalitha was incarcerated in jail in connection with a corruption case, and the subsequent delirious scenes of celebration after she was released, bear testimony to the filmic spectacle of contemporary Tamil politics. At the time of writing this chapter, the terrible floods that devastated Chennai in December 2015 proved occasion for pitching the Chief Minister as a saviour through posters showing her rescuing little children from flood waters.

Jasodhara Bagchi (2010, 159) remarks upon the 'simultaneous privatization and institutionalization of motherhood' as one of capitalist patriarchy's most 'spectacular ploys'. 'Patriarchy, whether in its most traditional or modern form, constantly tries to glorify motherhood as the most prized vocation for women.' (159) Writing about the deployment of the ideology of motherhood to the burgeoning nationalism and quest for identity, Bagchi examines what she terms the 'investiture of motherhood' (163) at a critical juncture in Bengal's social-political and cultural history. The marrying together of the loving, warm quintessential Bengali mother, and the force and power of the mother goddess Shakti (variously known as Durga, Kali and Chandi) produced a composite mother figure that was emblematic of the nation. The mother(land) was thus constructed as an object of worship. Mother as mother nature—fecund, fertile, fruiting and flowering—is also woven into the discourse of Bengali nationalism. Thus, the iconic poem *'Vande Mataram'* from Bankim Chandra's *Anand Math* celebrates the motherland as goddess and as verdant natural space. The celebration of the mother-son bond fitted neatly with the ideology of patriotic nationalism while making the mother a long-suffering victim of the depredations of marauding 'others' who had reduced her to a shadow of herself. The Bengali male's frustration and guilt at the sight of his mother(land) laid to waste comes through powerfully in the poetry and prose of the period as does the vision to restore her glory. Bagchi (2010) argues that the mythicization of the Bengali mother did little for the empowerment of the ordinary Bengali woman in terms of the daily exploitation she experienced (refer to the contrast between Woman as symbol and women as agents made earlier in the chapter). The social oppression of daughters and daughters-in-law within the patriarchal order continued and motherhood came to be appropriated as a symbol of 'order' rather than challenge and contestation. Whether the outlier and non-Hindu 'other' finds a place within this ideological universe is also a question that needs to be answered. As Gabriel (2010, 344) remarks, '*Bharat Mata*/Mother India is signalled both as (mythic) national Mother Goddess, and as (historical) Hindu, upper caste, upper class, north Indian, sexually and morally "respectable".' Thus, even though the maternal body of the nation is a metaphor, 'the power of this metaphor derives from the literal social structures of caste, class, religion, social status, etc., that bind it, validate it and give it meaning and authority.'

The mapping of the mother's body with the body of the nation is a theme that recurs in contemporary popular culture, and is used by the media machinery of the state to disseminate ideals of patriotism and national unity. An animated short film that played extensively on the national broadcaster Doordarshan during the 1970s and 1980s showed a teacher drawing the outline of a woman clad in a sari on the blackboard, inviting the children to identify the figure. A child comes up to the board, says '*Maa*' and writes the word in Hindi. This is followed by another who says '*Ai*' (Marathi for mother), and soon the board is covered with different scripts and the soundtrack with multiple voices articulating the word for mother in several Indian languages. The figure of the woman then transforms into the outline of a map of India, and the many voices then start to sing '*Saare jahan se accha*', Iqbal's paean to Hindustan (India) as the '*gulistan*' (garden) where many birds sing their distinctive tunes. The simple and powerful message of the film—India/Bharat/Hindustan is our mother, we are her children even though we speak a multiplicity of tongues—was internalized by a generation of television-viewing children who grew up to shape and partake of the neo-liberal resurgent India where consumerism and jingoistic nationalism coexist and complement each other. Short animated films of the period still enjoy a dedicated following on YouTube, notably Vijaya Mulay's '*Ek, Anek, Ekta*' (1974), which brings home the simple, if not simplistic, message that there is 'strength in unity' and 'unity in diversity'. Diversities that result in deprivation and discrimination can be written off and neutralized by invoking the image of a transcendental 'mother nation' to whom all children are equal in theory, if not in practice. In his analysis of Mani Ratnam's film *Roja* (1992), Nicholas Dirks (2011) quotes from Susan and Shiv Visvanathan's article in a special issue of *Seminar* on secularism:

> Our childhood in the fifties was something beautiful. It was a period of innocence where every child was proud to be an Indian. There was something secure about a world in which Gandhi was in heaven and Nehru in command. Every citizen was a craftsman, every child an apprentice in the most exciting craft of all, the process of nation-building.

However,

> But as the nation became the *nation-state,* something got bureaucratized. What was a vision, a living language, froze into a dead grammar.... The corset tightened as the nation-state became a *national security state.* (Visvanathan and Visvanathan 1992, cited in Dirks 2001, 165)

Reading the films *Mother India* and *Deewar* enables us to read the story of the nation as it transited from an 'area of hope' (to invert Naipaul's phrase) to one of darkness, corruption and contradictions.

Mother and Motherland in Hindi Cinema: Illustrations from select films

The post-independence cinematic project reflected the hopes and aspirations of a newly liberated nation and the promise of an egalitarian social order held out by Nehruvian socialism. It deployed the figure of the mother both as the repository of tradition and 'culture' as well as an emblem that transcended narrow boundaries of family and kin and embraced the entire nation as one family. Mehboob Khan's iconic *Mother India* (1957) exemplifies the nation-building project with the figure of the mother who becomes a symbol for the nation. No discussion on motherhood and representation in Indian cinema can proceed without reference to *Mother India*, a remake of Mehboob's earlier film *Aurat* (1940). The title, ironically, was borrowed from Katherine Mayo's notorious booklet of 1927, which painted a sordid picture of the moral degradation and perversion of Indian men, and the atrocities committed on the bodies of Indian girls and women. It made a case for the unworthiness and incapacity of Indians for self-rule and was denounced by critics and nationalists as a scurrilous piece of colonialist propaganda. Mehboob's film set out to contradict and correct this notion, and paint Indian womanhood in heroic hues. A lavishly illustrated brochure that was specially prepared to contextualize the film for international audiences, waxed eloquent on the ideal of chastity as a 'sacred heirloom' of the culture and tradition of this ancient land, demanding the most painful sacrifice; even the sacrifice of one's own child by a righteous mother. The Indian woman, it was asserted, considered her home a temple, her husband a god, her children his blessings, and her land a great mother. The woman is an 'altar'; her chastity and character virtues to be worshipped (cited in Thomas 1989, 20) Thus, the very integrity of the collective she represents is measured by her worth. The broken and brutalized creature created by Mayo is replaced by a goddess worthy of worship.

The film's narrative plots the transitions in the life of Radha, a village woman, from a coy bride to an impoverished widowed mother to a revered community matriarch, and her life-long struggle against poverty, indebtedness and exploitation. The film opens with the inauguration of a dam in the village at the hands of Radha, now a withered old woman. As she recalls her past, the narrative goes back in time, showing us a coy, demure Radha as a young bride. Married to the loving and attentive Shamu (Raaj Kumar) she soon finds herself and her family at the mercy of the unscrupulous and lecherous moneylender Sukhi Lala who lusts after her. Even though he fails in his attempt, he still manages to cheat her out of her wedding bangles (*kangan*), which are ultimately forcibly recovered by her son Birju. Shamu, in a desperate attempt to get out of the debt trap gets badly injured and loses both arms. Filled with shame and a sense of impotence, he leaves his wife and little children, and is not heard of again. Struggling against monumental odds Radha attempts to rebuild her life, and works the fields with her young sons. The sons grow up into young men: the stolid, stable and temperate Ramu (played by Rajendra Kumar) and the wild, tempestuous Birju (Sunil Dutt). Birju is a rebel, an 'angry young man', challenging social mores and traditional authority. His behaviour and his teasing of the village girls leads to community outrage and the family's lands are set ablaze. Radha is trapped in the fire, but is saved by Birju. His desire to avenge his mother's humiliation and the family's impoverishment at the hands of Sukhi Lala, and the exploitative feudal order he represents results in him becoming an outlaw and a bandit on the run. The climactic moment of the film takes place when Birju and his gang take their revenge on Sukhi Lala, and abduct his young daughter Rupa who is about to be married. Unable to withstand or condone this attack on the honour of a daughter of the village, Radha warns Birju that she will shoot him if he does not release Rupa. Birju retorts that as she is his mother she will never be able to kill him. Radha guns him down, and Birju dies in her arms. As the flashback ends, the film catapults us back into the present; Radha opens the gates of the dam and a gush of water flows out to irrigate the fields where she has toiled all her life.

Mother India is one of the all-time box office hits in Indian cinema. Released just after the tenth anniversary of India's independence, the film had a high profile release with screenings in the country's capital New Delhi, attended by both the President and the Prime Minister. It was India's first submission for the Best Foreign Language Film category at the Academy Awards in 1958, where it was nominated. Thomas (1989), whose analysis I draw upon heavily in this discussion, observes that the film highlights crises within kinship morality, both by focusing on contradictory pulls and demands within the domain of kinship as well as the contradictions between kinship loyalties and loyalties to larger social collectives. (15) Thus, Radha is torn between protecting her honour and chastity as the ideal wife by rejecting Sukhi Lala's advances and feeding her starving children. Later, her role as a devoted mother comes into conflict with her role as a village elder and custodian of the honour of its womanhood when her favourite son nearly violates the *laaj* (honour) of a daughter of the village (which as per North Indian kinship is tantamount to an act of incest). As a mother, she is simultaneously nurturant and destructive; she embodies both Durga and Kali. Thus, it brings to the fore the 'dual nature' of the feminine principle discussed earlier in the chapter. Thomas draws attention to the range of mythic feminine icons exemplified by Radha, the ardent *premika* (lover) of Krishna, whose name she shares; the chaste Sita, captured by the demon king Ravana, who remains inviolate and proves this through an ordeal by fire; Savitri, the *pativrata*; Lakshmi, the goddess of wealth and plenitude, to whom Sukhi Lala ironically compares her; and, as earlier mentioned, Shakti in both benevolent and destructive forms, upholding order and destroying that which subverts it. (17) Radha is also *Bharat Mata*; her story is the story of a nation coming out of colonial subjugation and making a brave new world for itself. The corrupt exploitative old order exemplified by Sukhi Lala is marked by the pauperization of the peasantry, natural disasters, flood and famine unleashed by uncontrollable natural forces where men are weak and helpless (like Shamu, who is reduced to an unproductive dependent whose hands are literally cut off) and women at constant risk of violation.

Birju challenges and attempts to overthrow the old order through acts of lawlessness and violence but is doomed to failure because they violate the law of *dharma* (righteous conduct), based as it is on a well-calibrated scale of hierarchy and authority and a strong notion of duty. The law abiding son Ramu (named after Lord Rama, the *maryada-purushottam*, the upholder of righteousness), who embodies stoicism, patience and respect for authority is ultimately the one who emerges triumphant from the ordeals of a difficult childhood and becomes a respected figure in the village. The story of the freedom movement is narrated in terms of Gandhian *ahimsa* and self-control demonstrated by Ramu versus the violent and extreme tactics of Birju. Even though it is the lawless son who wins back the mother's *kangan* (bangles) from the moneylender, they are bloodstained and thus only serve to perpetuate the saga of violence. Closure to the tale is brought about by opening the gate of the new dam by Radha. The dam which symbolizes the new order based on scientific rationality and the application of technologies of progress and change is inaugurated at the hands of the matriarch, the repository of the values and traditions of the timeless community. Thomas aptly remarks, 'oppression is ousted and the hazards of nature overcome by modern technology, but the purity of traditional values—symbolized by female chastity—must still bless, and ultimately legitimize, technological advance. Mother India must open the dam.' (19)

The hope and optimism of the post-Independence era was gradually eroded as the national party, the Congress, riven by succession wars, split in 1969. Indira Gandhi once dismissed as a '*goongi gudiya*' (dumb doll) by rival factions within the political establishment emerged as a powerful leader who had the dubious distinction of abrogating hard-won political freedoms by imposing a state of national Emergency in 1975. Escalating unemployment, endemic poverty, industrial strife, crime and the rise of the 'underworld', insurgency, political unrest and a general climate of disillusionment with institutions saw the emergence of a new kind of film text; the 'anti-hero' or the 'angry young man' as embodied in the person of the new superstar of the day, Amitabh Bachchan. (Virdi 1993) *Deewar* (The Wall, 1975) directed by Yash Chopra and scripted by Salim-Javed is the tale of the wronged hero, who grows up in a climate of crime and urban brutality and sees the daily humiliation and deprivation of his mother who he vows to avenge. As in *Mother India*, the mother has to make a moral choice between a law-abiding son and a law-defying one. Once again, it is through her pain and sacrifice of a beloved son that the moral order and the writ of society and state is re-imposed.

94 Embodying Motherhood

The film deals with the issues of urban poverty, injustice, class conflict and gender against the backdrop of the social unrest of the 1970s. (Virdi 1993) Set in a teeming urban landscape far removed from the rural heartland of Mother India, it tells the story of the brothers Vijay Verma and Ravi Verma (played by Amitabh Bachchan and Shashi Kapoor), sons of the trade unionist Anand Verma. Cornered by a ruthless management, Anand is forced to betray the interests of worker comrades to save the lives of his family. Shamed and disgraced, he flees the town, leaving his wife Sumitra Devi (Nirupa Roy) and young sons to fend for themselves and face the brunt of the angry community. Vijay's arm is branded with the words 'mera baap chor hai' (my father is a thief), a permanent reminder of his father's helplessness and impotence. Unable to withstand this hostility they try to make a new life in Bombay, where, like countless other impoverished migrants, they live on the pavements and eke out an existence through manual work. The mother works as a labourer at a construction site and Vijay becomes a shoe-shine boy. Ravi is sent to school and adopts a normative path. As the years pass, Vijay, who takes up work as a labourer at the dockyard and earns a reputation as a fierce fighter against the local mafia, is drawn into the company of another mafia don who inducts him into his business. Before long, Vijay becomes a millionaire and the family moves into the very mansion where the mother once toiled as a construction worker. Meanwhile, Ravi becomes a police officer, and before long the two brothers become adversaries: one a smuggler and criminal, and the other an enforcer of the law. When the truth about Vijay's lavish lifestyle is revealed, Ravi and his mother decide to leave and shift to the modest dwellings of a government official. In a confrontational scene that has become a part of movie lore, Vijay taunts Ravi for his idealism and asks what they have got him apart from a meagre salary, a rented flat and two pairs of uniforms. Ravi looks at him squarely in the eye and utters one of the most unforgettable lines in Hindi cinema: 'Maa. Mere paas maa hai' (I have mother). Vijay's attempts to get out of the circle of crime and settle down with his pregnant girlfriend Anita meet a bloody end when Anita is murdered by Samant, the villain of the piece. Vijay kills Samant, thereby sealing his own fate as a wanted criminal. The film moves to its inexorable climax when Ravi is forced to hunt down his own brother, with the implacable injunction from his mother that when he aims the revolver, his hands must not tremble. While tasking her younger son to bring the criminal Vijay to justice, her motherly love cannot be contained as she gathers the fatally wounded son into her arms. He draws his last breath in the sanctuary of his mother's lap, a return to a place that is safe, comforting, womb-like. (Lal n.d.)

As in *Mother India*, the mother in *Deewar* is torn between two sons: the 'nationalist', normative police officer who upholds the writ of the state, and the lawless 'anti-national' smuggler who subverts it. But, unlike in Mother India, the power to redress the abrogation of *dharma* is wielded not by the mother, but by the 'good' son. It is he who appropriates power to discipline and punish, to restore the status quo. The mother must suffer the pain of the loss of one son at the hands of the other, even though it is he who shared her trials, tribulations and humiliation by the virtue of being the first born and a surrogate father to his younger sibling. His 'transgressive love', as Virdi terms it, for his mother, who remains always the epicentre of his attention and fantasy, comes through sharply in the famous temple scene. As his mother struggles for her life, the atheist Vijay, who never entered the temple all his life, finally does the unthinkable and thus 'saves' her from his own ungodliness. Yet she cannot 'belong' to him once it is clear that his path deviates from *dharma*. It is the good son who, in the words of Vinay Lal (n.d.) 'speaks in the voice of patriarchy, as the defender of the family and the social order, and also as the reincarnated husband, with all the "rights" that accrue to the husband.' Ravi thus represents the inexorable social order with which she must ally herself. '*Mere paas maa hai*' is an affirmation of the primacy of the institution of family and kinship within a normative order, overriding the dangerous domain of affect and unbridled emotion. The dual nature of the goddess as one who both gives and demands life is played out here as well, except that the goddess hands over her powers of life and death to the son who now 'owns' her.

Mother India and *Deewar* are perhaps the most powerful examples of a cinematic tradition that represents and narrates the mother, opening up *dharmic* dilemmas that force the viewer to reflect upon the cultural heft of her role as well as the spaces of agency available to her within the bounds of patriarchy. Later examples of 'mother-and-son(s)' melodramas include the hugely popular *Amar Akbar Anthony* (Manmohan Desai, 1977) and *Karan Arjun* (Rakesh Roshan, 1995). *Amar Akbar Anthony* is the story of long-lost brothers who are raised in different faiths, yet, through a series of fantastical twists and turns, are reunited with their birth mother. The film repeatedly highlights the primal call of the mother beckoning her sons across religious, spatial and social divides, and finally uniting with them through the most elemental symbol of kinship: blood. In an unintentionally hilarious scene, the protagonists are linked through an utterly implausible serial blood transfusion reclaiming the integrity of their identity as sons of one mother(land), despite their religious differences. At the same time, the mother is portrayed throughout as a devout Hindu, highlighting the capacity of Bharat Mata to accommodate diversities. *Karan Arjun* (1995) invokes the power of the mother (Durga) to call back her sons even across the abyss of death in order to avenge her humiliation at the hands of her ruthless brother-in-law Durjan Singh. The names Karan and Arjun derive from the *Mahabharata*, thus blending into the narrative the connotation of a *dharma yuddha* (holy war) to be fought by the reincarnated brothers Ajay and Vijay (the 'victorious ones') to avenge the wronged mother Durga. It is the call of the now insane and rambling mother that unites the orphans Ajay and Vijay to overcome their initial enmity and fight for a common cause. In her discussion of the film, Gabriel (2010) reminds us of its referencing of the legendary figures of the epic *Mahabharata*. Kunti, mother of the Pandavas, bears the terrible pain of witnessing the deadly rivalry between Karna, her unacknowledged first-born, conceived out of wedlock and Arjun, her legitimate son. Social pressures prevent her from declaring Karna as her son, thus she is unable to make him cross over to the 'right' side and fight the great war with his brothers. Instead, he sides with his friend Duryodhan (Durjan) and dies on the battlefield at the hands of his uterine brother. The war of the *Mahabharata* ends in an empty victory for Kunti's sons, secured at the cost of precious lives of kinsmen, children, and ultimately, the whole clan. The narrative of the Partition of India, which similarly caused a bloodbath between communities, also comes to mind. The project of the nation as mother is to unite brothers, to bring the outlier into the fold and erase the faultlines born out of a traumatic Partition which turned into genocide. The '*ideological* power of the figure of the mother to conjugate the nation harmoniously' (354) is thus emphasized; Karan and Arjun reincarnated as Ajay and Vijay fight on the same side, the 'right' side and *Maa* Durga is avenged.

In the films discussed above, the absent husband/father is a common feature suggesting that the sons must assume the mantle of protection of the mother and at the same time hold her at the centre of their moral universe. Widowhood is social death precisely because it throws the body of the woman open to exploitation and abuse in a social system where marriage is the only rite of passage sanctioned to her. At the same time, it confers upon a mother 'a position of ultimate superiority as the sole author of her children' (Gabriel 2010, 355) who must then rise to defend her, take up arms at her bidding and avenge the loss of her status as wife. In so doing, the son then becomes the effective owner and controller of her agency, arrogating to himself the powers of the patriarch.

The important point here is that, while the son (of the nation) thus actually derives his identity from the mother-nation, this is elided by his assertion of 'fatherdom', an ethico-legal right over the transgressive femininity of the mother. The assertion of this right thus marks the son's self-identity at the very moment of granting identity to the mother (by becoming the father). (355)

In the political arena a similar narrative was seen when the widowed Indira Gandhi came to be identified as a modern-day Durga, the mother of a seething mass of humanity. Her son Sanjay was widely seen as an extra-constitutional authority who exercised great control over his mother and was being groomed as her successor. His untimely end in a freak accident resulted in the quiet, publicity-shy brother Rajiv gradually assuming the mantle of Mrs. Gandhi's heir. In the wake of her violent assassination in 1984, he was sworn in as Prime Minister. The mid-1980s signalled a renewed romance with technology under the leadership of Rajiv Gandhi; the computer became the symbol of the new age and the Information Technology revolution opened India to the world.

Global Bollywood: Some reflections

The 1990s saw India shedding the shackles of a self-imposed isolationist economic policy and heralding the era of economic liberalization, opening up of markets and trans-national flows of human and economic capital. The 'culture industry' and the burgeoning of TV, satellite and cable networks exposed Indian audiences to a whole new world of entertainment options. The 1990s also saw the growth of right-wing 'hindutva' mobilizations by urban middle classes, the greatest beneficiaries of liberalization and globalization. Bollywood cashed in on the global moment, reinventing itself for a new and increasingly consumerist audience. It emerged as a site for a significant diasporic engagement feeding on sentiment and nostalgia and creating possibilities for the creation of a 'global' Indian identity. We observe the celebration of a fetishized great Indian family and a jingoistic nationalism undergirded by a 'benevolent patriarchy'. (Bhattacharya Mehta 2010, 2) The great joint Indian family became the site in which the free market and reactionary politics coalesced creating a fantasy world of benevolent bucolic *babujis* (fathers), trendy yet traditional mothers, dutiful daughters and the mythic *pind* (homeland). This lost paradise blended seamlessly with a world of unbridled consumption and desire that had become tantalizingly accessible to a generation of Indians at home and abroad. Sooraj Barjatya's *Hum Aapke Hain Kaun* (1994) was the defining 'family film' of the 1990s, with its happy extended family whose members are willing to sacrifice their own desires for the larger good. Examining the two-pronged process of homogenization in mainstream Indian cinema, Dutta (2000) suggests that conservative, fundamentalist forces at home erase spaces of difference and construct a monolithic representation of gender and nation; at the same time, the process of globalization isolates filmmaking from a historical or social context. The commercial powerhouse of 'Bollywood' cinema threatens to obliterate alternate images and representations. The films of directors like Karan Johar and Aditya Chopra, and the global appeal of stars like Shahrukh Khan consolidate the image of the new global Indian, at home in the world yet rooted to *Bharatiya Parampara* (Indian tradition). As Bhattacharya Mehta writes, 'Films with diasporic contents such as *Kabhi Khushi Kabhi Gham* have propagated an extreme yet immensely successful formula of patriarchal control over post-global modernity and have pushed Bollywood's ideology to the far-right.' (2010, 9) The tag line of Johar's *Kabhi Khushi Kabhi Gham* (2001) reminds us that 'it's all about loving your parents'! (Both Johar and Chopra, it is pertinent to mention, are second generation filmmakers whose fathers were well-established in the industry. They are, therefore, well-networked and enjoy family-like ties and reciprocal rights and obligations within the 'extended family' of the Hindi film industry.)

It is the theme of fatherhood that emerges with a new force and confidence in Bollywood's 'negotiation of nation-ness' (Sen 2010, 147) in the post liberalization era. The role of the mother diminishes to merely a supporting one. The 'globalized' mother may have graduated from the simple cotton sari to an embellished designer creation, but her attitudes and values remain resolutely wedded to maintaining the status quo and the patriarchal structures that support her status as a wife and the adoring mother of her male children. The generational metamorphosis of Amitabh Bachchan from the angry young hell-raiser of *Deewar* (1975) to the conservative pater familias of *Mohabbatein* (1999) and *Kabhi Khushi Kabhi Gham* (2001), deliciously ironical as it is, is of a piece with the cultural nationalism of the contemporary 'global' Bollywood film presided over by the powerful father figure with a wife confined firmly within the spaces of the domestic and affective as an 'ideal' woman ought to be. Mother India exists as a mere appendage to the Father who presides over the world of business, commerce and politics and is in perfect alignment with a masculinist world order premised on military domination, environmental degradation and marginalization of different subjectivities (Sen 2010).

Aditya Chopra's *Dilwaale Dulhaniya Le Jayenge* (1995) traces the co-option of the free-spirited, brazen Londoner Raj (played by Shahrukh Khan) into the world of North Indian Hindu family values as represented by Baldev (Amrish Puri), father of Simran (Kajol). Raj has already won over Simran; it is the father whom he must now woo and win over. Women exist merely as the currency through which kinship relationships are transacted by men; the transfer of 'ownership' of Simran from Baldev to his childhood friend's son in Punjab and thereafter to Raj who proves himself 'worthy' to win the bride are only feebly contested and challenged by the women in the family. When Simran's mother does in fact urge Raj to elope with Simran the offer is refused by Raj who wants to do the 'honourable' thing and marry Simran with Baldev's blessings. Similarly in Karan Johar's *Kabhi Khushi Kabhi Gham* (2001), the pater familias Yash (Amitabh Bacchhan), who radiates wealth, modernity and style, proves himself to be nothing more than an 'unreconstructed autocrat' (Gopal 2010, 28) when he asks his (adopted) son Rahul to leave the house for daring to marry a lower-middle-class girl against his will. Nandini, the mother has no choice but to watch her beloved son being cast out of the house and must suffer the separation until eventually a chastened Yash makes amends. Because it is 'all about loving your family', reactionary stances cannot be challenged; order cannot be compromised. The mother is rendered a cipher in this battle of men. Meheli Sen (2010, 149) argues that Bollywood's renewed investments in tradition and the family in the moment of the 1990s skilfully deployed the figure of the new Hindu father epitomized by Amitabh Bachchan as both the 'carrier of "tradition"' as well as a 'powerful repository of "modernity"', which in this specific context refer to popular understandings of globalization and neo-liberalism. Through a close reading of three films, *Mohabbatein, Ek Rishta: The Bond of Love* (2001), and *Baghban* (2003) she attempts to show the inter-connections between the resurgence of a masculinist Hindu nationalism and revivalism and the valorization of an authoritarian father who also holds the key to the limitless possibilities of modernity and globality. As the conflicted son of *Deewar* becomes the supremely confident father of a globalizing moment, *Bharat Mata* remains the symbol that grants him legitimacy even as her agency is systematically eroded.

Riaz (2013), in her analysis of the portrayal of screen mothers, draws an interesting comparison between Radha in *Mother India* and what would appear to be her polar opposite, Sheetal (Dimple Khanna) in the 2005 film *Pyaar Mein Twist* (Hriday Shetty). Sheetal is a widowed mother of an adult daughter, and has an unabashed love affair with Yash (Rishi Kapoor). The resistance to this by their respective children, the social pressure to give up the relationship and sacrifice personal happiness for the family is ultimately overcome, and the couple unites in the end with the blessings of their children. However, despite Bollywood's attempt to 'update' the portrayal of the mother, Riaz shows that the traditional values of the self-sacrificing, nurturant mother, who willingly sets aside her own needs and desires, are very much alive and kicking. Striking a more optimistic note, Sucharita Sarkar's discussion of the portrayal of Shashi (Sridevi), in the 2012 film *English Vinglish* reveals how the shy, retiring housewife found her voice and confidence when she joined an English language learning class while visiting relatives in the US. Shashi's friendship with a multicultural group of fellow learners, including the Frenchman Laurent with whom she strikes a special rapport, and her gentle rejoinder to her husband who cannot imagine her as anything but a domestic goddess, highlight the journey from 'sacrifice to selfhood'. While never actively contesting her status as wife and mother, Shashi certainly questions being taken for granted by the family she loves. The tradition-modernity binary highlighted by Mishra (2002) is clearly visible: 'Modernity is disavowed even as it is endorsed; tradition is avowed even as it is rejected.' (Mishra 2002, 4, cited by Sarkar n.d., 7)

A gentle critique of what we may term 'designer patriarchy' is also seen in Zoya Akhtar's *Dil Dhadakne Do* (2015). The Mehras—a rich, successful 'power couple'—with a clearly dysfunctional marriage and strictly social and economic compulsions to keep it going, are forced to review their lives and values as well as the needs and desires of their children. The hollowness of conspicuous consumption, social status and gender stereotyping are wittily exposed through the voice of a non-human with a supremely nuanced understanding of human society with all its follies and foibles: the family dog, Pluto! The trophy wife (Shefali Chhaya), who dotes on her only son and would rather not engage with her brilliant and talented daughter, is forced to confront the hollow sham that her marriage has become and make a choice about supporting her daughter's desires and goals. The fact that the film ends with Aysha, their daughter, walking out of a marriage of convenience and pursuing her heart's desire, with the support of her parents, indicates that mainstream cinema is ready to make bolder choices and give space to new voices—that *parayi* can hope to become *apni*. (Johri 2013)

Motherhood, Vulnerability and Alternative Subjectivities: Challenging homogenization

What are the spaces within which motherhood can emerge as a counterpoint to hegemonic discourses of masculinity? I argue that it is in relation to the experience of alternative identities and subjectivities that the creative and empowering dimensions of motherhood can be explored. The 2008 comedy *Dostana*, for instance, which dealt with homosexuality in a farcical and slapstick way, nevertheless cocked a snook at the heteronormative society. Sam and Kunal, heterosexual males, pretend to be in a gay relationship for certain material reasons. When Sam's mother (Kiron Kher) visits them, all hell breaks loose. The mother's exaggerated horror at gay love and, over time, her acceptance of her male *bahu* (daughter-in-law) are rendered hilariously. However absurd the film, it did succeed in holding up a mirror to love, sex and heteronormativity, and the subversion of these norms by the mother who accepts her child's choices and orientation.

The experience of mothering a child with disability is also a critical space for engagement with difference and challenging dominant paradigms about 'ways of being'. *Taare Zameen Par* (2007) directed by Aamir Khan, for instance, sensitively told the story of a child whose learning difficulties were construed as intractable disobedience and distractedness, and was packed off to a residential school to discipline him and make him conform to the urban middle class ideal of the hardworking, high-achieving son of the family. While the mother understands the needs and compulsions of her child (*'tujhe sab hai pataa, meri maa'*), she has to comply with the wishes of her husband. Her inability to resist the force of middle-class conformity and the writ of the father is addressed through the person of a deeply empathetic male teacher, who becomes a kind of 'male mother', drawing the child out of his shell and helping his talent flower. The therapeutic role he takes on is a deeply nurturant one, complementing the role of the mother and posing a strong critique to the values and practices adopted by the father.

In the film *Paa* (2009), directed by R. Balki, the female protagonist gives birth to her child after being jilted by her ambitious lover, the scion of a political family. She trains as a medical doctor and with the steadfast support of her own mother raises her son, who suffers from a rare genetic disorder, Progeria (accelerated aging), and whose physical difference brings in its wake immense challenges. Yet her acceptance of her child's difference, and the quality of mutual joy and enrichment they bring to the relationship save the film from slipping into maudlin sentimentality. The mother is depicted as vulnerable yet strong, empowered and empowering. The twist in the tale occurs when a terminally ill Auro conspires to reunite his mother with his newly discovered father. By reclaiming his patrimony and restituting her wifely status, he completes his duty as a good son. In a curiously quirky casting coup, the role of the thirteen year old Auro is played by Amitabh Bachchan and Amol, the dynamic young politician, by Bachchan's real life son Abhishek. The child, thus, literally and metaphorically becomes the father of the man. Despite its eventual co-option by patriarchy, the roles of the mother and grandmother are refreshingly spunky and unsentimental, and reflective of a strong and supportive mother-daughter relationship under the most trying circumstances. Here, the unwed and pregnant daughter is far from being a *parayi*. It is rather the unstinting and unconditional support of the mother that helps her cope with her difficulties and celebrate her motherhood.

My Name is Khan (2010) tells the story of an Indian Muslim man confronting ethnic and racial discrimination in post 9/11 America. Khan's 'simple' mind cuts through the conflicts and contradictions of our times, foregrounding the universal truths of humanity and decency. Khan's mother, shown in an all-too-brief flashback, is an ordinary small-town Muslim woman with extraordinary empathy for her 'Rizzu' (Rizwan). The life lessons she teaches him, her belief in his inherent abilities, and her celebration of his small achievements reflect her acceptance and celebration of his 'difference'. Khan's Hindu wife, Mandira, undergoes the trauma of losing her only son to a racial attack because she is married to a Muslim, an object of hate in the terrible aftermath of the 9/11 attacks. Her trauma and grief at the hideous act, and her gradual coming to terms with its irrationality highlights the quality of forgiveness and acceptance, without which the cycle of violence can never cease.

In the 2015 film *Margarita with a Straw*, directed by Shonali Bose, young Laila who has cerebral palsy comes of age and explores her sexuality. Her relationship with her mother, whom she calls 'Ai', is portrayed with deep sensitivity. Ai's understated care-giving, her support for her daughter's ambitions and dreams, and ultimately her reconciliation with her daughter's sexual choices and private life provide Laila with the strength and capacity to emerge out of the shadow of her disability and live her life to the full. The twist in the tale is when the care-giver role is reversed. Laila's mother is diagnosed with terminal cancer, and it is the disabled daughter who now assumes the role as care-giver, along with her father. The inevitability of disease and death, the mutual bonds of dependence in which we are all implicated, and the ever-changing, contextual nature of ability/disability are the themes that run through the film. Like *Paa*, the character of *Ai* in *Margarita with a Straw* is not an idealized and mythologized depiction of a sacrificing and long-suffering mother. She is a mother who labours, loves, scolds, affirms her child's personhood and thereby emerges as a complete and complex personality in her own right. Despite the many limitations of the film and its blithe disregard for the deeply embedded structures of oppression that operate in the lives of disabled women, the mother-daughter relationship is rendered with warmth and empathy.

Conclusion

In the above highly selective reading of cinematic texts, I have attempted to paint with broad strokes a narrative of the embodied mother and the national body. In *Mother India*, she is the Earth Mother of a wounded and vulnerable new nation who rises phoenix-like to reclaim and reinstitute a moral order harnessing the best of western (masculinist) science and homegrown patriarchal constructs of chastity and honour. *Deewar* also takes up these themes, revealing the contradictions and fissures in the order, and the personal, emotional cost that must be borne by the maternal body, the toil and drudgery of raising children alone, the fragility and ephemerality of 'good times,' and the unspeakable choice of surrendering the rebellious yet most-beloved son to uphold the writ of (patriarchal) society and state. Under the conditions of cultural and political homogenization and a world-order premised upon masculinist domination, the mainstream Hindi film mother lost her iconic status, and became a mere shadow of the father figure who represents a unique blend of globality and Indianness. In the political arena, this coincided with a dominant majoritarian idiom and the growth of the Hindu right. The emergence on the national and international stage of the Hindutva machismo, epitomized by the current Prime Minister Narendra Modi in the wake of a landslide electoral victory in the General Elections of 2014, has signalled an important moment in cultural politics. Mr. Modi's perceived comfort and ease on the international stage, skilful media management, and the confident assertion of his Hindu identity have been remarked upon by political commentators. The frenzy and fanfare that accompanied his recent visits to the USA, Australia, Europe, Canada and other countries, and the enthusiastic response amongst the Indian community settled there, echoed in the loud chants of *'Bharat Mata ki Jai'* (Long live Mother India) that punctuated his (Hindi) speeches. This vividly illustrated the resonance and power of the father figure calling upon his scattered kinsmen to return to their roots, 'make in India' and remake the 'Hindu Undivided Family'.

Alongside these, sites of resistance and new narratives have also emerged within mainstream cinematic spaces; representations of the embodied experience of motherhood rendered with empathy and honesty is a task that a new generation of Bollywood filmmakers (which includes a number of women filmmakers) is well-equipped to take on. As viewers who are both women and mothers, we eagerly await new and thoughtful narratives that make space for all genders, alternative sexualities, different abilities and subjectivities—for mothers who embrace and empower humankind in all its variety, and play an active and agentic role in reconstructing the discourse of 'Woman'.

References

Bagchi, Jasodhara. 'Representing Nationalism: Ideology of Motherhood in Colonial Bengal'. In *Motherhood in India: Glorification without Empowerment*, edited by Maithreyi Krishnaraj. New Delhi: Routledge, 2010, pp. 158–85.

Bhattacharya Mehta, Rini. 'Bollywood, Nation, Globalization: An Incomplete Introduction'. In *Bollywood and Globalization*. London: Anthem Press. pp. 1–14.

Dirks, Nicholas. 'The Home and the Nation: Consuming Culture and Politics in *Roja*'. In *Pleasure and the Nation*, edited by Rachel Dwyer and Christopher Pinney. New Delhi: Oxford University Press, 2011, pp. 161–85.

Dutta, Sangeeta. 'Representations of Women in Indian Cinema', *Social Scientist* 40 (3,4), pp. 71–82. Accessed at http://www.jstor.org/stable/3518191. Accessed 16 February 2015.

Dube, Leela. 'On the Construction of Gender: Socialization of Hindu Girls in Patrilineal India'. In *Anthropological Explorations in Gender: Intersecting Fields*. New Delhi: SAGE Publications, 2001.
Gabriel, Karen. *Melodrama and the Nation: Sexual Economies of Bombay Cinema 1970–2000*. New Delhi: Women Unlimited, 2010.
Gokhale, Shanta. 'The Mother in Sane Guruji's *Shyamchi Ai*'. In *Motherhood in India: Glorification without Empowerment*, edited by Maithreyi Krishnaraj. New Delhi: Routledge, 2010, pp. 228–56.
Gokulsing, M. and W. Dissanayake. *Indian Popular Cinema: A Narrative of Cultural Change*. Hyderabad:Orient Longman, 1998.
Johri, Rachana. 'From *parayi* to *apni*: Mothers' Love as Resistance'. In *South Asian Mothering*, edited by Jasjit K. Sangha and Tahira Gonsalves. Bradford: Demeter Press. 2013, pp. 17–32.
Kakar, Sudhir. *The Inner World: A Psycho-Analytic Study of Childhood and Society in India*. 3rd Edition. New Delhi: Oxford University Press, 2008.
Kasbekar, Asha. 'Hidden Pleasures: Negotiating the Myth of the Female Ideal in Popular Hindi Cinema'. In *Pleasure and the Nation*, edited by Rachel Dwyer and Christopher Pinney. New Delhi: Oxford University Press, 2011, pp. 286–308.
Krishnan, Prabha. 'In the Idiom of Loss: Ideology of Motherhood in Television Serials-*Mahabharata* and *Ramayana*', edited by Maithreyi Krishnaraj. In *Motherhood in India: Glorification without Empowerment*. New Delhi: Routledge, pp. 106–157.
Krishnaraj, Maithreyi (ed.). *Motherhood in India: Glorification without Empowerment*. New Delhi: Routledge, 2010.
Lal, Vinay. 'Deewar (The Wall)' (http://www.sscnet.ucla.edu/southasia/Culture/Cinema/deewar.html. Accessed 17 February 2015.)
Lakshmi, C.S. 'Mother, Mother-Community and Mother-politics in Tamil Nadu' In *Motherhood in India: Glorification without empowerment*, edited by Maithreyi Krishan raj. 2010. New Delhi: Routledge, 2010, pp. 186–227.
Mishra, Vijay. *Bollywood Cinema: Temples of Desire*. New York: Routledge, 2002.
Pinney, Christopher. 'Introduction: Public, Popular and Other Cultures' In *Pleasure and the Nation*, edited by Rachel Dwyer and Christopher Pinney. New Delhi: Oxford University Press, 2011, pp. 1–34.
Riaz, Amber Fatima. 'Selfless to Selfish' In *South Asian Mothering*, edited by Jasjit K. Sangha and Tahira Gonsalves. Bradford: Demeter Press, 2013, pp. 165–175.
Sarkar, Sucharita From Sacrifice to Selfhood: Representations of the Mother in Hindi Films. Accessed from www.academia.edu. (n.d.)
Sen, Meheli. '"It's All about Loving Your Parents": Liberalization, Hindutva and Bollywood's New Fathers'. In *Bollywood and Globalization*, edited by Rini Bhattacharya Mehta and Rjeshwari V. Pandharipande. London: Anthem Press, 2010, pp. 145–68.
Shah, Shalini. 'On Gender, Wives and "Pativratas"', *Social Scientist* 40 (5, 6). 2012, pp. 77–90.
Starr Sered, Susan. '"Woman" as Symbol and Women as Agents; Gendered Religious Discourse and Practices'. *Women and Religion: Critical Concepts in*

Religious Studies Vol. 1, edited by Pamela Klassen, Shari Golberg and Danielle Lefebvre. London and New York: Routledge, 2009, pp. 9–33.

Thomas, Rosie. 'Sanctity and Scandal: The Mythologization of Mother India', *Quarterly Review of Film and Video* 11 (3), 1989, pp. 11–30.

Virdi, Jyotika. 'The "Fiction" of Film and "Fact" of Politics: *Deewar* (Wall, 1976)', *Jump Cut* 38, pp. 26–32.

Virdi, Jyotika. *The Cinematic ImagiNation: Indian Popular Films as Social History*. New Brunswick: Rutgers University Press, 2003.

Wadley, Susan S. 'Women and the Hindu Tradition'. In *Women in India: Two Perspectives*, edited by Jacobson Doranne and Susan S. Wadley. New Delhi: Manohar, 1986, pp. 113–39.

4

'More than a Mother': Autism, motherhood discourse and lived experience*

Introduction

The over-determined construction of the mother as a repository of unquestioning devotion and the source of unending care becomes particularly salient in the context of mothering a child with a developmental disability. Across cultures, the central role attributed to the mother in determining the developmental pathways of her child results in the mother often being blamed for her child's atypical or non-normative development. There is a powerful discourse of mother-blaming that stigmatizes the supposedly neglectful, self-centred mother, especially if she happens to be a professionally qualified, working one. This is particularly the case in the context of challenging disorders like autism, which impact the core capacities of language, communication and sociality that define and establish competent personhood and being 'human'. Autism is a complex neurobehavioural disorder that includes impairments in social interaction, developmental language and communication skills combined with rigid, repetitive behaviours. It ranges in severity from a mild condition that somewhat limits an otherwise normal life to a devastating

---

*This chapter is a thoroughly revised and considerably expanded version of the essay 'Motherhood as Ideology and Practice: The Experiences of Mothers of Children with Autism Spectrum Disorder' first published in *An Anthropology of Mothering* edited by Naomi Watts and Michelle McPherson (2011); Toronto, Demeter Press.

disability that may require life-long or institutional care.[1] A 'spectrum disorder', its manifestations vary from severely withdrawn, non-verbal children who seem to shun human contact to extremely talkative yet naive individuals who often behave very inappropriately in social situations.

Ever since autism was identified as a distinct disorder by the Austrian psychiatrist Leo Kanner in 1943, the condition has been inextricably linked to faulty mothering. The term 'refrigerator mother', coined by Kanner and taken to an extreme by scholars and practitioners like the University of Chicago professor and well-known writer Bruno Bettelheim, became an epithet that blamed and stigmatized a whole generation of autism mothers in the West, who were seen as lacking in the 'natural' maternal capacities of love and nurturance, and were thus responsible for the withdrawal of the child into his/her inner world. While many mothers bore the brunt of this label, others actively challenged and contested it. Their critiques and experiential accounts provided correctives to the prevalent 'expert' theories and professional practices. Social policy academic and autism mother Mary Langan (2011, 194) observes that the 'distinctive contribution of parental voices to the emerging discourse about autism… has received remarkably little attention.' However, recent works tracing the history and evolution of autism address the pivotal role played by parents in influencing the autism discourse. (Grinker, 2007; Feinstein, 2010; Silverman, 2012)

The growing salience of autism as a diagnostic category across the world in recent years has been driven by the globalization of western bio-medical and psychiatric discourses and the availability of information on the internet and other technologies. While the refrigerator mother concept had a specific socio-historical context and genealogy, mother-blaming emanates from cultural understandings of 'good' and 'bad' mothers, and thus, mothers across the world are made to feel responsible for their child's disability in specific, gendered ways. Autism mothers across the world, including India, have been at the forefront in creating and disseminating awareness about the condition, creating networks for mutual support and public understanding, challenging the hegemony of the medical and psychiatric professions, and fighting for the acknowledgement and celebration of their child's personhood and unique way of being in the world. This chapter examines how scientific and lay discourses simultaneously vilify and glorify the autism mother as both the pathological 'bad mother', who in a sense has made her child autistic, as well as the crusader who is 'more than a mother', struggling against all odds and thus, redeeming herself and her child. Between these bipolar discourses exists the lived reality of women struggling with the challenges of mothering a child with autism—experiencing physical, emotional, psychological and financial stress; attempting to juggle her multiple roles and responsibilities while seeking to love; and understand and do their best for the child. How do mothers make sense of the condition? How do they construct the child's 'personhood' and represent it to the world? How does the child's disability shape mothering ideology and practice? These questions assume added salience in the context of a condition like autism, which stigmatizes and isolates the child and the mother alike.

I begin with an examination of the evolution of autism as a diagnostic label, and its historical misrepresentation as being somehow caused by cold, disengaged mothering. I then give an overview of how mothers themselves engaged with and transformed this discourse, giving valuable insights into the embodied difference that autism represents as well as challenging received notions. Shifting the focus to the Indian situation, I go on to discuss the experiences of urban Indian mothers of children with autism drawn from the ethnographic research that I conducted with families (Vaidya 2008), as well as provide reflexive insights based upon my own experiences as the mother of a child (now a young adult) with autism. A discussion of the major findings of the research from a gendered perspective, with specific focus on the feminization of care, has been published earlier. (see Vaidya 2015) I attempt to show how the lived experiences of mothering a child with disability open up possibilities for engagement with multiple subjectivities whilst affirming a shared humanity.

Autism and the Refrigerator Mother

In 1943, the US-based Austrian psychiatrist, Leo Kanner, published his now-famous paper 'Autistic Differences of Affective Contact' based upon clinical work with 11 children who, according to him, displayed an *'inability to relate themselves* in the ordinary way to people and situations from the beginning of life.' (1943, 242, Kanner's italics) Kanner used the term 'autism' (from autos, self) to describe the condition. Just a year after the publication of Kanner's paper, another Austrian, Hans Asperger, independently published a dissertation in German concerning 'autistic psychopathy' in childhood. The four children he studied were highly intelligent and verbal, like 'little professors'. Yet, they too, like Kanner's patients were socially impaired and often mercilessly teased and bullied by their peers. Asperger's work, however, remained largely unknown to the English-speaking world for several years. Autism was also equated with 'childhood schizophrenia', a misleading term, as, unlike schizophrenics, autistic individuals did not appear to have hallucinations or delusions. Kanner believed that autism was an innate disorder present since birth. Unlike schizophrenics, autistic children did not withdraw from the world; rather, they were unable to participate in it, in the first place. However, Kanner did draw attention to what appeared to him as a genuine lack of maternal warmth and spontaneity, and the apparent inability of parents to engage their children or indulge them in play, leaving them neatly 'in refrigerators which did not defrost'. Indeed, he once remarked in an interview in 1960 that the parents of autistic children must have probably defrosted just enough to produce a child! (cited in Douglas 2014, 4)

Both Kanner and Asperger observed that parents of the children they studied tended to also be aloof and distant, and that even distant relatives displayed certain odd or abnormal traits. With the benefit of hindsight it appears that their observations provided evidence for what scientists are increasingly recognizing today as a genetic component in autism, much on the same lines as that in schizophrenia or bipolar disorder. (Grinker 2007, 72) However, given the intellectual climate of the time, the observations on cold parents were taken as evidence that parents, and mothers in particular, actually were the cause for their child's condition. The fact that many mothers were actually highly educated and professionally qualified added another nail in the coffin. What was actually at play was the process of 'referral bias'; educated, upper-class families were far more likely to take their children for consultations with psychiatrists than working class or poor ones!

The 'refrigerator mother' theory, which speculated that highly educated, professionally successful and therefore unnaturally cold and disengaged mothers somehow contributed to triggering off the autistic symptoms of these children, was of a piece with the prevailing psycho-analytical discourse current at the time and was lapped up by the medical establishment as well as the general public in the 1950s and 1960s. Bruno Bettelheim, Chicago University Professor, child development specialist and renowned writer was one of the best-known proponents of this view and exercised a huge sway over the public imagination. He firmly established autism as a disorder of parenting (specifically mothering) which required a 'parentectomy' or removal of the child from the pathological home into a nurturing therapeutic milieu presided over by the all-knowing 'expert'.

An Austrian refugee and former prisoner of the notorious Nazi concentration camps, Bettelheim came to America and became the Director of the Sonia Shankman Orthogenic School in Chicago in 1944. The School undertook the care and rehabilitation of emotionally disturbed children and was to become the 'field site' for the propagation of Bettelheim's ideas about the causes and treatment of autism. Feinstein explains that it was Bettelheim's experience in the Nazi camps that prompted him to make 'a dreadful and damaging mental leap' (Feinstein 2010, 54–55) in which he equated the behaviour of autistic children with that of the inmates of Nazi camps and their mothers with the camp commanders. In his most famous book on autism, sombrely titled *The Empty Fortress* (1967), Bettelheim wrote that much like some of the prisoners in the camps who showed absolutely no overt reaction to their most cruel experiences and defensively withdrew from the world, autistic children too withdrew in response to the 'emotional pain' and 'depletion of the self' that they experienced at the hands of their mothers. Infantile autism, he claimed, was 'a state of mind that develops in reaction to feeling oneself in an extreme situation, entirely without hope.' (57)

He proposed that in contrast to the parents of non-autistic children, parents of autistic children were themselves psychologically impaired and thus, reacted abnormally to their child's normal behaviour; this led the child to respond negatively by withdrawing from interaction. The parent would react to the child's unresponsiveness pathologically and thus, would ensue a cycle of rejection and withdrawal that resulted in the child retreating into what Bettelheim termed 'chronic autistic disease'.

As mentioned earlier, Bettelheim believed that the only way the disease could be treated was by separating the child from the parents. The Orthogenic School which he headed was promoted as one such place where a child would be 'healed' from the psychic wounds inflicted by his parents and be exposed to a caring, nurturing environment that would enable the distorted 'self' to flower and develop. *The Empty Fortress* attempted to show how three severely autistic children were effectively treated by Bettelheim through psychoanalysis and 'milieu therapy', a new buzzword of the time. The book received an enthusiastic reaction and much critical acclaim, and Bettelheim's stature as a kind of 'sage' who had experienced and survived the horrors of the depths to which humanity could sink, vested him with an authority to 'transform' the lives of children damaged by their own parents. Waltz (n.d., 2) remarks that his use of 'emotionally stirring language and potent metaphors built a dramatic narrative of autism'; the metaphor used in the title capturing the idea of 'the essential emptiness, otherness or non-humanness of people with autism; the idea of a "real" self that is missing, estranged or asleep in people with autism; military metaphors; and the concept of autism, or the person with autism, as an enigma or puzzle.' The heroic endeavours of the iconic father figure in the shape and form of Bettelheim himself would redeem these lost souls from the damage inflicted by bad mothers. The positioning of the therapist as a heroic figure is patriarchal to the core and underscores the vulnerability of the affected person in relation to the voice of expertise, seeking to vanquish the 'abnormal' and discounting the lived experiences of mothers and children.

Weusten (2011), in her discussion on the narrative construction of motherhood and autism in America and Europe, remarks upon the seamlessness with which the theory of the failing refrigerator mother fits neatly into the prevalent public discourse about 'bad mothers' which was strongly influenced by psychoanalytical and pedagogical theories of authors like John Bowlby and Donald Winnicott. These theories were premised upon a gendered binary opposition between the public, masculine sphere and the feminine, private sphere wherein the father carried out the 'outside' work and enacted the role of breadwinner, whereas the mother's domain was the private sphere of home, bearing and rearing children. The ideology of 'separate spheres' is at the very heart of the modern, industrial nuclear family, and the 'ideal' family is portrayed as a 'harmonious, stable, nuclear household with an economically successful father and an angelic mother.' (Cancian 1989, 17, cited in Wharton 2005) The emphasis on the woman as homemaker created a 'myth of motherhood' in which maternal instinct was conceptualized as an inborn feminine trait rather than as a socially learned and contextually specific practice. 'Intensive mothering' requires mothers to focus most of their time and energies on child development, nutrition, education, hobbies and play so that the child gets the best possible start in life. (Hays. 1996, cited in Bradley 2007) The 'refrigerator mother' demonized by (male) experts thus became the perfect target of blame for a child's atypical or abnormal development, as an 'abnormal' mother deficient in maternal instinct and caring practices. Weusten sums it up neatly:

In other words, discourse on the 'failing', 'refrigerator mother' of a child diagnosed with autism is born out of the discourse on the 'good', intensive mother of a neurotypical child. This mechanism of blaming illustrates how the two are underpinned by a hetero-normatively gendered, binary opposition between the masculine public sphere and the feminine private sphere. In addition, it illustrates a normative opposition between what is considered to be a neurotypical child and a non-neurotypical child—in this case, a child diagnosed with autism. The first category is rendered 'normal' while the latter is categorized as 'abnormal'. (Weusten 2011, 58)

Challenges and Contestations

Challenging the discourse of mother blame, experiential accounts of parents of children with autism emerged from the late 1960s onward. (Langan 2011) Clara Claiborne Park's *The Seige* (1967) published in the same year as Bettelheim's magnum opus called for a breakdown of the separation between parents and psychiatric profession, and presented a detailed account of 'a family's journey into the world of an autistic child'. Park wrote in moving detail of her experiences of raising Elly (a pseudonym for her autistic daughter), and her rejection of the pernicious and implausible theory that held her to be responsible for her child's condition. The fact that she was already the mother of non-disabled children gave her confidence in herself and her mothering practices. Interestingly, as Weusten (2011) points out, she challenged the patriarchal construct of the housebound, always-available, 'good mother' and emphasized the value of her own professional commitments as a teacher and scholar in actually helping her understand Elly better; and her experience as Elly's mother in turn helping her become a better teacher. (60) Park attempts to penetrate the wall of silence that surrounds Elly by attempting to enter her world. Through music and song, drawing and play, Park humanizes her child, acknowledges her as a complete (if different) human being. Douglas (2014, 9) suggests that Park's narrative repositions the cold 'refrigerator mother' as an engaged, curious and inventive one, 'gesturing to the wealth of mothers' knowledge about difference and human relationality as one that might humanize how we—all of us—live with difference within now-dominant biogenetic regimes.' These regimes include pre-natal testing and aborting of potentially defective fetuses, the desire to produce 'designer babies', and assisted reproductive techniques that privilege the 'normative' and attempt to weed out differences or anomalies. Ghai and Johri problematize the idea of the 'choice' exercised by women to abort a potentially disabled child and argue that the impossible burden of perpetual motherhood and unpaid care work within patriarchy constrains any real choice. By giving birth to and raising their children with disabilities, mothers in fact pose a challenge to the devaluation and marginalization of children whose minds and bodies work differently and whose capacities can be nurtured through the deep knowledge that caring practices engender.

As autism increasingly came to be recognized as a neuro-developmental condition whose basis was probably biological or genetic, the earlier psychogenetic theories were discredited and debunked within Anglo-American psychiatry. However, they continued to flourish in countries like France and Italy where psychoanalytical theory was the mainstream discourse in the realm of mental health. In countries like South Korea too, autism is associated with faulty mothering and termed 'Reactive Affective Disorder'. (Grinker 2007) Feinstein (2010), in his comprehensive history of autism, writes about the pioneering role played by autism parents in redefining and calibrating the contemporary understanding of autism and in devising appropriate diagnostic and pedagogic strategies based upon these understandings. The work of Lorna Wing, child specialist, autism expert and mother of a daughter with autism is particularly remarkable. Her conceptualization of the 'triad of impairments' that characterize the condition, and her popularization of the path-breaking contributions of Hans Asperger to the English-speaking world, brought about a qualitative shift in autism research and practice.

Writing of parental perspectives on autism in America and the UK, Langan (2011) discusses their contributions to ongoing debates and controversies, challenging the culture of mother-blame, and mobilizing for mutual support, generation of public awareness and creation of services during the period from the 1960s to 1980s when autism was considered a rare and unfamiliar condition. National advocacy organizations were established; attempts were made to integrate children into the community; and civil society and local groups were involved in providing assistance and support to families in crisis. From the 1990s onwards, a profusion of family narratives in the form of novels and autobiographies, television documentaries and internet sites emerged. The proliferation of autism diagnoses in the West, probably on account of greater awareness and better diagnostic methods fuelled the idea that there was an autism epidemic, and this was caused neither by genetics nor flawed parenting, but by environmental toxins. Vaccines became the villain and big pharma, the target, as 'pop' theories regarding the purported link between certain kinds of vaccines and the onset of autism circulated. These theories were never scientifically proven but continue to excite heated debates. 'Anti-vaccine moms' like Hollywood actress and autism mother Jenny MacCarthy, who wrote the bestseller *Louder Than Words: A Mother's Journey into Healing Autism* (2007) became a poster-girl for unorthodox treatments to 'defeat' autism. These ranged from special diets to vitamin supplementation, chelation (removing heavy metals from the blood) and hyperbaric oxygen, and lately, stem cell therapy. However, none of them has yet been proved to provide a cure. Over the years, the consensus emerging within the therapeutic community suggested that the underlying cause for autism was most likely genetic, and that behavioural interventions were more likely to improve the quality of life for persons with the condition.

As a growing number of adults with autism emerged in public view and became self-advocates around the new millennium, the 'neurodiversity' perspective emerged from within the ranks of autistic people themselves. Neurodiversity challenges the bio-medical, disease-cure framework, and argues for an acceptance and celebration of autistic difference as part of the diversity that characterizes humankind, an embodied difference which is not in any way inferior to that of 'neurotypical' people. Autistic activist and self-advocate Jim Sinclair's moving piece 'Don't Mourn for Us' (1993) urges parents to accept that autism is an intrinsic part of who their child is, and that to wish away the autism would be to deny the very existence of their child. From 'damaged goods' without a voice to assertive subjects asserting their 'right to be different', the emergence of autistic self-advocacy is certainly a heartening development and is in no small measure due to the efforts of families to secure their children's rights and entitlements to appropriate education, rehabilitation and care. However, for the vast majority of families struggling with the demands of caring for a child with autism and other developmental disabilities, the issues of life-long care and ensuring a life of dignity for their loved one are critical and often intractable. We now turn to autism and motherhood discourses in India and map how motherhood ideology structures practices and how mothers attempt to redefine their child's subjectivity as well as their own. We attempt to illustrate how patriarchal perspectives on the mother as defective or lacking are balanced by the counter-narrative of selfless sacrifice and the attempt to become 'more than a mother'.

Autism, Motherhood and Lived Experience in India

Unlike the scientific and cultural fascination that has existed around autism in the west (see Straus 2010 for an overview) in India it is still a relatively marginal category that frequently gets equated with intellectual disability or mental retardation. However, the 'internet revolution' in contemporary India has opened the floodgates; information (sometimes dubious and unsubstantiated) about the latest theories and therapies is readily available for those who can access the web. Knowledge and awareness about autism as a distinct syndrome with clearly defined diagnostic criteria has certainly increased over the years in the medical and psychiatric community, yet it is largely underdiagnosed or misdiagnosed in all but a few urban pockets. Unlike other disabilities, it does not have a local 'name'; people presenting with its symptoms are frequently classified as intellectually disabled (*manda buddhi* in Hindi) or mad (*paagal*). The number of people likely to be affected with autism in India is also not clear. As a result, quick and accurate diagnoses are hard to come by, and the paucity of services of children diagnosed with the condition makes it even harder for families to manage the demands of caring for such a child. The following sections draw upon fieldwork conducted during the course of my doctoral research. (Vaidya 2008) The research was conducted in the metropolis of Delhi. With its multispeciality public and private hospitals and a well-developed and active NGO sector, the capital city is a place where families from different parts of the country come to 'show' their children and find answers to their questions about the child's atypical development. It would be appropriate to begin the discussion with a biographical note.

On a hot summer morning in the year 2000, I journeyed across the city of Delhi with my hyperactive three-year-old clutched tightly against my chest. Navigating unfamiliar streets we finally reached our destination: a dingy building in an urban village in South Delhi, home to Action for Autism, a parent-driven NGO that works with autistic children and their families. Struggling up the steep flight of stairs I was filled with a deep sense of foreboding. I had brought my little boy for an assessment on the advice of my paediatrician as he displayed a pattern of development startlingly different from other children his age—a pattern that seemed to fit a diagnosis of autism. The cheery bustling atmosphere in the Centre took me completely by surprise; they were preparing for their Annual Day and the place was filled with colourful cardboard cutouts of trees and trains. A friendly therapist observed him and made her assessment quickly. Yes, it was quite clear that he displayed the symptoms of autism. Yes, there would certainly be improvement with early intervention and a supportive environment. No, there was no 'cure'.

The diagnosis brought home the sobering realization that this was a reality we would have to negotiate with throughout our lives, and that the condition was simply not going to 'go away' like a viral fever or an attack of measles. With this knowledge, we tried to prepare ourselves and our children for the future. The journey so far has been an eventful one. Reflecting upon my experiences as a parent of a child with a developmental disability, I realized the urgent need to document and study the experiences of other families like mine. The narratives I gathered during the course of my fieldwork are retold even today, umpteen times, in different voices. I am frequently approached by parents who are referred by friends and colleagues for advice and assistance, and their stories almost invariably corroborate the ones I gathered in the field.

The endeavour to transform the nature and scope of my experiences from parent of an autistic child, whose academic discipline happened to be Sociology, to those of a researcher in Sociology undertaking a study of families of autistic children, was a problematic one. While my child's disability affected me personally and emotionally, it also fascinated the social scientist in me. Much of what I had studied in the areas of child development, socialization, development of selfhood and identity seemed inadequate to explain the developmental path my child was taking. Merely finding a 'name' for his condition was not enough. It was not an organic condition like diphtheria or polio that was caused by viruses or bacteria, nor was it a disorder like mental retardation or *manda buddhi*, which was culturally recognizable and would have been received by family and community with sympathy. The behaviour displayed by my child and others like him, more closely resembled the category of *paagalpan* or madness, a far more stigmatizing label. Calling it by an English name like 'autism' made it seem even more strange and alienating. The situation that families like mine found themselves in, vis-à-vis the community, was a break-down of inter-subjectivity. The situation was further compounded by the demands for conformity and rejection of difference by an elitist educational system and a competitive urban social milieu where children's academic achievements and extra-curricular triumphs were the 'trophies' displayed by middle-class parents in the quest for upward social mobility.

A child's autism may be conceptualized as a window through which to view processes of change in the urban middle-class family. Popular journals, newspapers and television features have been telling us that modern Indian families are changing in many ways; women are taking up careers, the 'joint family' is breaking down, elders are being neglected, the number of latch-key children is growing. We read reports of 'high-achieving' children exhorted by parents to excel in academics, sports and the arts. We see reality shows and talent hunts on television where children as young as four are made to sing, dance, act, laugh and cry on demand, with scant regard for their tender age and psychological vulnerability. We also see the valorization of the joint family (albeit in a trendy new *avatar*) in recent blockbuster Bollywood films and prime-time television soap operas which have a large audience amongst the urban middle class. These depictions in popular culture apparently fuel the notion that the all-encompassing, nurturing joint family has been rent asunder by the pervasive impact of modernization and the growth of individual aspirations. Serious sociological analysis on such apparently sweeping changes is, however, thin on the ground, perhaps because it is too close to home, and part and parcel of the milieu in which sociologists themselves live and work.

A difficult circumstance like a child's disability acts as a 'critical event' or a breach in the fabric of 'normalcy', challenging existing rules and regulations and bringing to light the weaknesses in the social fabric. It is in a sense a natural laboratory in which to view the changes supposedly taking place in the urban family, specifically with regard to the changing role of the mother. The choice of topic for this project was the outcome both of biographical factors and a keen interest in the changes taking place within families in a metropolis that I have been living in for most of my adult life.

My research was informed by a feminist epistemology and methodology (see Gorelik 1991; Klein 1983) Thus, I challenged the 'objective' splitting of subject and object, of the researcher and the researched. The methods of data collection employed included in-depth, narrative interviews, observation and participant observation. The methods were not really separable but flowed into each other, and were geared towards capturing in all its rich detail, the ebb and flow of daily life, the constant demands and challenges of mothering an autistic child. Additionally, through 'intersubjectivity', I compared my research and experiences as a woman and shared it with my respondents, who then added their opinion.[2] (Klein 1983) The following sections examine some of the common themes that emerged in the course of the ethnographic interviews with mothers pertaining both to the day-to-day, nitty-gritty realities of care as well as the ideological underpinnings and cultural constructions which serve as the prism through which mothers make sense both of their child's 'difference' and their own roles and responsibilities.

The Challenges of Mothering a Child with Autism

A consistent observation that was noted during fieldwork was the unending hard work involved in mothering an autistic child. This work includes actual physical care, cooking the kind of food the child will eat, ensuring that enough nutrition is being put into his/her system, cleaning, bathing, dressing, toileting, transporting from place to place, 'working' with the child (i.e., following the educational guidelines prescribed by teachers/therapists), keeping the child comfortable at home, leisure activities after school, and putting the child to bed, among other tasks. Added to these activities, parents have to run the household, work, shop, fulfil social obligations, care for other children and other family members, attend to each other's needs (emotional, physical, sexual), and to their own personal routines and health.

Strains such as these also pull on parents of regularly developing children in the context of an urban milieu with shrinking familial networks. However, autism, with its variation in manifestation and complexity, poses certain unique challenges. A mother may want to pick up groceries on the way back from school with her child, but the sensory over-stimulation of a crowded market-place may result in the child having a screaming fit. Parents may need to attend another child's Parent-Teacher Meeting, but due to the absence of a care-giver for the child, one of them may have to stay at home. A hyperactive autistic child may run pell-mell at a wedding or social gathering, requiring one parent to attend to him/her throughout, while the other converses with the guests and relatives. Such adjustments are part and parcel of parenting young children, but parents know that the children will soon mature and not need constant physical monitoring. However, with a developmentally disabled child, such assumptions cannot be automatically made. The unpredictability of symptoms can also be disconcerting. A child who normally enjoys his evening at the swings in the park may suddenly develop an aversion to the new colour they have been painted, or may be so attracted by a crying baby that he may suddenly hit them to make them cry harder, laughing uncontrollably at the result. The predictability, the routine that everyday life is inscribed in, is often breached by the enigma that is autism. These breaches rip apart the fabric of daily functioning and constantly demand 'patchwork' to repair them. Most narratives and observations of life with an autistic child highlight the need for constantly thinking on one's feet, being vigilant and not allowing one's guard to slip. Underlying the day-to-day strains is the omnipresent realization of the life-long nature of the condition and fears for the future: 'what will happen when I am gone?' A mother put it poignantly:

> The slogan you are given is, 'zero expectations, one-hundred percent hope', but is it possible to live a life without expectations? When he has a good day, it's a good day for us. When he has a bad day it's a bad day. Is dealing with his tantrums from day to day what our life is all about? Are we going to do this all our lives? You keep wanting to get used to it, but can't.

Perspectives on Mothering

Mothers' experiences were conditioned by their children's disabilities. Disablement being a devalued identity, these mothers had difficulty not just in establishing the personhood of their children, but also their own worth as mothers. Even though they had to work equally hard, if not harder than regular mothers, in the material and non-material work of nurturing, they had to fight hard on behalf of their children to 'win' their personhood. Their narratives demonstrated the extra work they had to do to 'prove' themselves as 'good' mothers in a social setting where the achievements of one's children are the currency by which a mother is valued.

As we discuss throughout the book, becoming a mother is culturally regarded as an Indian woman's defining goal, a key 'act' in her life, the fulfilment of her womanly destiny. As we have discussed in the previous chapter, scholars like Wadley interpret it as a transition from the subservient wifely role to one of control, even danger, making the mother an object of reverence and even fear. (Wadley 1986) While authors like Kakar (1978) have detailed the intense physical and psychological bonding that exists between mother and child (particularly the male child), Kurtz (1992) refers to 'multiple care-giving' as being the norm rather than the intimate dyadic relationship as Kakar highlights. As Chaudhary (2004) observes, the Indian child is in contact with multiple mothering presences, a practice rooted in the joint family ideal that persists in urban, nuclear ones. She refers to a 'packaged' form of traditional care through visits to kin, one's own mother, friends and neighbourhood. In her analysis of the way mothers talk to their young children, she highlights how mothers invoke several 'others', in the form of kin, both present and absent, thereby creating a densely peopled universe for their children.

Conversely, the mothers in this study pointed out that the presence of a disability like autism, with its occasional extremely challenging behaviours, made it socially embarrassing and difficult for them to develop and sustain contacts with relatives and friends. They felt themselves isolated and pushed into a corner, unable to explain their child's difficulties, often resulting in adverse comments on their own mothering abilities and practices. If not 'refrigerator mothers', they were certainly seen as incompetent ones. Although most of them informed of the immense emotional support they received from their own mothers, their experiences with their in-laws were sometimes quite different. The 'blame game', particularly with respect to paternal grand parents often caused strained relations, leading the couple to retreat into their shell and further isolate themselves and the child. This further impeded better understanding and acceptance of the child's disorder, thus creating a vicious cycle. Mothers informed that they had become 'hypersensitive' to comments and questions in the early days following diagnosis, and would react adversely to words like '*paagal*' or 'mental', which they now realize were not used with any intent to hurt, but rather due to the lack of knowledge or information. They, therefore, preferred to seek solace and support from friends and other families like themselves, if available, however, the pressures of urban life also made this difficult to do. Their narratives revealed certain core themes in the manner in which they constructed and conceptualized their roles. These include the over-determined conceptions of 'mother's love'; the notion of the mother as the 'voice' of her autistic child; precedence of the needs of the autistic child; the pressures of constant mothering; and the opportunity to become 'better persons' because of the special responsibilities they are entrusted with.

Mother's Love

'Mother's love' (*mamta*, as expressed in Hindi) is believed to transcend all bonds. A child with severe impairments, who is reviled, rejected or ridiculed by the world around him, is unconditionally loved only by the parents and particularly by the mother. The strength of this sentiment was poignantly felt when mothers used the expression 'after all, you too are a mother!' to express their solidarity, trust and confidence in me as a researcher. In their work on the cultural construction of motherhood in urban India, Chaudhary and Bhargava (2006a; 2006b) discuss the meanings imputed to the concept of *mamta* and motherhood. *Mamta* is construed as indestructible, continuous and natural, involving self-sacrifice, devotion, forgiveness, and self-realization through unity with one's child. The narratives of the mothers in the present study suggest that while the world may reject the autistic child, a mother could never forsake it. Love and care were conflated. This could be observed in the jibes that mothers directed to 'uncaring' or 'irresponsible' mothers. I recall the case of a child whose mother had taken a transfer to another city leaving the child in the care of the father: 'How much can the poor father do? It's the mother's responsibility, after all,' was the common refrain. I often heard remarks like 'she doesn't know how to handle the child properly' and 'she doesn't work hard with the child', in connection with particularly difficult children. While these over-determined conceptions of the centrality of the mother's role in shaping the child's development apply equally in the case of regularly developing children, they were magnified in the case of a disabled child.

The construction of the 'good mother' is also reinforced by the emphasis laid by medical professionals, therapists and educators on maternal coping being the key to the child's outcomes, as I discussed earlier in the chapter. Mothers also had powerful role models in the form of the Special Educators and therapists working with their children, who were also mothers of disabled children. The mothering role thus also included that of teacher, companion, therapist and advocate, much more than what is expected in the case of regularly developing children. The pressure of living up to this ideal is intense. Women would often give voice to their frustrations, anxiety and irritation, something they could not do with their family members, for fear of their feelings being misunderstood. Tension was often released through humour. Mothers would poke fun at their children's eccentricities, and the sessions would end in peals of laughter. During the course of the interviews, mothers confided feelings of ambivalence and revulsion they sometimes experienced, and the guilt that accompanied these feelings. To my utter discomfiture, some mothers frankly expressed the wish that their children would not outlive them, not because they did not love the child, but because they loved them so much.

Mother as the 'Voice' of the Autistic Child

As Autism impacts communication, language and social skills, mothers saw themselves as the child's voice, the medium through which the child was rendered intelligible to the world and vice-versa. The child's personhood and his participation in social life were also constructed through talk. Mothers would delve into great detail on family activities, and the things their children were doing. They would talk about the new foods the child was eating, the appreciative comment made by a visiting relative on how much the child had improved, or a funny incident in the school or playground. Mothers also narrated their ongoing battles to secure acceptance and dignity for their child with kin, neighbours, shopkeepers, rickshaw-drivers, school authorities and salespersons. They recounted their initial feelings of discomfiture, embarrassment and shame, which over a period of time changed to anger at people's insensitivity or a 'don't-care' attitude. A mother recounted an incident when she yelled at a shopkeeper for calling her son '*paagal*' (mad): 'you are mad, not he. Is he hitting you? Abusing you?'

Precedence of the Needs of the Autistic Child

The needs, routine and welfare of the autistic child frequently took precedence over those of other family members, and the mother's own concerns, commitments and health. Mothers particularly felt they were doing an 'injustice' to their other non-disabled children, not paying enough attention to their husband's emotional and sexual needs, and were unable and often unwilling to maintain social contacts with kin, friends and colleagues. Mothers found scant time to socialize with friends, and to devote to health, fitness, personal development, leisure activities and sexuality. Their interactions with other mothers of children with autism were sometimes the only spaces where they could share their feelings and be understood. Talking with their own mothers or other relatives would often result in the reiteration of the 'tragedy'; they would often end up feeling worse than before.

Constant Mothering

Mothers confided that there were moments in which they felt so burdened by the demands of constant care that they felt like escaping or even committing suicide. Such feelings were particularly intense in the early years, and resulted from the shock of the diagnosis. Most of the mothers informed me that they eventually overcame these feelings of desperation and had become used to the child's condition. Some of them, however, admitted to being 'pushed to the brink' on numerous occasions. Homebound, with busy husbands, far away from their natal homes, with few friends or acquaintances to share their plight, these mothers epitomized 'urban angst', isolation and loneliness.

Becoming 'Better Persons'

The narratives suggested that while mothering a child with autism is indeed a challenging, exhausting, sometimes frustrating, and always a demanding job, it can also be interesting, fulfilling, and even uplifting. For some mothers, the child's autism resulted in their giving up career plans and staying at home; however, some mothers also converted 'adversity into opportunity' by getting involved in fields like therapy and special education. While their endeavours in this field were primarily oriented to help them work better with their own children, it also resulted in them networking and building relationships with other children and families.

Several mothers said that having a child with autism had made them 'better human beings', made them more patient, accepting, kind and helpful. Some said that their child's autism had enabled them to meet and interact with remarkable people—other parents, teachers, activists and autistic people who despite their difficulties adjusted to the demands of 'our' world—as a young mother of an autistic girl put it: 'Until she came into our lives I was just any other ordinary housewife. Because of her, I have come to know how strong I am, that I can contribute something to the society.' Speaking for myself, the research was an attempt to turn personal adversity into a positive opportunity, using the emancipatory tools of social science theory and methodology. (Vaidya 2010)

Entrapment and Empowerment: Case studies of mothers of children with autism

The 'mothering ideology' that emerges from the narratives places a premium on mothers' coping and caring skills, and draws on the cultural representations of the selfless nature of motherhood celebrated in myth, folklore and popular culture. Confronted with the 'tragedy' of mothering a disabled child, she has to literally rise from the ashes and find her salvation in untiring care and sacrifice, becoming 'more than a mother'. It can be said that the role of the autism mother magnifies and intensifies some of the issues which define mothering in patriarchy: intensive focus on mother care, mother-love, mother blame, exhaustion, lack of a personal identity independent of motherhood. The autism mother becomes responsible for carrying much more than the double-burden that average mothers do, and brings to light the inescapability of maternal plight in patriarchy. This model can simultaneously produce entrapment and open a pathway for empowerment, as can be seen in the case studies presented below. The case studies of Preeti and Kavita, mothers of children with autism, highlight the complex and sometimes unexpected intersections of personal biographies, social structure and gender relations in an urban milieu that is simultaneously homogenizing and yet accords spaces for breaking free of traditional hierarchies.[3]

Preeti's Story

Preeti, a personable young woman, was in her early 30s when I first interviewed her. Her husband was a corporate executive and they were an upwardly mobile, upper-middle-class couple, staying in a well-furnished apartment in Delhi. Preeti gave up her job and became a full-time mother after the birth of her son R. As an infant, R was extremely demanding and needed constant attention. Preeti recalled,

> Everyone used to say, 'Give him a good massage, bath, feed him… and see how he'll sleep.' But as soon as I used to put him down, he would wake up at once. He never used to leave my breast. People used to say, 'This mother and child live in their own world. They are immune to what is going on around them….'

Although his early milestones (head-holding, creeping, crawling) were within the 'normal' range, his lack of speech even after his first birthday worried her. He started attending a neighborhood play-school, but his play-group teacher was baffled at his inability or unwillingness to join in play activities. She described him as 'abnormal', and eventually he was withdrawn from the school. He would throw terrible temper tantrums, scream and cry continuously, and display self-injurious behaviour. His father attempted to discipline him by hitting and shouting; this would frighten the child into submission but it deeply upset Preeti who became very protective. She would have serious arguments with her husband over the issue of management of the child. When the child turned three, they consulted at one of the country's leading hospitals, where they received a diagnosis of autism. They had no idea what autism was; it was only when they read the information booklets provided by the institution that they realized it was a life-long disability. The young couple was devastated. Preeti reported that she wept for months. However, she slowly tried to come to terms with this painful reality and do what she could to help her child. Her husband was caught up in the demands of his career; it fell to Preeti to devise ways and means of teaching, training, helping R to 'fit in'. She would entice neighbourhood children to come home and play with him by offering toys, snacks and balloons. They would play with his things but not with him, and he seemed oblivious to their presence. Disheartened, she gave up her attempts to help him 'mix' with his peers.

Due to the lack of educational opportunities available for autistic children in their home town, they moved to Delhi and enrolled the child at a Special Needs Centre. The child responded well to the therapy and started showing improvement; this filled the young parents with renewed hope. Preeti even trained as a special educator and worked part-time. But as the years rolled on, R's extremely complex difficulties took a severe toll on her energy, enthusiasm and optimism. Her daily activities revolved exclusively around his needs; she hardly ever went out to meet friends or family, and had minimal interaction with the neighbours. She would take R to school, get him home in the afternoon and spend the rest of the day attending to him. She felt that any time not spent 'doing things' or 'working' with R was time wasted. Yet when they were home together, she did not know how to engage him because he was 'not interested in anything—toys, books, TV, nothing.' Boxes of colourful and interesting toys lay unused in the playroom. He would often just sit in his room rattling a bottle filled with beans, jump vigorously on his trampoline or spend time looking out of the balcony at the children playing downstairs. He would oscillate between bouts of extreme anger and aggression, and depression and misery. At the time of the fieldwork, he was under very strong psychiatric medication. During his angry spells he would pull Preeti's hair and claw at her face, sometimes hitting or kicking so hard, that she would fall down. He was a big, strong, heavy child and could inflict considerable physical harm, especially when in a fury. His mother confided that her greatest fear was that he might injure or even kill her when he grew up: 'he'll be treated badly... people will lock him up, hit him.' She would sometimes lose her temper and self-control but then feel intense guilt and self-hatred because she knew that her son was not deliberately trying to hurt her, but rather was a victim of his disorder. She experienced feelings of frustration and rage, tenderness and pity: 'what else can you call it? Because he is not a complete human being.... Who can he take his anger out on except his mother? After all, even we vent our anger onto our mummy.' Torn between her concern about her child and her own feelings of misery and loneliness, Preeti's condition at the time I interviewed her was one of entrapment in the expectations of selfless motherhood. There was a sense of alienation in an anonymous urban milieu, and the politics of care that emerged from the gendered segregation of the 'homemaker/breadwinner' roles. Her plight underscores the paucity of services such as respite care and residential facilities where parents can admit children with extreme symptoms or high-support needs; wretched conditions that prevail in state-run facilities and the prohibitive costs and unregulated nature of privately managed ones push families in to a corner; urbanization, migration away from natal homes and disintegrating joint family networks combine to create an impossible situation where parents are, literally, the first and last resort, and the mother the primary provider of life-long care.

Kavita's Story

Kavita grew up in a small town in the eastern part of India. She belonged to a family of traders, and had a sheltered and happy childhood. After her marriage to a groom selected carefully by her family, she continued to lead a regimented existence as the daughter-in-law of a large joint-family household. Three years later, her daughter D was born. She was a very frail baby, susceptible to all kinds of infections. Kavita cannot recall anything conspicuously odd about her, except the lack of speech, but her in-laws assured her that she was just late in that department. Deafness was suspected because of fungal infections in the ear, but soon ruled out. Eventually, D was taken to Delhi to a well-known hospital for an evaluation. She was given a provisional diagnosis of autism and referred to a special needs centre for rehabilitation. Kavita and her husband had never heard of autism; and it was only after repeated visits and counselling did they realize the import of the diagnosis and that there was no 'cure'. Kavita does not speak much about what she went through at the time. Her response is tightlipped: 'What could I do? If it's "written on your forehead" then you have to just grit your teeth and bear it.... I felt suffocated inside.... I was just living each day mechanically.' (Translated from Hindi)

Lack of services and facilities in their hometown made them consider moving to Delhi. It was a very difficult decision for them to take because it meant leaving behind D's aged grandparents and the security of the joint household. Kavita's husband arranged for a rented accommodation close to the special school where they admitted their daughter. Kavita had to learn to live alone in a big city. It was at this juncture in her life that the sheltered, shy, young woman started coming into her own. She learned what she could about autism and management of her child. She learned to manage her household without any support: shopping, budgeting, negotiating with the outside world. She started interacting with other mothers and teachers at the child's school. Her dress and demeanour changed. She switched from her traditional *sarees* to the more practical *salwar-kameez*. Her once demure gait became a confident stride. She stopped being tongue-tied before the other 'stylish' (urban, English-educated) mothers in her child's school, and asserted her views and desires. She had to make do without conveniences like a washing machine or a domestic help for a while before they found their feet and stabilized financially. She expressed satisfaction that all the sacrifices they made were for the long-term welfare of their child. She was the focus of their existence.

> I'll say it in one line: if we would have stayed there, D was a gone case. I would be toiling in the kitchen all day.... She would just be wandering here and there. No matter how we live, how we eat, we are answerable to no one.... Look at the way we are sitting and chatting... it just wouldn't have been possible out there. (Translated from Hindi)

At the time of the fieldwork, D was approaching puberty. Kavita had planned to instruct her by actually demonstrating changing a sanitary pad during her own period, so that the child would be well-prepared. She was extremely vigilant about her daughter's safety and would not leave her unattended under any circumstances. Although their life in Delhi had worked out well for them, she was sure that eventually her husband would insist that they move back to their hometown and that she would have no choice but to comply. Like Preeti, she too desired another child, a 'normal' one, but feared the risks involved. 'She (her daughter) is all we have got. We have got to do whatever we can.' She did not share her husband's optimism that D would be cared for by the extended family after her parents were no more. She hoped to train her to look after her self-care needs so that she would not be a 'burden' on anybody.

Redefining Personhood and Agency

The experience of being a mother of a child with autism changed the lives of both women in profound ways. Kavita learnt to live alone in Delhi away from the sheltered joint-family situation. She negotiated with property dealers, shopkeepers and vendors. She learnt how to manage and teach her child. She interacted with other mothers and fathers. She became a mentor for families who travelled from the country's hinterland to seek help for their child, just as she had done. She described her transformation as '*saree se suit*' (i.e., from a traditional saree to a practical, modern salwar suit). The shy, silent woman found her voice.

Preeti, despite her superior education and training, financial stability, and strong, supportive ties with parents and extended family, withdrew into a constricted domestic space with her severely challenged child. Like Kavita, her world revolved around her child and his needs; however, it had become profoundly stressful and depleting. She had distanced herself from her friends, given up her hobbies, and neglected her health and physical appearance. Kavita's relationship with her daughter was marked by a sense of enjoyment of each other's company. She would follow her mother around as she did her household chores, often sidling up to her for a kiss or cuddle. D loved pretty clothes and make-up, and even though Kavita could not afford expensive cosmetics for herself, she would get them for her daughter. D's gentleness and docility would attract even complete strangers.

Their perceptions about their children's disability and personhood were conditioned by their experiences. I recall Kavita's spirited advice to a mother telling her to do the best she could for her child, and accept him as he was. Preeti's feelings about her son displayed great ambivalence because of the severity of his difficulties and his extreme dependence on her. He was therefore seen as a tormented creature to be loved because he was born of her body, but pitied because he was not a 'whole' human being, and feared because of the violence with which the disability manifested itself. The intensity of R's disability neutralized Preeti's socio-economic advantage; in a sense, it 'disabled' her as well. Kavita too was catapulted into a pattern of life quite different from the one she was socialized into, as a consequence of her daughter's special needs. It exposed her to new influences and conferred a sense of agency she may not have experienced had she borne 'normal' children and lived a 'normal' life in consonance with her status and upbringing. The 'spectrum' of autism also results in a spectrum of experiences and challenges, both for the people with autism and those who care for them.

Conclusion

In this chapter I have attempted to situate the discourses surrounding motherhood and the actual lived experiences and 'dirty work' of mothering, through the lens of a qualitatively different subjectivity and way of being in the world. Autism is believed to be one of the most challenging developmental disabilities, placing care-givers, particularly mothers, under tremendous pressure and stress. The day-to-day challenges that came through so dramatically in Preeti's story highlight the almost universal experience of stigma and mother-blame that have characterized the condition right from the time it was first defined and described. The unique challenges of persons with autism makes it very easy to perceive them as not-quite-human 'others'; outside the pale of 'normal' society and relationships. The overwhelming importance given to the mother in making her child a competent and normal human being thus resulted in the indictment of the autism mother as someone who caused her child to retreat from the world and reject the embrace of the normal social world. At the same time, it was precisely this reviled mother who engaged with her child's difference in creative ways; who fed, clothed, bathed and cleaned the child; attempted to enter his or her world; and also gave a crucial impetus to scientists, educationists and policy makers to redefine and remake an understanding of autism and societal responses to it

The affirmative discourses of neurodiversity and autistic self-advocacy are welcome developments, signalling respect and empathy for all forms of human difference. At the same time, the thankless, unending grind of intensive care in the case of persons with severe and profound difficulties cannot be papered over and need to be addressed. The conflation of 'love' with 'care' binds mothers in sometimes acutely depleting relationships; these can only be addressed by a humane political order that foregrounds the needs of its most vulnerable citizens—including persons with disability.

As a mother of a young adult with autism, I celebrate my son's difference and the value he adds to my life and the lives of those he touches, simply by being himself. At the same time, not a day goes by without wondering what will happen when I am gone, and whether there will be anyone else who will place him at the centre of their world. This chapter is an attempt at illuminating a slice of life that has so far received scant attention in the social sciences, and within feminist research. My location as a mother grappling with the same issues as my respondents opened a fertile ground for sharing intimate vignettes of daily life, and gave me an opportunity to meet, interact and network with other families like my own. It allowed me to share experiences, build solidarity, and dedicate myself anew to the task of building a caring society where children like ours may lead their lives meaningfully and with dignity. The mothering work performed by autism mothers under the unforgiving eye of patriarchy holds productive possibilities to break free from an ideology premised on the notions of lack, deficit, blame and shame by drawing attention to the mutual relations of care and dependency, in which we are all bound as human beings. Becoming 'more than a mother' can then translate into becoming a change-maker who sensitizes society to the value and potential of human difference and neuro-diversity.

Notes

1. Adapted from http://www.webmd.com/brain/autism/understanding-autism-basics accessed on 2 September 2015.
2. For a detailed discussion of the methodological and ethical dilemmas I encountered during the study, see Vaidya 2010.
3. Names have been anonymized and biographical details altered to maintain confidentiality.

References

Asperger, Hans. 'Autistic Psychopathy in Childhood'. In *Autism and Asperger Syndrome*. Translated by Uta Frith. Cambridge: Cambridge University Press, 1991.
Bettelheim, B. *The Empty Fortress*. New York: Free Press, 1967.
Bradley, Harrier. *Gender*. Cambridge: Polity Press, 2007.
Cancian, Francesa. 'Love and the Rise of Capitalism'. In *Gender in Intimate Relationships*, edited by Barbara J. Risman and Pepper Schwartz, Belmont: Wadsworth, 1989, pp. 12–25.
Chaudhary, Nandita. Listening to Culture. New Delhi: SAGE Publications, 2004.
Chaudhary, N. and P. Bhargava. 'Mothers and Others: Kamla's World and Beyond', *Psychology and Developing Societies* 18(1), pp. 77–94.
Chaudhary, N. and P. Bhargava '*Mamta*: The Transformation of Meaning in Everyday Usage', *Contributions to Indian Sociology (new series)* 40(3), 2006b, pp. 343–73.
Duelli Klein, R. 1983. 'How to Do What We Want to Do: Thoughts About Feminist Methodology'. In *Theories of Women's Studies*, edited by Gloria Bowles and Renate Duelli Klein. London: Routledge, 1983.
Douglas, Patty. *Autism's 'Refrigerator Mothers': Identity, Power and Resistance* Comparative Program on Health and Society (CPHS) Working Paper Series (2013–14). Munk School of Global Affairs, University of Toronto.
Feinstein, Adam. A History of Autism: Conversations with the Pioneers. Oxford: Wiley-Blackwell, 2010.
Ghai, Anita and Rachna Johri. 'Pre-natal Diagnosis: Where do We Draw the Line?' In *Disability Studies in India: Global Discourses, Local Realities,* edited by Renu Addlakha. New Delhi: Routledge, 2013, pp. 97–121.

Gorelik, Sherry. 'Contradictions of Feminist Methodology', *Gender and Society*, 5 (4), 1991, pp. 459–77.
Grinker, R. R. *Unstrange Minds: Remapping the World of Autism*. New York: Basic Books, 2007.
Hays, Sharon. *The Cultural Contradictions of Motherhood*. New Haven: Yale University Press, 1996.
Kakar, Sudhir. *The Inner World*, New Delhi: Oxford University Press, 1978.
Kanner, L. 'Autistic Disturbances of Affective Contact', *Nervous Child*, Vol. 2, 1943, 217–50.
Kurtz, S.N. *All the Mothers are One: India and the Cultural Reshaping of Psychoanalysis*. New York: Columbia University Press, 1992.
Langan, Mary. 'Parental Voices and Controversies in Autism', *Disability & Society*, 26:2, 2011, pp. 193–205. DOI: 10:1080/09687599.2011.544059
MacCarthy, J. *Louder than Words: A Mother's journey into Healing Autism*. New York: Dutton, 2007.
Park, Clara Claiborne. *The Siege: A Family's Journey into the World of Autism*. Boston: Little, Brown and Company, 1967.
Sinclair, Jim. 'Don't Mourn for us'. *Autism Network International* 1:3. 1993. http://www.autistics.org./library/dontmourn.html
Silverman, Chloe. *Understanding Autism: Parents, Doctors and the History of a Disorder*. Princeton: Princeton University Press, 2012.
Vaidya, Shubhangi. 'A Sociological Study of Families of Autistic Children in Delhi' Unpublished PhD thesis, Jawaharlal Nehru University, New Delhi, 2008.
Vaidya, Shubhangi. 'Researcher as Insider: Opportunities and Challenges', *Indian Anthropologist*, 40:2, 2010, pp. 27–38.
Vaidya, Shubhangi. 'Developmental Disability and the Family: Autism Spectrum Disorder in Urban India'. In *Disability, Gender and the Trajectories of Power*, edited by Asha Hans. New Delhi: SAGE Publications, 2015.
Wadley, S. 'Women and the Hindu Tradition'. In Doranne Jacobson & Susan S. Wadley, *Women in India: Two Perspectives*. New Delhi: Manohar, 1986.
Waltz, Mitzi. 'Metaphors of Autism, and Autism as Metaphor: An Exploration of Representation' Downloaded from https://www.inter-disciplinary.net/ptb/mso/hid/hid2/waltz%20paper.pdf. (n.d.)
Weusten, Josje. 'Narrative Constructions of Motherhood and Autism: Reading Embodied Language beyond Binary Oppositions', *Journal of Literary and Cultural Disability Studies* 5:1, 2011, pp. 53–69.
Wharton, Amy S. *The Sociology of Gender*. Oxford: Blackwell Publishing, 2005.

5
Capitalist Encounters: The motherhood pact*

In previous chapters, we have traced some of the ways in which the maternal has been mapped out in history and culture, and examined representations of maternal roles through mythology, religion, literature and cinema. How do prevalent configurations of motherhood interrelate with the effects of capitalism, globalization and the ensuing westernization that follows in its wake? Urban areas in India have been at the forefront of such effects, in the aftermath of public policies of economic liberalization, and the 'opening up' of India's economy to global markets. Some of the influences of the recent shifts to a capitalist economy are most palpable in terms of the shifting roles of women and definitions of mothering, especially amongst the urban middle and upper classes, and lower-class rural migrants to urban areas. I argue here that despite alterations in the performance of maternal roles, the substantively contractual nature of the motherhood 'pact' has remained stable due to the unshakeable and dominant patriarchal ideologies which continue to determine women's destinies. Notwithstanding customary perceptions that increasing westernization would bring potential 'liberation' to women based on changing cultural practices, the advent of globalization and capitalism may, in fact, interact with prevailing notions of womanhood and motherhood in unexpected ways, not all of which are necessarily emancipatory.

---

*A few of the ideas discussed in this chapter have previously been briefly explored by the author in a chapter written for self-learning material for the MAWGS programme and published by Indira Gandhi National Open University, 2013 ('Maternal Bodies in Urban India', MWG 004, Gendered Bodies & Sexualities, 193–208).

A critical analysis of mothering in nations such as India reveals that the commodification of women's bodies previously sustained by patriarchal forces may only be exaggerated under the more recent influences of capitalism, substantiated by the increasingly contractual nature of motherhood.

In public and private spaces in urban India, motherhood roles occupied by women reflect the effects of a transforming 'global' economy and consumerism in specific and very telling ways. If motherhood is a 'pact' that women are compelled to consent to under patriarchy, the contractual aspects of such a pact are only exaggerated by the side effects of capitalism, which may be witnessed in the performance of motherwork especially as it pertains to childcare and education at the fulcrum of class and caste. The most acute consequences of such an interaction can be evidenced in the 'surrogacy industry'. I examine surrogacy here more as an extended metaphor for motherwork under capitalist patriarchy, based on the premise that the latter encourages a contractual concept of mothering, which is in consonance with the idea of surrogacy, and which represses the desire for maternal autonomy, sexuality and aesthetic.

Performing Motherhood on the Private/Public Stage

Various dimensions of the inter-linkages between capitalism, patriarchy and motherhood have previously been examined in a range of feminist scholarship, which includes earlier works by Nancy Chodorow, and more recent contributions by Barbara Rothman and Neil Gilbert. In the past, feminist discourses around the world have associated oppressive aspects of motherhood with the public/private dichotomy since motherhood, within patriarchal parameters, is delimited primarily within the boundaries of the private where oppression can be more easily cloaked and resistance, stifled. In capitalist economies that define human resources in terms of their use-value, the emphasis on the public sphere and consequent de-valuation of the private sphere further adds to the denigration of the roles of women as mothers. Manisha Sethi, for instance, describes the consequences of 'the rise of public market economy' under capitalism as 'the emphasis on overt political action, capitalist labour process and devaluation of women's procreative activity'. (Sethi 2002, 1546) The relationship between motherhood ideology and lived realities is consequently determined by these larger structures that impinge upon women's lives in and outside the home.

Evocative of Judith Butler's conceptualization of 'gender performativity',[1] the motherhood pact calls for a certain kind of 'mother performance', one which upholds patriarchal ideology, reduces the notion of female autonomy and overvalues adherence to societal norms. As discussed in previous chapters (especially Chapter 1), the process of the transformation of independent, self-sufficient female religious icons to secondary consorts, wives and mothers started early on in Indian history. In the theatre of patriarchy, women continue to enact prescribed roles in order to avert tragic endings to their personal narratives and ensure their survival.

In the contemporary scenario where capitalist economy, globalization and 'culture' meet to create a curious mix of values, such performances take on a specific tenor. In urban middle-class households, entrenched value systems ensure that the roles of mother and father continue to be constructed as primary care-giver and primary provider, respectively. Complicated further by economic exigencies which push women to work outside the home, the triple burden of childcare, housework and paid labour falls almost entirely on women and mothers. Although extended families may provide some degree of respite in the form of shared work and support structures for childcare, they also often fortify the already embedded normative expectations of women's primary roles as housewives and mothers. Moreover, the personal anxieties engendered by collective/communal living in traditional family structures may also counter the advantages of shared housework and childcare support. The demand for continuously augmented incomes generated by capitalist patriarchy implies that earnings provided by women are both welcomed and designated as a 'side-income' so that the balance of power between men and women remains undisturbed. Thus, it is still largely expected that the man will bring home more than the woman, and provide the bread and butter for the family.

Public work spaces and inter-personal interactions outside the boundaries of the family unit, at the same time, open up notions of financial and sexual autonomy, and threaten to disturb the carefully preserved notion of the desexualized mother. The ostensible tolerance of women's sexual agency outside the four walls of the marital bedroom does not, however, radically upset the cultural expectations imposed within the inviolable private sphere. We have discussed, in the first two chapters, how the desexualization of the maternal figure helps to concretize the dichotomy of the nubile, sexually available woman and the sexually inviolable mother. Rather than upsetting this binary, the modern public/private dichotomy in fact further facilitates and ingrains such a dualistic notion of women's roles, so that the private sphere remains a site that upholds the so-called 'traditional family values', such as women's subordination or even subservience to the husband and in-laws, particularly in their roles as wives, mothers and caregivers. When women venture into the public arena, they are perceived as risking/abandoning the carefully constructed persona imposed on them by the patriarchal accord, such as that of the desexualized mother. This explains why in the case of middle-class urban women, only certain, relatively 'non-threatening' professional avenues, such as that of teacher, assistant, nurse, secretary, etc., continue to be deemed most appropriate from the perspective of the 'respectable' family. The recent shift in definitions of 'respectability', 'values' and 'tradition' brought about by exigencies of modernization and globalization, and the consumerist lust engineered by capitalist economies implies that the (financially limiting) boundaries of tradition and culture will be more frequently breached in favour of lucrative careers and autonomy. Such a trend is evidenced in an increasing number of women venturing into a variety of other fields, such as work in multinational corporations (MNCs), and experimenting with working hours previously considered unacceptable, for instance, the all night shifts of international call centres. Consequently, the motherhood pact and other contractual arrangements between women and patriarchy are brought into a state of flux by the exigencies of capitalist patriarchy.

The maternal 'pact' is thus informed by the clear-cut separation between the private, which becomes the cultural signifier for traditional morality, and the public, which is seen as a space permeable by modernization. In such a severance, only those western liberal values, which can be reconciled with middle-class Indian notions of respectability in the interest of personal economic prosperity, become tolerable. Reconciliations between the private and the public occur alongside a tweaking of cultural norms, a process which does not radically upset the bedrock of traditional moralities, or impact culturally prescribed motherhood roles. It does result, nonetheless, in complex representations of women and mothers, collectively and aptly described by Shilpa Phadke as the 'modern urban middle-class progressive respectable woman'. (Phadke 2005, 68) Phadke, in an incisive analysis of middle-class female sexuality, opines that 'Middle class sexuality, then, is respectable not only because it operates within socially sanctioned norms but also because it recognizes the need for what is private to remain hidden from the public gaze. For women, being respectable involves understanding this dichotomy and playacting the scripts of sexual femininity in public, while making it clear that private spaces cannot be transgressed.' (74) Phadke makes a convincing argument for the need to analyse the roles of consumption and desire in the context of marriage, since the majority of middle-class married women continue to remain impacted by marital codes imposed by a class system that itself is the product of capitalist and patriarchal forces. It is apparent, therefore, that the image of the caged, sexually invisible woman trapped in maternal and domestic responsibilities is placed under constant pressure by capitalist and consumerist demands. Such demands, with their ever-widening penumbras of desire and greed, create the need for women whose labour can be exchanged for money, and whose bodies can at times be commodified and exploited, as in the case of the sexual objectification of female bodies in popular media, or the use of the maternal body as resource for surrogacy.

The Reproductive Contract: Surrogacy as sign of the times

In continuation of our earlier contention regarding the contractual aspects of the performance of motherhood under heteronormative patriarchy, surrogacy becomes an apt metaphor for the pact of motherwork performed by women, in return for social acceptability and economic compensation. This is not to assert that all women are surrogate mothers, in this particular sense, but rather that a certain kind of idealized mothering, which locates women's bodies as breeding ground for the propagation of patriarchal progeny, is privileged over alternative models of autonomous mothering, which it suppresses. The motherhood pact is thus a cultural compulsion, just as much as the daughter or the wife pact is, under capitalist patriarchy—reminiscent of previous observations made by First Wave feminists such as Simone de Beauvoir as well as Marxist feminists like Monique Wittig.[2]

Given the contractual underpinnings of motherhood roles under patriarchy, it is not surprising that surrogacy (along with other Assisted Reproductive Technologies) has become, in India, a contested ground for feminists, medical practitioners, governments, judiciary, potential parents (many of whom reside outside India), and surrogate mothers. As the ultimate 'maternal contract', surrogacy provides an avenue for capitalist forces to enlist resources (female bodies) to provide labour (reproduction) at cheap rates (monetary compensation): 'As such, the stage is set for a flourishing market based on capitalist principles of profiteering, deployed to cash in on patriarchal values.' (Sarojini and Nayak 2013, 179)

The provision of cheap resources and labour by women of a post-colonial nation to those in flourishing western economies further muddies the capitalist waters by adding a neo-colonial aspect to the mix. As a result, surrogacy has mutated into an India-based 'industry' (with ironic links to the current jingoistic 'make in India' slogan), attracting many US and European clients to visit India for the purpose of 'reproductive tourism', and instigating a recent (2015) representation by the government to the Supreme Court to ban commercial surrogacy for foreign clients. (*TOI* 2015) Ellen Goodman describes surrogates as a 'new coterie of international workers who are gestating for a living.'(Goodman 2008) Since surrogate mothers are, for the most part, economically deprived women, whose earnings may be used to provide for their other children, the debate around surrogacy has no easy answers. While on the one hand, ethical concerns about the use of poor/third-world women's bodies for feeding wealthy/western women's demands for tailor-made children have become the subject of postcolonial feminist critique, there is an equally strong defence of the medical advances of ART on the basis of their capacity to bring hitherto unavailable emotional fulfilment to parents who may be otherwise unable to have children. Shulasmith Firestone, who commented that 'procreation is at the origin of the dualism' (Firestone 1971), was in line with Beauvoir and others, among the foremost feminists to call for a biological revolution which would do away with the 'unequal power distribution' at the heart of the biological family. According to her, this could be achieved if women revolted against the naturalization of gendered reproduction.

> So that just as to assure elimination of economic classes requires the revolt of the underclass (the proletariat) and, in a temporary dictatorship, their seizure of the means of *production*, so to assure the elimination of sexual classes requires the revolt of the underclass (women) and the seizure of control of *reproduction*: not only the full restoration to women of ownership of their own bodies, but also their (temporary) seizure of control of human fertility—the new population biology as well as all the social institutions of child-bearing and child-rearing. (Firestone 1971)

Firestone constructed a romanticized view of new population biology as an expression of reproductive autonomy, in an early Marxist feminist revolutionary attempt to upset the power hierarchy, which she believed rested on the inherent difference and inequality of gender anatomy. Three decades later, feminists are still contending with the ethical concerns raised by surrogacy, complicated as they are by global capitalism. Ellen Goodman emphasizes the inescapable commercialization of international surrogacy in which third-world women's wombs become the temporary rental accommodation for first-world women's foetuses:

> Frozen sperm is flown from one continent to another. And patients have become medical tourists, searching for cheaper healthcare, whether it's a new hip in Thailand or IVF treatment in South Africa that comes with a photo safari thrown in for the same price. Why not then rent a foreign womb?
>
> ...
>
> It's the commercialism that is troubling. Some things we cannot sell no matter how good 'the deal.' We cannot, for example, sell ourselves into slavery. We cannot sell our children. But the surrogacy business comes perilously close to both of these. And international surrogacy tips the scales. (Goodman 2008)

It is not the purpose of this chapter to weigh in on either side of the debates surrounding surrogacy, which have been adequately addressed by feminist ethnographers and sociologists.[3] Rather, in continuation of our ongoing exploration of the cultural imprint of the sign of mothering and its implications for women, we wish to locate surrogacy as a trope within the particular socio-cultural context in India, in order to throw light on how motherhood ideology continues to be manufactured under a dominant hetero-normative patriarchal structure. Apart from the ethical conundrums that surrogacy raises for feminist scholarship, it is equally important to mark out its influence as a culturally constructed signifier in the context of the ongoing commercialization of women's bodies. As such, it is symbolic of a larger endemic cultural malaise which normalizes the notion of the maternal body, and specifically the womb-on-rent, as resource under patriarchy. Rented out, outsourced, owned and discarded, the womb-on-loan reinforces the concept of the woman's body as territory to be acquired, conquered, bought and sold, consequently limiting its rights and underscoring its responsibilities towards its patrons. As pointed out by Chayanika Shah, the surrogacy debate is made complicated by 'the disconcerting use of the language of "rights" and "choice" by the promoters of these businesses on behalf of the women going in for these technologies.' (Shah

2009) Such a language of 'rights' and 'choice' dodges the deep-rooted economic or other compulsions under which maternal pacts such as that of surrogacy operate, and glosses over the inherently contractual nature of maternal identities performed by women under capitalist patriarchy. Surrogacy is not a novel notion invented by modern science, although medical advancements in this field can certainly be credited to the latter. The prevalence of surrogacy in Indian ethos, culture and religion helps to 'sell' the idea to first-time surrogate women who can justify their participation in a commercial venture on the basis of a culturally sanctioned practice. As noted by various feminist scholars, examples of surrogate mothers abound in ancient Hindu religion and folklore, thus enabling a moral justification for what may otherwise be at risk of being perceived as an 'immoral' act. In Krishna's narratives, Rohini is the surrogate birth mother of Krishna (after Kansa destroys the first seven embroyos of Devaki, and the eighth is magically transferred to Rohini's womb). Subsequently, she too is substituted by the ultimate surrogate-mother Yashoda who adopts the baby Krishna.[4] Similarly, in-vitro narratives about the pregnancies of Gandhari and the birth of Draupadi reveal that the literary trope of the child born from a mother's womb other than the one in which it was conceived was commonplace in Hindu mythology. As we have seen in Chapter 1, the waning of the worship of fertility goddesses as all-important and self-sufficient creators of life in pre-Vedic times, and the growing idea of the mother as vessel for the birth of a divine male held sway in post-Vedic mythology, with its ever-increasing patriarchal bias under Brahminical Hinduism. The transmogrification of the mother from divine source of all life to a resource for reproduction of patriarchal kinship structures, measureable in terms of its use-value and disposable if found use-less, is achieved early on in Indian history and sustained through dominant cultural practices over time. The patriarchal collusion with capitalist impulses can thus be traced back to ancient times, pre-dating the onset of modern capitalism. It reveals, therefore, an early conception of the female body as cache-resource for exploitation and profit under patriarchy, and the impulse for profiteering based on class, caste and gender inequity.

As woman's function gradually becomes one of supporting the patriarchal family and kinship structure by providing progeny on demand, 'barrenness' becomes the worst albatross around the married woman's neck. As we have seen in previous chapters, the stigma of barrenness has led, in mainstream cinema, to a groundswell of commercially successful films in which the barren woman, unable to conceive, visualizes her future as one worse than death. Just as much as reproductive ability (especially the ability to produce male children) bestows unforeseen privileges on the maternal body, its lack marks the body as deficient and flawed. Meanwhile, the cultural projection of machismo on to male partners ensures that the husband/potential father is kept carefully outside of the ambit of reproductive responsibility. In so doing, he retains his privilege to supplant the marred body of the barren woman with future, healthy wives, a theme that has been repeatedly used in Bollywood cinema, as also discussed in Chapter 3. In a recent and apparently more 'forward-looking' trend, the rejection of the wife on grounds of infertility is replaced by romanticized accounts of surrogacy, so that what gets swapped is not the wife-as-person, but the womb-as-body-part, as for instance in films such as *Doosri Dulhan* (1983), *Chori Chori Chupke Chupke* (2001), and *Filhaal* (2001). The option of surrogacy becomes here the panacea for the social dishonour attracted by 'barrenness', a convenient, morally acceptable resolution over the older, outright rejection of the 'deficient' wife. However 'modern' such a perspective may claim to be, what it glosses over is the unequivocal objectification and commodification of maternal bodies in all cases.

Given this cultural context, it is not surprising to see that the idea of the surrogate mother, supported by medical advancements, has gained ground in urban India, since it sustains the clear divide between female sexuality (read, no immoral, sexual act is expected of the surrogate mother) and reproduction (read, female as vessel), leaving undisturbed the patriarchal idealization of the desexualized mother. Surrogacy thus re-inforces the concept of the maternal body as vehicle, rather than that of woman as agent, since any 'agency' exerted by the concerned women is necessarily regulated within a framework of compulsion. As a 'contractual arrangement' it further unveils the position of woman-as-potential-mother as the obligatory party in a social contract that demarcates mothering as paid labour, underscoring what Amrita Pande calls the 'transient role and disposability of the women, not just as workers but also as mothers'. (Pande 2010, 977) In her study of a group of surrogate women from Anandpur, Gujarat, Pande equally underlines the presence of a Foucauldian 'resistance' on the part of the surrogate women, as for instance, in terms of their interrogation of the compensation they receive:

> The production of this mother-worker subject, however, does not go unchallenged. What we see instead is a continuum of resistance that includes both narratives as well as individual and collective actions... the Foucauldian enclosure (surrogacy hostel) becomes a space for resistance and networking. The hostels constitute a gendered place, one that generates emotional

links and sisterhood among the women. This intensive contact allows the surrogates to share information and grievances with one another and to sometimes come up with strategies for future employment and even acts of collective resistance. (970–71)

However, and despite Pande's emphasis on the notion of a Foucauldian resistance, it is clear, even from her own study, that the choices exerted by economically deprived surrogate women are hemmed in by circumstances dictated by class and gender limitations. Evidently, the small rewards won by surrogate women (such as negotiation of brokerage fee) are overshadowed by their unwitting location (based on class and caste factors) within larger disciplinary spaces that subject them to constant surveillance so that they remain prisoners of destinies which they could not help but choose. Elsewhere, Pande describes 'alternative constructions of motherhood' (Pande 2013, 141) by surrogates based on their recognition of their own roles and their bodily ties to the children they produce through 'the real blood of pregnancy and birth and sweat of their labor'. (143) Notwithstanding such altered re-definitions of motherhood brought about by the complex relationships of surrogates to children, these do not manage to 'completely subvert patriarchal assumptions about relatedness and "ownership".' (144) Thus, in Pande's own terms, the child may be 'a product of its gestational mother's blood' but remains the 'father's "property".' (145) turning us away from any hurried romanticization of surrogacy as a revolutionary form of mothering, and sustaining, in fact, the perception of the objectified maternal body as vessel for patriliny.

The Mother-Nation Pact and Emerging Sexual Identities

Such a contemporary sexual objectification of the maternal body may be read as contiguous with an older and prevailing nationalist discourse, which posits active sexuality on the side of the patriotic male citizen and embodies the mother-nation in the form of a passive receptacle of masculine erotic desire (see previous discussions of the nation-mother in the first three chapters). For instance, in her study of the cartographical representations of India as 'Mother India', or 'Bharat Mata', Sumathi Ramaswamy notes that the projection of the nation in the form of mother enables the male citizen to imagine the mother-nation as the recipient of his erotic desires, whereas the body of the mother-nation remains a passive sexual object.

> The bodyscapes of Mother India . . . erupt within the interstices of a nationalist discourse where the erotic, the patriotic and the cartographical converge in imagining the nation as an entity worth living, and dying for.... They invite the citizen-subject who gazes upon them to relate to the nation not as some abstract, dead geographical space, but as a near-and-dear person, his personal goddess, his vulnerable mother, even a beloved lover. (Ramaswamy 2001, 109)

In a postscript, Ramaswamy further adds that such a popular cartographical practice is one in which, 'while the male citizen is interpellated as the active subject of the body politic, the female citizen is virtually erased as an active subject to be replaced by the idealized, stylized and ultimately passive figure of Mother India propped up by a map of the nation.' (110) Nationalist discourse, hinging on a de-sexualized and idealized motherhood, thus led to the production of dichotomous gendered sexualities in which notions of honour became invariably mapped onto the mother's body. As noted by Mary John,

> ...for too long, it was not women's sexual experiences that were at stake, but the elaborate codes of honour that were/are inscribed on female bodies. Women bear the marks, sometimes, violent marks, of caste, ethnic and national imaginations. Not only have middle-class, upper-caste women been the ground on which questions of modernity and tradition were framed, they are the embodiment of the boundaries between licit and illicit forms of sexuality, as well as the guardians of the morality of the nation. But women are also 'reproductive beings'. It was, we well know, the dangerous sexuality of the non-mother that motivated the social reform legislation of the 19th century. (John and Nair 1999, 1)

In more recent times, the increasing influence of capitalist values and demands amongst the middle classes has become largely responsible for opening up spaces where women's sexual agency and desire are beginning to make themselves visible, albeit in a performative and largely unstudied ways. The traditional idealizations of the de-sexualized mother, as seen in eponymous images of Mother India, Bharat Mata, and others, earlier deployed to suppress any evidence of active sexual desire on the part of mothers, are being countered by the association of an active sexuality attributed to the 'westernized' working woman, as evident in contemporary popular media such as films and television serials. Such a binary serves to keep alive stereotypical representations on what are deemed as oppositional cultural fronts. Notwithstanding the transition from a passive sexual object to an active, desiring subject, what is significant to note is the ideological de-linking of mothers (and the de-sexualized domestic sphere) from working women (and sexually charged public spaces), a dissociation which continues to mark the absence of sexuality in the discourse of motherhood by allowing it to surface only outside of the home, and beyond maternal roles.

Mothers in Labour

Besides influencing the discourse of sexuality, capitalist patriarchy also determines the nature of work performed by mothers from different class and caste backgrounds. As we have previously noted, prevailing notions of morality and respectability are the determining factors of women's public roles among the urban middle classes. In the case of working women, their 'supplementary' income is equally delimited by the kind of work that is deemed to be permissible, determined as it is by social perceptions of jobs defined as threatening or non-threatening in the ambit of patriarchal values and established gender hierarchies across classes. Thus, while motherwork is 'valued' but unpaid labour (seen rather as divinely attributed duty to be fulfilled by women), paid work outside the home is projected as a necessary evil to be endured due to economic compulsions.

We may note, here, that the de-valuing of work done by mothers has been similarly underscored by feminist scholars in western capitalist societies. For example, Nancy Chodorow's observation that 'whatever their marital status and despite evidence to the contrary for both married and unmarried women, women are generally assumed to be working only to supplement a husband's income in nonessential ways' (Chodorow 1979, 90), may ring equally true in the analysis of work performed by middle- and upper-middle-class mothers in India. Women who mother are often rewarded with a deceptive sense of power over the domestic sphere, which includes a sense of control over their own lives and that of their children. However, dominant patriarchal parameters that define the boundaries of the domestic, as well as place limits on the control exerted by women, warrant that women behave in certain ways and perform pre-determined roles to assure the preservation of old sexist values thinly disguised in the garb of new westernized materialism.

The work of overseeing children's education naturally dovetails into such established perceptions of what constitutes 'motherwork'. Given Indian cultural traditions, this encompasses both formal education and the much more nebulous areas of moral, social and religious instruction imparted to offspring. Seen as the 'womb' of moral and religious values, the mother is expected to fulfil her obligations in this area as a primary, inevitable responsibility. Not surprisingly, drawing upon established cultural and religious iconographies, the media continues to posit the 'good' mother as someone who puts aside her own needs and always makes time for those of her husband and children, especially in her role as educator, and moral and spiritual guide of the latter. In this regard, urban Indian middle-class idealizations of certain aspects of mothering are not that far removed from western counterparts. We may discover striking similarities, for instance, in commentaries about western middle-class motherhood, such as that offered by Heather Hewett, which seem to be as applicable in India as anywhere else: 'In Euro-American culture, enduring images of the "good" mother (always defined against the "bad" mother) emphasize qualities of selflessness and self-denial.' (Hewett 2009, 126)

Similarly, Henrike Donner, in her study of education and the roles played by middle-class mothers in Kolkata, West Bengal, concludes that 'the discursive construction of a child's "needs" is linked to the intimate knowledge gained within a relationship only the mother possesses. Even if homework is set by the school in the first place, it is only the mother who can make the child perform.' (Donner 2008, 143) She goes on to add that 'in theory, only the mother and her child are involved in schooling and the mother is free to devote herself fully to school-related activities.' (144) The insistence on the mother as the 'natural' source for the child's formal as well as informal education sustains the patriarchal family structure, which is hugely dependent upon the successful transaction of the maternal pact. The weight of culturally determined expectations ensures the freezing of maternal roles and their unquestioning acceptance by women. The transformation of the mother into the fount of patriarchal family values further assures women's collusion in patriarchal social structures. It ascertains that women's identity remains linked to the guardianship of privileged moralities at the expense of a subduing of women's sexuality. It may be worth noting here that despite the fact that capitalism, on the one hand, devalues motherhood and its location within the private sphere, on the other hand, it requires the mother to fulfil her role as the dutiful guardian of the domestic sphere, since the traditional values upheld by the mother also serve to perpetuate the profit-making consumerist culture which keeps the focus on fathers as primary providers while making invisible the unpaid work of women as mothers. Traditionalism and capitalism, thus, no longer remain at odds with each other, but become allied in sustaining the common goal of the oppression of women and mothers as a class whose labour feeds into a materialistic culture which benefits men and women unequally.

Besides being assigned the work of propagating patriarchal values among future citizens of the nation, mothers are also expected to perpetuate, through the act of reproduction, the very race of future wage-earners on which capitalist patriarchy is dependent. In this regard, the juxtaposition of two analyses of motherhood in very different cultural and historical contexts brings to light an interesting commonality. In their discussion of questions of motherhood and race in imperial Britain, Amos and Parmar (2001) observe that,

> ...women were being defined as the breeders of race, bearing and rearing the next generation of soldiers and workers of the imperial race.... Such a development of an ideology of women as mothers duty bound to reproduce for the race went alongside the development of an imagery of them as vulnerable creatures who needed protection not only at home but also in the colonies. (26)

Similarly, but in a much-removed context, Samita Sen, while examining questions of motherhood and labour in West Bengal in the late 19th century, calls attention to the relationship between the idealization of maternal values and the notion of nation-building through race-building:

> The idealisation of womanhood as the repository of tradition and the construction of the domestic sphere as the proper and rightful domain of women, involved a general valorisation of motherhood.... This idealization found support in the notion that children were crucial for nation-building and for 'the maintenance of the race'. (Sen 1999, 148)

She further adds that 'if the ignorant and careless housewife was a threat to the social order, the neglectful and indifferent mother spelt national disaster.' (148) It is evident then, that notwithstanding cultural differences, capitalist patriarchy profits from the sustenance of those traditional notions of motherhood which idealize women's reproductive role and consequently enable the utilization of women as the reproducers of future wage-earners.

Systemically, such prevailing notions of motherhood and reproduction then serve to sustain regulatory concepts of nation, race, class and caste, from which patriarchy reaps its benefits, and within which the work and contributions of women as mothers remain a 'free' (unpaid) commodity. It serves capitalism, therefore, to nurture and idealize notions of traditional motherhood while de-valuing the private sphere so that while a certain ideology of motherhood is upheld, women themselves remain subservient and contained within domesticity.

Deconstructing Motherwork across Caste and Class

Even though the devaluation of the work performed by mothers cuts across class and caste boundaries, mothers from lower classes and castes pay a much heavier debt to patriarchal exigencies, as becomes evident in the work done by domestic maids and nannies in urban areas in India. Here, a different kind of 'surrogacy' operates in which poor women take on mothering work in return for monetary compensation. In middle-class and upper-class urban Indian households, it is commonplace to find that routine care of children is very often entrusted to the much-in-demand female help or *ayah*. Often, the *ayah* or *didi* (older sister) tends to be a young, rural migrant woman hired for the purpose of housework and childcare in return for salary, a room and boarding. Depending on the degree of work undertaken, it is not unusual to witness the transformation of these 'ayahs' from maid to nanny to surrogate mother, as they take on almost all of the childcare duties from changing diapers, bathing, and feeding, to accompanying their wards to parks, playgrounds, birthday parties and excursions. In an interesting parallel, while surrogate mothers who are birth mothers function as 'wombs-on-hire', but must forfeit any relationship defined by 'care' of the child, the nannies or 'ayahs' serve as non-biological surrogate mothers with exclusive childcare duties, with a clear understanding that they are permitted no other claim over their wards. Owing to differences in caste and class, and the fact that the surrogate 'mothering' is based on a financial transaction, emotional bonding between the 'ayah' and the child is severely curtailed. In a comment which may easily apply to surrogate mothers who provide their wombs for reproduction but are forbidden from developing emotional attachment to the child they give birth to, Maithreyi Krishnaraj's remarks that 'when care-givers do mothering, the care-taker gets emotionally attached to the child. Yet, she is not entitled to full ownership because there is a money transaction involved.' (Krishnaraj 2010, 23) Compare this with Amrita Pande's study of surrogate mothers in Anandpur, Gujarat, and her commentary on the patronizing nature of the discourse used to 'train' women to become the perfect 'motherworker': 'The discourse of disposability and transience emphasizes detachment from the child and keeps the negotiating power of the surrogates in check.' (Pande 2010, 980) As may be evident from these comparisons, both types of surrogacy entail a surrender of rights—either biological or emotional—further ensconcing the notion of the maternal body as a transient carrier vessel for patriarchy.

While married *ayahs* function as surrogate mothers for urban women, their own children are often left behind in the villages, to be looked after by their mothers, mothers-in-law or older siblings. Relationships between these rural migrant women and their biological children are often restricted to annual trips back home. A couple of them, whom I talked to, confided that the children hardly accept them now as their mothers, so habituated are they to the grandmother or older sister or aunt in the village. While the responses have been mostly matter-of-fact and dry-eyed, one cannot fail to perceive the deep sense of resignation and fatalism that belies their coolness. The situation of care-workers is thus similar, in several ways, to that of surrogate mothers, allowing us to see surrogacy (both as reproductive transaction and care-giving) as a culturally promoted trope under capitalism.

Ironically, the traditional joint-family structure, which functions as a rural childcare support system for poor women migrants, is also often the one that decides if and when a young woman must migrate to the big city in search of paid domestic labour. The earning, or most of it, is usually sent home to feed the family. More often than not, choosing a partner, getting married, bearing children or later being parted from them are not decisions that the lower-class/lower-caste migrant woman makes for herself. Educational opportunities, marriage and freedom of movement are also often determined by complex caste hierarchies. By exerting strict control over marital alliances, these caste-based social regulations restrict the mobility of women and their offspring, within or across caste barriers, in order to maintain control over communal property. The female body, especially in its capacity to produce future offspring, remains the site of territorial battle and violence, perhaps not such a shocking contrast to the images of the waif-like, cosmetically enhanced women and mothers pervasive in contemporary Indian and western media.

The 'surrogacy metaphor' can thus be seen as operating at various levels of maternal practices. It holds, at its core, the surrender of desires and rights, and the exercise of 'choices' within pre-determined frameworks. In the case of domestic maids, the notion of 'mothering-as-contract' bonds these women in imperceptible ways to those who employ them, despite obvious class and caste differences. Regardless of the disparities in personal freedoms, *ayahs* who perform the roles of surrogate mothers in well-to-do metropolitan homes seem to mirror the restrictions of the maternal pact imposed upon women across classes—both playing out roles defined for them by their families, which themselves reflect the larger, male-dominated social and economic structures, of which they are a part. As seen above, women from lower castes and classes are doubly exploited by capitalist patriarchy and by the urban mothers who employ them. Patriarchally prescribed delimitations of motherhood across class and caste barriers ensure differently configured victimizations of women as mothers. Whether they are performing their roles as reproducers of wage-earners and guardians of patriarchal moralities for future generations, or as surrogate mothers involved in domestic chores such as childcare, women's mothering work remains externally defined, as well as unpaid or under-paid. On the one hand, such a linkage may invite one to speak, in a circumscribed way, of a gender identity that cuts across caste and class barriers to manifest itself as a common product of capitalist patriarchy. On the other hand, however, it would also lead us to observe that capitalist patriarchal structures facilitate the complicity of mothers from upper classes in the double exploitation of their counterparts from less privileged classes and castes.

As contested by Manisha Sethi, in her discussion on women's roles of the Hindu right, gender identity is irreducible to any singular relationship with other identities such as that of caste and class:

> ... gender identity does not exist as primordially or eternally fixated but is invented, created, resisted and subverted at the fulcrum of multiple identities. Identities do not exist as disparate compartments with one particular identity say that of community dominating and overriding all other as that of caste or gender at particular moments. Rather these identities are worked in and through each other and indeed may be spoken [of] in gendered terms. (Sethi 2002, 1551)

Such an observation becomes evident in the roles played by the middle-class and upper-middle-class urban women whose motherhood roles are predicated upon the demands and needs of capitalist patriarchy, and those of the rural women who act as surrogate mothers to upper-class urban children. While the exploitative relationship between patriarchal structures and urban mothers may be less visible than that between the latter and their rural household help, the gendered identities of both get posed at the fulcrum of patriarchy, capitalism, class and caste in order to influence their destinies in specific directions.

Motherhood and the Familial Contract

In this context, the role of the family as the unit within which the destinies of mothers get inscribed is worth examining. In urban cultures, which have traditionally acted as the buttress of patriarchal values over the years, and are now swaying under capitalist forces, the heterosexual family unit, in its nuclear or extended form, idealized throughout history and by contemporary politicians and governments across the world, continues to shackle women by offering them prefabricated metaphors of femininity and motherhood, instead of liberating them through shared work, exchangeable roles and responsibilities, and communal relationships. When asked her opinion about 'family relations' vis-à-vis women, Luce Irigaray's response was unequivocal: 'As far as the family goes, my response will be simple and clear: the family has always been the privileged locus of women's exploitation.' Regarding the power of mothers within the family, she goes on to add, that 'this power exists only "within" a system organized by men.... historically, within the family, it is the father-man who alienates the bodies, desires and work of woman and children by treating them as his own property.' (Irigaray 1985, 142–43)

In contrasting vertical paradigms of motherhood against potential lateral relations between women, Juliet Mitchell relates 'the shift from the importance of giving birth to the importance of caring for offspring' to the shift 'from kin to class society and an economy of surplus profit in which capital not people increases...' (Mitchell 2007, 185) In increasingly capitalist economies such as those of urban India, such a shift is easily perceivable in the increasing dependence of women from the upper middle classes (especially working women) on their poorer rural sisters, who take on some of the burden of childcare. It is significant to note, however, that despite class and caste inequities, and the unequal onus of motherhood work placed on women from lower classes and castes, it is still primarily women who share childcare responsibilities, thus leaving the gender divide intact. In Joyce Trebilcot's early pathbreaking anthology on mothering, Rivka Polatnick had argued that 'the allocation of childrearing responsibility to women… is no sacred fiat of nature, but a social policy which supports male domination in society and in the family.' (Polatnick 1983, 37) More than three decades after feminists like Polatnick made similar observations about women's and men's responsibilities towards childcare, such a conclusion still rings true, cautioning us against any hasty moves towards post-feminist complacencies. Thus, while women, as mothers, remain trapped in the gender hierarchy of socially and culturally sanctioned maternal roles, both wealthy and poor women continue to perform destinies prescribed by capitalist-driven, caste-based and male-dominated economies. As Juliett Mitchell wryly observes, 'the economically rich or becoming rapidly rich countries or the economically successful within poorer societies are opting for one-child or child-free status per two adults; the condemned of the earth continue to have children, which means the wealthy can replace their children from elsewhere.' (Mitchell 2007, 176)

Conclusion

We may surmise, then, that the demands of contemporary capitalism and consumerism continue to impact the constructions of urban motherhood in ways which do not necessarily disturb the underlying sexist attitudes of traditional patriarchal societies, and extant constructions of motherhood. Under capitalist patriarchy, motherwork takes on the nature of a pact in which mothering remains in consonance with the concept of surrogacy, with its attendant clauses pertaining to rented wombs, resource, labour, use-value, transience, disciplining and detachment. Concurrently, notions of maternal autonomy, desire and sexual agency are repressed.

This is not to say that there are not many women who have charted out their destinies outside of these parameters. In contemporary urban India, at least, the patterns are fast changing, and the number of such women is growing multifold. Fortunately, for many women in India, which is an India clearly in transition, growing social acceptance of women's contributions and equality, emergent educational and employment opportunities, as well as an increasing participation by men in childcare and parental responsibilities, are all positive signs for the future. On the other hand, dominant right wing ideologies constantly reinforce the boundary walls at which female ambition, creativity and autonomy must check its bags, and wait for escape routes to emerge. Significantly, those who are able to break free from repressive cultural demands are usually those who have managed to seek out for themselves educational and professional opportunities, which lead to some level of economic and personal independence. Current configurations of motherhood roles in urban India are an indicator that the tussle between resignation to socially acceptable but unjust norms, and resistance against these through a re-negotiation of traditional ideologies with contemporary materialist values is very much alive. An ongoing critical interrogation of the collusion between patriarchal values and capitalist forces in the context of class- and caste-based delineations of motherhood may be the initial step in the re-creation of a different set of parameters where women, and women-as-mothers, can begin to envision their lives, and define themselves as 'women' and as 'mothers' in entirely new and liberating ways. Some possibilities of stepping outside of the patriarchal pact of motherhood, and to imagine it in alternate ways, especially by means of language, creativity and a specifically maternal aesthetic, have been suggested in previous chapters, and will be further explored in the final chapter of this book.

Notes

1. Judith Butler develops this notion extensively in *Gender Trouble*, 1990.
2. See The Second Sex by Simone de Beauvoir (1949) and Monique Wittig's essay 'One is Not Born a Woman' (1981, trans).
3. For debates on surrogacy, see Firestone (1979), Berkhout (2008), Goodman (2008), Pande (2010; 2013), Shah (2009), and others.
4. See previous discussion of the Krishna narrative in Chapter 1; see also Wendy Doniger (1975).

References

Amos, Valerie and Pratibha Parmar. 'Challenging Imperial Feminism'. In Feminism & 'Race', edited by Ed. Kum-Kum Bhavnani. Oxford: Oxford University Press, 2001, pp. 17–32.
Berkhout, Suze G. 'Buns in the Oven: Objectification, Surrogacy and Women's Autonomy', *Social Theory and Practice* 34 (1), 2008, pp, 95–117.

Butler, Judith. *Gender Trouble*. New York: Routledge, 1990.
Chodorow, Nancy. 'Mothering, Male Dominance, and Capitalism'. In *Capitalist Patriarchy and the Case for Socialist Feminism*, edited by Zillah R. Eisenstein. New York: Monthly Review Press, 1979, pp. 83–106.
Donner, Henrike. Domestic Goddesses: Maternity, Globalization and Middle-class Identity in Contemporary India. London Ashgate Publishing, 2008.
Doniger, Wendy. *Hindu Myths: A Sourcebook*. Translated from the Sanskrit. Harmondsworth: Penguin, 1975.
Firestone, Shulasmith. *The Dialectic of Sex*. New York: The Women's Press, 1979. Chapter 1 reproduced at https://www.marxists.org/subject/women/authors/firestone-shulamith/dialectic-sex.htm. Accessed 19 June 2015.
Gilbert, Neil. *A Mother's Work*. New York: Yale University Press, 2008.
Goodman, Ellen. 'The Globalization of Baby-Making', *New York Times*, Friday, 11 April 2008. http://www.nytimes.com/2008/04/11/opinion/11iht-edgoodman.1.11908760.html?_r=0. Accessed 19 June, 2015.
Hewett, Heather. 'Mothering Across Borders', *Women's Studies Quarterly* 37. 3/4, 2009, pp. 121–39.
Irigary, Luce. *This Sex Which is Not One*. Translated by Catherine Porter. Ithaca: Cornell University Press, 1985.
John, Mary E. and Janaki Nair. 'Sexuality in Modern India: Critical Concerns', *Voices for Change* 3:1, 1999, pp. 1–8.
Krishnaraj, Maithreyi (ed.) *Motherhood in India: Glorification Without Empowerment?* New York: Routledge, 2010.
Mitchell, Juliett. 'Procreative Mothers (Sexual Difference) and Child-free Sisters (Gender).' In *The Future of Gender,* edited by Jude Brown. Cambridge: Cambridge University Press, 2007, pp. 163–88.
Pande, Amrita. 'Commercial Surrogacy in India: Manufacturing a Perfect Mother-Worker' *Signs*, Summer, 2010.
Pande, Amrita. 'The 'Sweat and Blood" of Womb Mothers: Commercial Surrogates Redefining Motherhood in India'. In *South Asian Mothering,* edited by Jasjit Sangha and Tahira Gonsalves. Bradford: Demeter, 2013.
Phadke, Shilpa. 'Some Notes towards Understanding the Construction of Middle-class Urban Women's Sexuality in India', In *Sexuality, Gender and Rights,* edited by Geetanjali Mishra and Radhika Chandiramani. New Delhi: SAGE Publications, 2005, pp. 67–81.
Polatnick, M. Rivka. 'Why Men Don't Rear Children: A Power Analysis', In *Mothering: Essays in Feminist Theory,* edited by Joyce Trebilcot. New York: Rowman & Littlefield, 1983.
Ramaswamy, Sumathi. 'Maps and Mother Goddesses in Modern India', *Imago Mundi*, Vol. 53, 2001, pp. 97–114.
Rothman, Barbara. 'Motherhood under Capitalism', In *Consuming Motherhood*, edited by Janelle Taylor, Linda Layne and Danielle Wozniak. New Jersey: Rutgers University Press, 2004, pp. 19–30.

Sarojini, N. B. and Preeti Nayak. 'Surrogacy'. MWG 004: *Gendered Bodies & Sexualities* (MAWGS Self Learning Material). IGNOU, 2013, pp. 173–92.

Sen, Samita. 'Motherhood, Mothercraft and the Maternity Benefit Act.' Women and Labour in Late Colonial India. Cambridge: Cambridge University Press, 1999, pp. 142–76.

Sethi, Manisha. 'Avenging Angels and Nurturing Mothers: Women in Hindu Nationalism', *Economic and Political Weekly* Vol. 37, No. 16, 2002, pp. 1545–552.

Shah, Chayanika. 'Regulate Technology, Not Lives: A Critique of the Draft ART (Regulation) Bill', *Indian Journal of Medical Ethics*, Vol. 6, No. 1, 2009. Accessed 19 June 2015, http://www.ijme.in/index.php/ijme/article/view/433/786.

Times of India. http://timesofindia.indiatimes.com/india/Foreigners-may-be-barred-from-commissioning-surrogacy-in-India/articleshow/49418285.cms. 16 October 2015.

6
Of 'Unfit' Mothers: Disability, stereotypes and contestations*

Introduction

The themes of deficiency and lack, good and bad mothers, the burden of care and the valorization of the mothering role that have been explored in previous chapters, acquire a new dimension when we take into account a different kind of embodiment, namely, disability. While Chapter 4 explored the experiences of mothers of children with disability, this chapter attempts to explore the lived experiences of disabled mothers as they attempt to negotiate the multiple marginalization of being women with non-normative bodies or minds in a patriarchal and 'ableist' world.[1] The bringing forth of new life from one's body through the processes of conception, gestation and birthing, sustenance through lactation and nurturing, and the practices of care, are surrounded by webs of meaning that shape and transform the embodied experience of mothering. When the mother in question is a disabled woman, the discourse of motherhood gets even more complicated. Sexuality, conjugality and motherhood are associated with normative, desirable, fertile bodies,

---

*Some of the ideas in this chapter were discussed in the teaching-learning Study Unit *Disability, Sexuality and Motherhood* (Vaidya 2013) prepared by the author for the MA programme in Women's and Gender Studies offered by the School of Gender and Development Studies, IGNOU.

Note: This is a modified version of the paper *Women with Disability and Reproductive Rights: Deconstructing Discourse* published in *Social Change*, 45:4 December 2015, pp. 517–33.

whereas the disabled body is regarded as defective, undesirable and thus, devalued. The very juxtaposition of 'sexuality', 'motherhood' and 'disability' thus becomes a contradiction in terms. Motherhood denotes care giving, while disability suggests a person in need of care herself, and thus, being unfit to assume the caring role for another, especially of one as vulnerable as an infant.

The multiple discrimination faced by women with disabilities and their erasure from discourses around sexuality and reproduction will be explored with the help of empirical studies from different parts of the world. The implications of the experiences of motherhood for the gender identity of disabled women, which challenge feminist understandings of reproductive and care work as potentially oppressive and disempowering, shall also be discussed. Two well-known cases in India, frequently cited in the context of the debates on sexual and reproductive rights of institutionalized women with mental disabilities, will also be highlighted. In the 'Pune Hysterectomies Case' (1994) intellectually disabled women in a state-run institution near Pune underwent the surgical removal of their wombs supposedly as a social service to prevent unwanted pregnancies and the inconvenience of managing menstrual periods. The second case, commonly known as the 'Nari Niketan' case, pertains to the pregnancy after the custodial rape of a young, intellectually disabled woman in a women's shelter in Chandigarh in 2009, and the debates with regard to her right to give birth to the baby in the light of her marginal and precarious status as a destitute disabled woman and the victim of a sexual assault. It would be appropriate to begin with a broad understanding of the concept and experience of disability.

Defining Disability

While current scholarship regards disability as an axis of oppression and discrimination, along with other well-established categories like gender, class, caste, race and ethnicity, it has by and large been relegated to the realm of medicine and psychiatry and the 'helping' or service-oriented fields of social work, special education and rehabilitation science. Disability has historically been viewed as a 'problem' or aberration in need of fixing or remediation, suggesting that something is missing or lacking. Persons with disability are likely to face discrimination in the areas of education, employment, political participation, sport and leisure, and in the domains of sexuality, marriage and parenthood. Needless to say, women with disability face the double jeopardy of being female and disabled in a patriarchal social order. Addlakha (2008a) writes that the multiple barriers (physical, social, attitudinal, economic, legal, etc.) experienced by persons with disabilities magnify manifold in the case of women with disabilities, rendering them a stigmatized and neglected category. The disabled body is also a source of shame and embarrassment, discomfort and ill-being, contributing to a sense of alienation with the environment. (Addlakha 2013) It is 'the spectre of incontinence, leakages, smells and spillages that engenders anxiety and fear in society as a whole'. (Seymour 1998, 19 cited in Addlakha 2013, 221)

Disability prevalence has a direct correlation with poverty. Parts of the world where access to primary health care, proper nutrition, sanitation and clean drinking water are deficient are likely to have children and adults at a higher risk of becoming disabled. At the same time, the developed world with its relatively advanced systems of health care and public welfare systems, increased life expectancy has resulted in a number of age-related disabling conditions. (Goodley 2011) The Census of India (2011) counted 26.8 million persons with disability, spanning eight disability categories. 11.8 million, i.e., 44 per cent are women; 8.2 million of these live in rural areas and 3.6 in urban ones. It is widely acknowledged that this figure is a gross underestimation of disability prevalence and that faulty enumerative practice, social stigma and the differential meanings attributed to the category result in the official figures not capturing the actual reality.

'Disability' is not a homogeneous category and encompasses different kinds of bodily variations, physical, sensory, intellectual and learning impairments which may be either congenital or acquired. Disabilities may be temporary or permanent, static or progressive and may be acquired at any stage in the life-course. Despite the ubiquity of disability, its very existence is considered an abomination or an anomaly in many cultures, and persons with disability are usually at the receiving end of pity, revulsion, superstition and fear. The arrival of a disabled child in the family may be regarded as a 'fate worse than death', more so if the child is a girl (Ghai 2002), and the acquisition of a disability by a 'non-disabled' person is viewed as a personal tragedy, probably the result of sins committed in lives past or present.

The aversion and fear that the non-normative body evokes amongst the 'normals' can be interpreted as the latent or repressed fear of the frailty and fragmented nature of the body itself, and the contingent and shifting nature of 'normalcy'. The person with disability is at once the 'Other' and a reflection of the self, an ambiguous or 'liminal' entity whose humanness can neither be fully affirmed nor categorically denied.

The experience of disability across cultures and through history has by and large been viewed in negative terms. Persons with disability have been viewed as accursed beings or victims of fate—a burden to be stoically borne by the affected individual and the family. Negative social attitudes are internalized by disabled persons themselves; their self-concept suffers, and they come to view themselves as inferior and inadequate. Disability is frequently deployed in cultural representations as a metaphor to connote moral flaws or weaknesses; everyday language is replete with disability metaphors.

Disability and Feminism: The need for a productive engagement

The disability-rights movement and the interdisciplinary area of disability studies, which emerged in the UK and USA in the 1970s and 1980s, overturned the conventional understanding of the category of disability from an individual affliction or deficit to a 'social' product. It brought to light the consequence of disabling environments, and social and attitudinal barriers which exclude persons with impairments from participating in the life of society and thus, marginalize them. The 'social model' of disability, which is the theoretical and ideological fulcrum of the disability-rights movement and the discipline of disability studies, thus focuses on identifying and transforming 'disabling' practices and policies so that people with impairments enjoy full human rights and are not discriminated against on the basis of biological or physiological differences.

The similarities with the core ideas of the women's movement are too obvious to be missed, as both challenge biological determinism and the social differentiation of persons based upon their sexual identity or their ability/disability. In her programmatic paper, 'Integrating Disability, Transforming Feminist Theory', Rosemarie Garland-Thomson (2010/2002) asserts that many of the issues raised by disability studies have been grappled with by feminists for a long time, and that feminist theory can offer deep insights, methods and perspectives. Equally, issues that preoccupy feminists, such as reproductive technology, the ethics of care, bodily differences, the construction of the subject and 'the particularities of oppression', are intricately intertwined with disability. (2010, 353) She describes feminist theory as 'a self-conscious cultural critique that interrogates how subjects are multiply interpellated: in other words, how the representational systems of gender, race, ethnicity, ability, sexuality and class mutually produce, inflect and contradict one another.' (355) She proposes that by including what she calls the 'ability/disability system', feminist theory can productively engage with complex issues such as the medicalization of the body, the privilege of normalcy, sexuality, multiculturalism and the social construction of identity. (355) The disability system, she writes,

> ...excludes the kinds of bodily forms, functions, impairments, changes, or ambiguities that call into question our cultural fantasy of the body as a neutral, compliant instrument of some transcendent will.... Thus the disability system functions to preserve and validate such privileged designations as beautiful, healthy, normal, fit, competent, intelligent—all of which provide cultural capital to those who can claim such status, who can reside within these subject positions. (356)

As we shall see in this chapter, the personhood and agency of women who are deemed 'the other' on account of their bodily imperfections and differences are thwarted and denied in the context of their sexual and reproductive needs and rights. In this context, Kallianes and Rubenfeld (1997) point out that the women's movement has a long history of fighting for women's rights to self-determination and bodily integrity, and supports their rights to make decisions about their bodies, sexuality and childbearing. Yet, according to disabled feminists neither the women's movement nor the disability-rights movement has adequately addressed reproductive freedom for disabled women.

Disability rights movements worldwide have focused on the rights of persons with disability to full inclusion and participation in all aspects of social life. The major thrust has been on removing physical and architectural barriers, provision of services, education and employment. However, when it comes to the specific issues of women with disabilities, particularly their experiences of sexuality, conjugality and parenthood, both the disability rights movement and the women's rights movement seem to talk past each other as Ghai (2002) and Addlakha (2013) have forcefully highlighted. While the disability movement in India is largely male-dominated, the women's movement has not paid adequate heed to disability as an axis of discrimination and marginalization. Recent scholarship (Addlakha 2008a, 2008b, 2013; Davar 1999, 2001; Dhanda

2000, 2008; Ghai 2002, 2003, 2015; Hans and Patri 2003; Hans 2015; Limaye 2003, 2008, 2015; Mehrotra 2013; Nayar 2013, 2015 to name a few) has sought to address this lacuna. The collection of essays edited by Asha Hans (2015), *Disability, Gender and the Trajectories of Power* situates itself against the backdrop of changing gender relationships and a global human rights regime exemplified by treaties such as the United Nations Convention on the Rights of Persons with Disabilities (2006) and the Convention on the Elimination of All Forms of Discrimination Against Women (CEDAW), which aim to bring about a just social order. While mainstream social science in India is yet to engage with disability with the same urgency as other categories of oppression such as caste, gender and class, there is no denying that disability is no longer a soft issue wrapped in the tissue of charity but rather a political category that speaks the language of rights.

The term reproductive rights broadly refers to the rights of women and men to be informed and have access to contraception, have a safe and legal abortion, control her fertility and not to be forced to undergo an unwanted pregnancy. (TARSHI, 2010) However, in speaking of disabled women, reproductive rights have a broader connotation. Morris (1995) writes that having sexual relationships, family relationships, bearing and rearing children, and making a home are all considered important human and civil rights, which if denied to non-disabled women, would cause an outcry. (76) However, since women with disabilities have traditionally been seen as undesirable sexual partners and incapable mothers, for them, reproductive rights also include the right to engage in consensual sexual relationships, and bear and rear children. While the women's movement focuses on societal expectations and pressures on non-disabled women to marry and become mothers within patriarchal structures, and in a sense aims to liberate women from these expectations, ironically, women with disabilities are routinely denied their 'right' to become mothers if they so desire by the disablist attitudes and values of mainstream culture and society, and even by the legal system in some cases. Women with disabilities thus view their reproductive rights as more than just the right to choose not to bear a child; they include the right to being recognized as sexual beings, to bear children even if the child is also disabled, to be seen as fit to mother and to refuse the use of genetic technologies. In the Indian context, Addlakha (2007) observes that the focus of disability policy is confined to medical rehabilitation, provision of education and employment. The rights of persons with disabilities with regard to sexuality, conjugality, family life and parenthood remain unacknowledged and unaddressed. The Working Paper by TARSHI (2010) also highlights the bleak situation of people with disability in India with regard to sexuality and reproductive rights.

Disability, Sexuality and the Female Body

Women with disabilities are regarded either as asexual beings incapable of becoming sexual companions or as hyper-sexual and unregulated ones who must therefore be put out of sight so that their sexuality can be controlled and contained. Writing about her experience of growing up as a disabled girl in a Punjabi family, Anita Ghai (2002) tells us that the restriction imposed on male and female cousins sleeping in the same room was not observed in the case of disabled girls, sending the clear message that they were not sexual beings in the same way as non-disabled girls of their age. Disabled activist Malini Chib (2015) writes that the personal and sexual needs of disabled women are constantly hidden and ignored because they fail to live up to the constructed ideal of the womanly body being the embodiment of sexuality. They are socialized into feeling ashamed about their bodies and thus deny their sexual feelings and needs. Whereas the truth is,

> ...disability does not hamper a person's emotional need to be touched and loved on an emotional and physical plane just like everyone else. Our sexual organs are not damaged or affected, and hence we do long for and are able to enjoy pleasurable sexual experiences. (105)

In her recent autobiographical narrative Shivani Gupta (2014) writes with depth and feeling about the road accident that left her paralysed in her early 20s and her experiences of romantic love, marriage and intimacy. Her narrative captures the ambivalent feelings and insecurities about her changed body, its needs and limitations and the ongoing struggles with a world that regards disabled bodies as defective and worthless.

Stereotypes in popular culture also reinforce the idea of the pitiable and tragic disabled woman. Bhambhani (2009) comments on the depiction of disabled women in popular Hindi cinema who inevitably 'sacrifices' her love; if the leading man still loves her it is because of her exceptional qualities that somehow manage to make us forget her disability. Running counter to this dominant narrative, a recent film by

Shonali Bose, *Margarita with a Straw* (2015) depicts the story of Laila, a young woman with cerebral palsy, and her search for love, sex and romance. Her experiments with sexuality including masturbation, purchasing sex toys, surfing pornographic websites, a lesbian love affair with another disabled woman, and casual sex with a male friend turn on their head the preconceived notions of the asexual and repressed disabled woman. The film received a mixed reaction: celebrated in some quarters for challenging traditional notions of gender, sexuality and disability, and criticized by others for over-sexualizing the disabled subject. An 'open letter' (Gera 2015) to the director of the film by a television actress Sonal Vengurlekar, widely publicized on social media, expressed shock and disgust with the film and opined that sex was the last thing on the minds of disabled women in India as they faced so many other barriers and obstacles in their lives. Vengurlekar pointedly asked whether the filmmaker would take the responsibility if 'sick' men would take it as a signal to molest and take advantage of disabled women. Here again we note the two extremes of asexuality and hypersexuality between which the construction of disabled sexualities fluctuate.

Empirical research by Addlakha (2007) provides an insight into the sexual needs, dreams and aspirations of young people in urban India with disabilities. It captures their ambiguous and conflicted feelings about their bodies and sexualities. Their poor body image emerges due to the lack of fit with culturally idealized images of healthy, strong, independent and beautiful bodies, resulting in low sexual self-esteem. This can also affect their mental health and their capacity to enter into fulfilling and pleasurable relationships. They may also avoid social interaction and intimacy, living a life of isolation and loneliness, lacking peer feedback. Since they have been taught to think of themselves as unattractive and undesirable, they may not take the risk of initiating and communicating sexual interest fearing ridicule and rejection. Living in institutions for disabled persons or restricted lives within the four walls of their homes further reduces their opportunities for social interaction and developing relationship skills.

Addlakha's (2013) interviews with adolescent girls in Delhi revealed, to a great extent, their agreement with mainstream standards of female beauty and behaviour; while strategically underplaying physical appearance and mobility, 'non-physical aspects of female personhood' such as modesty, loyalty, intelligence and moral uprightness are emphasized. With respect to efficiency in housework, the hallmark of competent femininity in the Indian context, Addlakha found that the girls did not develop much competence as they experienced 'a pervasive enforced invalidism and control by family members (often cloaked in the guise of benevolence).' (231) However, they were encouraged by their families to study and take up employment as a means of ensuring long-term security, particularly because they could leverage the reservation quota for persons with disability. Even though the possibilities of marriage and motherhood diminished due to social stereotypes, it was a valued goal, and the young women regarded themselves and others like them perfectly capable of becoming good homemakers, mothers and sexual partners. While respondents with total loss of vision or hearing wanted to marry people with disabilities like themselves, those with partial vision or hearing or mobility impairments wanted to marry non-disabled men. Sandhya Limaye's (2008) case-studies of two young hearing-impaired adolescent girls highlights how the 'communication bottlenecks' they face in a world which privileges hearing affects their self-concept and the pressures to 'fit in'. Radha and Hasina resent the restrictions and limitations imposed by their families owing to their gender and disability and actively strive to forge friendships and romantic relationships with other hearing-impaired people, revealing their need to engage with the world in the same way as their non-disabled peers.

Nandini Ghosh's (2013) ethnographic study of women with disability in urban and rural the Bengal contextualizes the situation of disabled women with reference to the Bengali feminine ideal, the *bhalo meye*. *Bhalo meye* is a 'good' woman, namely, a morally upright one; the pivot of her family who gets married and becomes a wife and mother. She symbolizes 'a woman with an unimpaired body and optimum capabilities, one who is seen as potentially capable of taking on increasing responsibilities to cater to the needs of her natal and affinal families, one whose productive and reproductive capacities blossom from adolescence to adulthood.' (205) Ghosh analyses the patterns of gender socialization within the family that constructs the disabled girl as different, lacking in capability and thus, devalued. The construction of the *bhalo meye* as a 'complete woman', and the internalization of patriarchal ableist norms, which emphasize physical beauty, desirability and femininity, result in a feeling of social exclusion and desexualization. At the same time, this places them in what Ghosh describes as a 'liminal space' of being neither a *bhalo meye* nor a *baje meye* (bad girl), burdening them with the fear of being labelled as 'loose' women and being shamed for having sexual urges and being disabled. (213) The construction of the disabled woman as unattractive, incapable and asexual thus denies them the possibilities

Of 'Unfit' Mothers   165

of fulfilling sexual lives and motherhood; 'The real tragedy is that it seems as if society cannot bear the sight of the disabled female self that dares to exercise agency in any way.' (218) This comment, we may argue, holds true for non-disabled women as well.

It is also observed that women with disabilities may be given away in marriage to men who are much older, widowers and those unable to secure non-disabled wives due to economic or social reasons. Mehrotra's (2004, 2006) ethnographic work in rural Haryana, a highly patriarchal society, finds that women with mild to moderate disabilities (which do not interfere much with their ability to perform reproductive and domestic tasks) have to work as much as other non-disabled women: fetching water from the well, cutting fodder, cooking and cleaning. Few concessions or allowances are made for their impairments, and if they receive any help or support it is through their natal kin. Domestic violence and wife-beating are common. Disabled men, on the other hand, find it easier to get wives due their structural superiority in the gender hierarchy. Mehrotra (2013) also brings out the role of a 'sorority' or sisterhood as it operates through highly feminized domestic spaces, allowing women to manipulate kin ties and draw upon physical and emotional support from sisters, sisters-in-law, daughters and daughters-in-law to manage the issues that arise out of their disabilities. She cites cases where disabled women are married off into the same family as their female kin and can thus rely upon their support. Elderly women with age-related disabilities similarly expect care from daughters-in-law and grandchildren.

A study by Khanal (2013) detailing the reproductive health experiences of disabled women in Nepal reveals that disabled women are more likely to get married with disabled men due to the perception that their common experienced of disability enables them to understand each other. However, a few disabled women also got married with non-disabled men because they were supportive, helpful and understanding of their disability. In some cases, disabled mothers were abandoned by disabled husbands, who later got married with able-bodied women at the behest of the man's family. The study revealed that disabled mothers experience violence within the family, both emotional as well as severe physical violence in some cases. Haldar's (2015) essay on married women with disabilities in West Bengal highlights the violence and exploitation that these women face. One of her informants who faced a disabling accident was told by her husband, even as she lay on the hospital bed, that he wanted a divorce as she would no longer be able to tend to his needs or give him sexual pleasure. In another case, a non-disabled man who married a disabled woman made it clear that his reason were strictly practical; he was jobless and therefore expected his wife to avail of the 3 per cent quota in jobs granted to persons with disability and take care of him!

Disability management within the structures of South Asian kinship is of a qualitatively different order from the framework of medicalization and segregation that has emerged in the West. At the same time, with the growth of urbanization, migration, the shrinking of extended family support and entrenchment of a neo-liberal capitalist order, traditional kin and community-based structures of support for the elderly, the infirm and the disabled are disintegrating. This has created a crisis of caregiving and placed an even heavier burden of female caregivers, most often mothers, as we saw in Chapter 4.

Domestic and sexual violence is a harsh reality in the lives of women with disability, especially because it is believed that they cannot resist their tormentors nor communicate what has happened to them on account of their disabilities. Women with mental or cognitive disabilities are at special risk. The horrific gang rape and murder of an intellectually disabled woman near Rohtak, Haryana in February 2015, where unspeakable torture was meted out to the victim was widely reported in the media but failed to generate the kind of public outrage and anger witnessed after the Delhi gang rape of 2012. The protests that took place were largely by the migrant community to which the woman belonged. With regard to sexual violence, the lot of disabled women like their non-disabled sisters in India is bleak indeed, and their disability marks them out as the 'other', subjecting them to further humiliation and inhuman treatment.

Disabled Mothers and 'Ideal Mothering'

We now shift the lens to the complex discourses of motherhood and how the embodied experience of disability enables us to consider it in new ways. It is in these discourses that societal and cultural attitudes towards disability and the 'othering' of women with disability resonate with great force. At the same time, through the lens of disability, we can reconceptualize mothering as an experience that confers agency on a person who is otherwise viewed only as a dependent. As givers of care, rather than mere recipients, disabled women attempt to assert or reclaim their identities as 'competent' women. This certainly complicates feminist critiques of the female body as a vessel or the receptacle controlled by men through which patriarchal structures reproduce themselves.

Becoming a mother is supposed to make a woman complete and fulfilled; a childless woman is referred to as a barren field (*baanjh* in Hindi). Her moral power in nurturing and training her children is acknowledged and celebrated. Thus, it is not merely the biological act of giving birth but the process of nurturing that constitutes the experience of motherhood. The mother as the source of selfless love and sacrifice is celebrated in myth and folklore. Under conditions of globalization, the 'super-mom', who seamlessly combines career and care, is the stuff of consumerist fantasy and the backbone of the advertising industry. Disabled women do not fit into these stereotypes. Moreover, the fear that a disabled woman can transmit her 'defects' to her child can adversely affect chances of her own marriage and those of her relatives.

The valorized mothering role across cultures leads to judgemental attitudes and suspicion towards women with disabilities who aspire to become mothers. Carol Thomas's (1997/2009) sociological study of 17 women with a variety of disabilities and chronic medical conditions in the UK reveals how these women are incorporated into the medical and social discourses around 'reproductive risks', to their own health and well-being and, more significantly, to their unborn babies. If they give birth to a baby with impairments, they are viewed as irresponsible and made to feel guilty. They also feel fearful about not being 'good enough mothers', and are under constant surveillance by professionals and experts who judge their performance as good or bad mothers and potentially wield the power to take custody of the child. The medicalization of pregnancy and childbirth under Western bio-medicine is starkly evident in the case of disabled women whose impairments are seen as additional complications to be managed by professionals and thus, feel a loss of control over their bodies when health professionals 'take over.' The 'unhelpful help' rendered by professionals who believe that they 'know best' can be highly disempowering for disabled mothers. In a nutshell, their reproductive journeys are 'strewn with social barriers of an attitudinal, ideological, and material kind.' (268–69) The devaluation of the disabled identity or 'disablism' is starkly evident in their narratives.

In their study of Norwegian women with a range of disabilities, Grue and Laerum (2002) employ a Foucauldian framework to show how these women resist the dominant discourse of disability as dependence by situating themselves within the discourse of motherhood, thereby constructing themselves as social actors capable of *providing* care and becoming responsible for the welfare of another human being.

When disabled women have children, they make themselves known as something other than disabled women, as dependent, rather than responsible for others. Becoming a mother and thereby entering the discourse of motherhood can be seen as a way of challenging and resisting widely held views in relation to what kinds of statuses disabled women are expected to have in society. (2002, 674)

Amongst the important themes highlighted by the authors was the empowering nature of the experience of motherhood and the difference it made to their perceptions of their bodies. They were not viewed merely as impaired bodies in need of medical treatment and improvement, but rather as valuable persons capable of producing new life. For those women who had been disabled since childhood, having a child meant that for the first time in their life they were given the status of adults and not just disabled people. Their motherhood enabled them to 'stage their lives as gendered persons, as women.' (676) Building upon Thomas's (1997/2009) discussion on the need for disabled mothers to show that they are 'good enough mothers' (see previous page), Grue and Laerum demonstrate the care and the stress that goes into the 'performance' of competent motherhood and the self-policing that these women do to make sure the performance is perfect. Sometimes, the harsh and unforgiving glare of society refuses to account for the practical difficulties they undergo and the strategies they adopt. The authors cite the case of a wheelchair-using mother with her toddlers at the beach. Because she could not run after them to keep them safe, she tied a long rope around the children and attached it to her wheelchair. As tying a leash on a child is considered unacceptable in that society, and only a 'bad mother' would do such a thing, someone reported to the police that she was mistreating her children! Disabled mothers must therefore always be mindful and vigilant of the fact that the safety, health, well-being and psychological adjustment of their children is evaluated against the backdrop of their disabilities and the blame for anything that may go wrong is likely to be laid at their door. The performance of mothering is thus a tightrope walk that is carefully negotiated and always tricky.

Malacrida (2009) in her qualitative study of 43 Canadian mothers with a range of disabilities—physical, cognitive and psychosocial—examines the contradictions and tensions embedded in the disabled mothers' performances of ideal motherhood and how women with disabilities reconcile the demands of ideal mothering against the realities of their disabilities. The 'ideal mother' is one who performs her multifaceted role as caregiver, teacher and playmate optimally and perennially. As such, it is a construct which can never be lived up to by mothers, thus, amplifying their sense of guilt and disempowerment. She attempts to show how disabled women perform motherhood in ways that will undermine or challenge the perceptions of others and the ways that normative constructs of femininity and motherhood structure their interactions with their peers, professionals and experts, and welfare delivery systems. She notes that 'women with disabilities go to creative and extraordinary lengths in order to be seen as complying with ideal motherhood, perhaps as a way to lay claim to a maternal and sexual identity that society denies them.' (99) The experiences of mothers with disabilities, as they negotiate the tensions of ideal motherhood, hold up a mirror to the challenges that the mothering ideology raises for all women, and the need for a feminist politics that will account for the lived experiences of all mothers and attempt to change it.

Regardless of their marital status, socio-economic positions or geographical locations, the stories narrated by Malacrida's respondents 'inevitably acknowledged how the women's mothering practices intersected with their awareness of the ideology of ideal motherhood.' (105) They spoke of how they felt judged and evaluated by non-disabled society, and thus had to become 'over-conscious' of their motherhood performance and of living up to the image. While most of the women spoke about the difficulties in performing ideal motherhood some of them, particularly the ones whose children also had disabilities, described their disabilities as enhancing their mothering as they could intuitively understand what their children were going through.

'Mother's intuition' is regarded as an important ingredient of the idealized mothering ideology. These mothers felt they could lay claim to it on account of their own disabled state. While narrating how their bodily differences often interfered with their performance of ideal motherhood, the mothers also demonstrated remarkably creative ways of getting around these barriers. One of the mothers who is housebound and unable to access public spaces, and thus unable to do many of the things with her son, like taking him to the park or playground, worked around the problem by providing free day-care facilities to her neighbours' children. In exchange, her neighbours help her out with her son, thus fostering strong community networks and support that help her provide all that an ideal mother is expected to. (111) While the women in Malacrida's study were well aware of how their status as disabled mothers prevented them from playing out the valorized role of the ideal mother in a variety of ways, they consciously performed 'compensatory mothering', by ensuring that their child was always clean, tidy and well-turned out or by pushing themselves beyond their limits in order to overcome the stigma attached to being a mother with disabilities. At the same time, hegemonic discourses of the 'good mother'—'always present, always capable and always nurturant' (113)—were internalized and never questioned by these disabled mothers who sought ways of working around their limitations to fulfil this role, with varying degrees of success. Malacrida speculates that it is perhaps the denial of sexuality and procreation as legitimate experiences for disabled women that make them so eager to be seen as conforming to such an over-determined construct which is fundamentally oppressive for all women, disabled or otherwise. Like the women in Grue and Laerum's (2002) study, Malacrida's respondents also experienced motherhood as ultimately a fulfilling and enabling experience, helping them to occupy the status of an adult women rather than dependents in need of care. For the women in her study, Malacrida reported that,

> ...pregnancy and motherhood were ways to lay claim to a full adult sexuality, and to erase their invisibility as gendered beings...being pregnant and engaging in motherhood had been empowering to them precisely because, for the first time in their lives, they were seen by others as fully functioning adult women. Intensive mothering and its performance thus provided these women a positive self-image and a vector into normative femininity. (114)

In the Indian context, Sandhya Limaye (2015) opines that mothers with disabilities, like their Western counterparts also face similar issues of stigma, pressure to conform to the concept of ideal motherhood and various kinds of oppression by family members. In her study of seven mothers with disabilities, she found that during their pregnancies the women experienced tension (reinforced by the attitudes of family members and doctors alike) that their child too would be born with impairments. After the delivery of 'normal' babies they felt a sense of great joy and satisfaction. Their parenting experiences revealed their struggles to cope with the stress of raising young children and their innovative strategies to cope with situations. For instance, a mother with visual impairment tying an anklet with a bell on her child's feet to know where the child went; another mother with hearing impairment rigging a bell with a light bulb near the bed so that she could be alerted by her mother-in-law in the next room when the child cried at night. The author highlights how the mothers draw upon support from their parents and in-laws, friends and the children themselves who were certainly affected by the negative perceptions of society towards their mothers, but, over time, came to accept their mothers' disabilities as a part of their lives. She underscores the need for disability organizations to provide services and supports for mothers with disabilities, particularly in rural areas.

While the studies discussed above delineate the ways in which disabled women attempt to exercise agency and empowerment through motherhood, the following section moves the debate to another entirely different social and situational context where agency over the body and consent for the things done to it are appropriated by medical, legal and social practices that challenge the very personhood and humanity of the disabled person.

Disability, Agency and Personhood: Case studies of institutionalized women

The reproductive capacities of persons with disabilities are perceived as a threat to the 'normal' society and various means have been used to control them. Tilley et al (2012) write of the history of sterilization of women with disabilities in several European countries, remarking upon its continuance with the tacit support of the medical system even in the present time. On 4 February 1994, hysterectomies or womb removal surgeries were conducted on 11 women inmates of a state-run home for the intellectually disabled in Shirur near Pune, Maharashtra. The young women whose chronological ages ranged between 15 and 35 years reportedly functioned at the level of three- or four-year-old children. The justification given for the procedures by the authorities at the facility was that they would safeguard the women from unwanted pregnancies, and also deal with the nuisance and bother of monthly periods. Activists launched a vociferous protest against what they believed to be a violation of the rights and bodily integrity of women under state control; they felt that conducting such a major surgical procedure was unwarranted and could not possibly guarantee the safety of the women from sexual assault. The Shirur facility was described by activists as horrific, reeking of urine and excrement, where inmates led bleak and dreary lives, devoid of any kind of stimulation or engaging activity. No training in self-help skills or basic literacy or vocational skills was imparted that would help them lead a dignified life. The girls and women suffered from anaemia, skin infections and other clear indicators of poor care and terrible hygiene. The absence of staff compounded the problem further. A report prepared by a group of non-governmental organisations, *In The Guise of Human Dignity* (1994) highlighted not only of the state of affairs at the Shirur centre but the attitude towards women with disability in general. The assumption that the removal of a disabled woman's womb is a solution to her sexual and reproductive problems is highly flawed besides being risky and painful for the woman herself. Given this sorry state of affairs it is hardly surprising that the women residents were seen as troublesome bodies to be managed and controlled rather than as persons with rights and entitlements to a dignified and comfortable life despite their cognitive limitations.

The voices of the affected women did not find a place in the discourse; it was the doctors, activists and administrators who battled out the ethical, medical and legal aspects and offered contradictory understandings. (see Sundar Rajan, 2005 for a thoughtful analysis on the issue) The activists' perceptions of the feelings and emotions of the women were countered by the versions of the officials running the facility who highlighted the difficulties experienced by the women in managing periods and the risks of pregnancy. The 'nullity of the subjects' (133) and the lack of engagement with their subjectivities and consciousness by experts who took decisions on their behalf is a testimony to the devaluation and dehumanization of the disabled subject. Sunder Rajan (2005) writes,

> It will be clear that in the debate over the hysterectomies, the government's most elevated defense of the practice was based on the 'alleviation of suffering' argument, while the activists' opposition to it drew from the human rights defense of the women's autonomy, liberty, integrity, and privacy. By extending and applying these constitutional rights to mentally retarded women, activists were making a radical claim for a subjectivity grounded in their *identity* with others (others as *citizens*), rather than their differences from them.... In a single stroke, the sterilization procedure wholly and comprehensively defined the identity of the inmates of the welfare home as 'mentally retarded women': as *women* in terms of the 'problems' of female sexuality; and as *mentally retarded*, in terms of their incapacity to make rational choices. The individual's spaces of selfhood, subjectivity, and citizenship are thus entirely usurped by the state and the exigencies of institutional 'care'. (145–46)

A report by *The Indian Express* (22 January 2008) published in *The Punekar*, revisiting the events of 1994, paints a much less dismal picture. The running of the centre was handed over to social workers in 1997. Conditions had improved—there was more staff available to run the home and the women who had undergone the procedure in 1994 were reported to be doing well, with no medical complications. The nun who was in charge of the centre felt that for some women with profound disabilities, a surgical removal of the womb was necessary and humane as they were just not able to manage their periods. For many non-disabled women too, monthly periods are frequently painful and debilitating, and if they wish to opt for womb removal they are free to do so. The jury continues to be out on the vexed issue of rights over bodily integrity and reproductive freedoms on the one hand, and the very real difficulties and dilemmas of caregivers of disabled persons (usually women) on the other, who must assist their charges in maintaining menstrual hygiene, changing soiled clothing and so on. The messiness and unruliness of the reproductive female body cannot be captured clinically within a medical or legal discourse; its reality as experienced by diverse women must be taken into account. The Chandigarh Nari Niketan case discussed below further complicates these debates.

The custodial rape and resultant pregnancy of an intellectually disabled 19-year-old woman in March 2009 at a government-run home for destitute women by the staff working in the facility created a public outcry, and raised several sensitive and contentious issues. The key issue was whether the young woman who suffered from several physical ailments in addition to her mental impairment, and had no family or any other means of social support, was fit to carry and give birth to a baby. The Chandigarh administration and the Punjab and Haryana High Court had to take a call on the legal issues of informed consent, and the ability of mentally disabled persons to make decisions about their futures and those of their unborn children (see Rastogi and Yadav, 2010)

A three-member committee was constituted by the director of the Government Medical College and Hospital to assess her mental condition; she was reported to be 'mildly mentally retarded' with the mental capacity of a nine-year-old. A multi-disciplinary medical board constituted a few days later and went into the details of the case. The board opined that the woman's physical ailments and impairments were such that they might be genetically transmitted to the foetus or might endanger the health of the mother. The mental condition of the woman was such that she was not deemed capable of understanding how she came to have a baby inside her. Her destitute status and the bleak future prospects of a child of a victim of sexual abuse were also considered. The board therefore recommended the medical termination of the pregnancy. The High Court however appointed yet another committee consisting of three doctors, including a psychiatrist with a judge as the coordinator. According to the committee there were no serious physical risks involved in the pregnancy; however they felt that the woman was not socially and emotionally capable of understanding what motherhood meant. She thought of her unborn baby as a future playmate and seemed quite unaware of the precariousness of her situation. The committee was unable to ascertain whether the woman's surroundings were conducive to her making an informed choice about herself and her unborn child. On 17 July 2009 the High Court ordered the Chandigarh administration that the pregnancy be terminated. The case took a new turn when a young woman advocate Tanu Bedi took an interest in the case and helped the young woman move the Supreme Court to seek the protection of her unborn child.

After listening to arguments on both sides, including medical experts who had earlier examined the young woman, the Supreme Court, in its order dated 28 August 2009, granted a stay on the decision of the High Court. The woman was permitted to go ahead with the pregnancy. Questioning the decision of the High Court to direct a termination of pregnancy without the consent of the woman, the Supreme Court opined,

> We disagree with this conclusion since the victim had clearly expressed her willingness to bear a child. Her reproductive choice should be respected in spite of other factors such as the lack of understanding of the sexual act as well as apprehensions about her capacity to carry the pregnancy to its full term and the assumption of maternal responsibility thereafter. (Para 10, p. 6.)

The Supreme Court also did not accept the invocation of the doctrine of *parens patriae* by the High Court. The doctrine of *parens patriae* has been evolved in common law and is used in situations in which the State must make decisions for those who are unable to take care of themselves or make informed decisions. Traditionally, this applies to minors or persons who may not be mentally capable of doing so. One of the major standards for exercising this jurisdiction is the 'Best Interests' test. In this regard, the Supreme Court remarked that the direction for termination of the pregnancy did not serve the purpose of ensuring the 'best interests' of the young woman. Neither was her life nor that of her unborn child in danger, as per the opinion of medical experts, and, most crucially, she did not consent. In this context, the Supreme Court judgement also made reference to the issue of discrimination against and violation of the human rights of persons with intellectual disabilities through the practices of eugenics, forced sterilization and abortion. (Para 28, p. 13) It is also pertinent to note that the woman's pregnancy was perilously close to the legal limit for medical termination, i.e., 20 weeks, and grave concern was expressed by the court that proceeding with a termination at such an advanced stage of pregnancy may cause physical harm to the pregnant woman.

The Nari Niketan case and the Supreme Court judgement upholding the reproductive rights of a disabled and institutionalized young woman is cited as a landmark in moving the discourse around disability and the lack of agency of the subject to one driven by a recognition of personhood and rights. The rights of persons with disabilities, who, as we have seen, are frequently treated as 'non-persons', to live within the community and receive appropriate assistance and support is underscored. Even if they live in institutions, labelling them as 'inmates' suggests that they are on par with prisoners in a jail or dangerous persons who deserved to be locked away from public view. Ironically, the institution mandated with her care and safety was the site of her violation, and its own employees actively colluded in the crime. The presumed inability of the young woman to understand the enormity of what had happened to her and the presumption that having the child could result only in further deterioration of her situation were compelling reasons for ordering a termination by the High Court. However, her resistance to the writ of the state over the fate of her unborn child prompted the legal system to review the ruling and restore the girl her rights over her body and reproductive decisions. Her disability was not deemed to disqualify her as a potential mother, at the same time it was acknowledged that she would need support and help in discharging her functions as a mother, and that it was the duty of the state to provide her with adequate and appropriate help. Accordingly, the court directed that the best medical facilities be made available to her to ensure a safe delivery and post-natal care, and thereafter, she be given all the necessary support and guidance to assist her in her maternal responsibilities. (Para 31, p. 14)

The young woman was deemed unfit to take appropriate decisions regarding the well-being of herself and the child she was carrying. The Supreme Court judgement observed that it was quite possible that a person with a low IQ or mental age, which indicated only academic capacities, could have the social and emotional capacities to be a good parent. (Para 28, p. 13) The equating of 'fitness to mother' to a western bio-medical construct, namely, the Intelligence Quotient, denies a whole realm of emotional experience, and is a reductive and simplistic way of measuring ability and competence. It exemplifies the application of the medical model of disability to the hilt and sidelines the role of social and community structures in fostering or impeding competence. It is also particularly ironic in a cultural context where nine-year-old girls render care to siblings and sometimes singlehandedly run households while their mothers go out to labour in fields or factories!

On 2 December 2009 a baby girl was born. Divya Tripathi's article in the *Frontline* (7 February 2014)[2] reports that both mother and child are doing well.

A special educator visits them regularly; the mother is being imparted basic self-help and vocational skills, and the child attends a playschool. The young woman, after initial hesitation, learned to handle and care for her child, and is an affectionate mother. The little girl receives affection and attention from the other residents at the home and is likely to be admitted to a residential school when she is older. The circumstances around her birth brought into view the pathetic condition of state-run institutions, and the need to make them more open and accessible to public scrutiny so that the routine and unreported abuse taking place behind their walls would be exposed and prevented. The circumstances around her birth, and the legal and medical debates that accompanied it brought to the fore the fraught and contentious issues of legal capacity, personhood and agency. These debates have become particularly significant in the context of the framing of a new legislation to replace the Persons with Disabilities Act (1995), harmonizing it with the United Nations Convention on the Rights of Persons with Disabilities (UNCRPD 2006) signed and ratified by India. The UNCRPD recognizes persons with disabilities as equal holders of all rights, and places them at the centre of all rights. This has a direct bearing on the reproductive rights and choices of women with disability and their potential to exercise their agency. At the same time, the need to extend care and support based upon a shared understanding of the essential interdependence of all human beings, male or female, able or disabled is also crucial. The challenges and opportunities of mothering as a creative and liberative practice that values and respects difference thus becomes salient.

Conclusion

The case studies across cultural contexts discussed above open up the experience of motherhood through a different kind of embodiment, namely, disability. The experience of disability complicates the understanding of motherhood as a 'natural' and normative rite of passage, signalling a girl's entry into the adult world, and her incorporation into a gender regime where her role as a reproducer and nurturer are paramount. The disabled, deficient female body is viewed as an abomination which is itself in need of care and incapable of giving or receiving sexual pleasure or bringing forth new life. While women with physical disabilities are regarded as 'asexual' and unattractive, women with mental or cognitive disabilities are seen to be sexually unregulated and vulnerable to abuse, and therefore in need of medical and social interventions ranging from sterilization to confinement in institutions where their sexuality and reproductive capacities may be tightly controlled and hidden away from the 'normal' world. Scholarship at the intersections of gender and disability studies has sought to illuminate the ways in which women with disabilities challenge these understandings and thereby complicate and enrich discourses on embodiment and motherhood. At the same time, hegemonic, patriarchal ideological constructs of 'good' and 'bad' mothering practices appear well-entrenched and internalized, and disabled women attempt to reclaim agency and feminine identity by conforming to these constructs to the best of their ability. The growing medicalization of disability in contexts like India has resulted in western constructs of ability and intelligence being uncritically applied. Disabled women's bodies become the objects of medical and legal discourses about reproduction and sexuality, often at the cost of lived, experiential realities and diverse socio-cultural contexts. This compels us to reflect upon the disciplining and punitive power of patriarchal social structures and the modern state over non-normative bodies, and will hopefully lend urgency and a critical edge to our understandings of what constitutes humanness and personhood.

Notes

1. Ableism refers to ideas, practices, social relations and institutions that are based on the assumption of able-bodiedness and therefore marginalizes and invisibilizes persons with disabilities.
2. These case studies have been referred to in the IGNOU teaching module *Disability, Sexuality and Motherhood* (see footnote on the opening page of the chapter).

References

Addlakha, Renu. *Gender, Subjectivity and Sexual Identity: How Young People with Disabilities Conceptualise the Body, Sex and Marriage in Urban India*, Occasional Paper, CWDS, New Delhi, 2007.
—— 'Introduction: Disability, Gender and Society', Indian Journal of Gender Studies Special Issue Vol. 15, No. 2, 2008a, pp. 191–207.
—— *Deconstructing Mental Illness: An Ethnography of Psychiatry, Women and the Family* New Delhi: Zubaan Books, 2008b.
—— 'Body Politics and Disabled Femininity: Perspectives of Adolescent Girls from Delhi'. In *Disability Studies in India: Global Discourses, Local Realities*, edited by Renu Addlakha. New Delhi: Routledge, 2013, pp. 220–40.
Bhambani, Meenu. 'Societal Responses to Women with Disabilities in India'. In *Disability and Society: A Reader*, edited by Renu Addlakha, Stuart Blume, Patrick Devlieger, Osamu Nagase and Myriam Winance. New Delhi: Orient Black Swan, 2009.
Chib, Malini. 'I Feel Normal Inside.Outside, My Body Isn't!'. In *Disability, Gender and the Trajectories of Power*, edited by Asha Hans. New Delhi: SAGE Publications, 2015, pp. 93–112.
Davar, Bhargavi. *Mental Health of Indian Women: A Feminist Agenda*. New Delhi: SAGE Publications, 1999.
—— *Mental Health from a Gender Perspective*. New Delhi: SAGE Publications, 2001.
Dhanda, Anita. *Legal Order/Mental Disorder*. New Delhi: SAGE Publications, 2000.
—— 'Sameness and Difference: Twin Track Empowerment for Women with Disabilities', *Indian Journal of Gender Studies* Special Issue Vol. 15, No. 2, 2008, pp. 209–32.
Garland-Thomson, Rosemarie. 'Integrating Disability, Transforming Disability Theory'. In *The Disability Studies Reader*, edited by Lennard Davis. Third Edition. New York and London: Routledge, 2010, pp. 353–74.
Gera, Sonal. TV actress Sonal Vengurlekar not happy with 'sexuality' in 'Margarita with a straw',writes open letter to Shonali Bose. Retrieved 25 April, 2015. indianexpress.com/article/entertainment/entertainment-others/tvactress

Ghai, Anita. 'Disabled Women: An Excluded Agenda of Indian Feminism', Hypatia–17:3, pp. XX-XX.

—— (Dis)Embodied Form: Issues of Disabled Women. New Delhi: Har-Anand Publications, 2003.

——. Rethinking Disability in India. New Delhi: Routledge, 2015.

Ghosh, Nandini. 'Bhalo Meye: Cultural Construction of Gender and Disability in Bengal'. In Disability Studies in India: Global Discourses, Local Realities, edited by Renu Addlakha. New Delhi: Routledge, 2013, pp. 201–19.

Grue, Lars and Kristin Tafjord Laerum. 'Doing Motherhood: Some Experiences of Mothers with Physical Disabilities', Disability & Society, Vol. 17, No. 6, 2002, pp. 671–83.

Gupta, Shivani. No Looking Back. New Delhi: Rupa, 2014.

Haldar, Santoshi. Tale of Married Women with Disabilities: An Oxymoron Reality? In DGTP, edited by Asha Hans. New Delhi: SAGE Publications, 2015, pp. 121–32.

Hans, Asha and Annie Patri (eds). Women, Disability and Identity. New Delhi: SAGE Publications, 2003.

Hans, Asha (ed.). Disability, Gender and the Trajectories of Power. New Delhi: SAGE Publications, 2015.

Kallianes, Virginia and Phyllis Rubenfeld. 'Disabled Women and Reproductive Rights', Disability & Society, Vol. 12, No. 2, 1997, pp. 203–22.

Khanal, Neeti Aryal. Status of Reproductive Health and Experience of Motherhood of Disabled Women in Nepal, Report submitted to Social Inclusion Research Fund (SIRF) Kathmandu, Nepal 2013.

Limaye, Sandhya. 'The Inner World of Adolescent Girls with Hearing Impairments: Two Case Studies', IJGS Special Issue Vol. 15, No. 2, 2008, pp. 387–406.

—— 'A Disabled Mother's Journey in Raising her Child'. In Disability, Gender and the Trajectories of Power, edited by Asha Hans New Delhi: SAGE Publications, 2015, pp. 133–54.

Malacrida, Claudia (2009). Performing Motherhood in a Disablist World: Dilemmas of Motherhood, Femininity and Disability, International Journal of Qualitative Studies in Education, 22:1, pp. 99–117.

Mehrotra, Nilika. 'Women, Disability and Social Support in Rural Haryana', Economic and Political Weekly, Vol. 39, No. 52, 2004, pp. 5640–644.

—— 'Negotiating Gender and Disability in Rural Haryana', Sociological Bulletin, Vol. 55, No. 3, 2006, pp. 406–26.

—— Disability, Gender and State Policy: Exploring Margins Jaipur: Rawat Publications, 2013.

Mehrotra, Nilika and Mahima Nayar. 'Women and Psycho-social Disabilities among the Urban Poor'. In Disability, Gender and State Policy: Exploring Margins. Jaipur: Rawat Publications, 2013, pp. 208–36.

—— 'Women with Psycho-social Disabilities: Shifting the Lens from Medical to Social'. In Disability, Gender and the Trajectories of Power, edited by Asha Hans New Delhi: SAGE Publications, 2015, pp. 72–90.

Mehrotra, Nilika and Shubhangi Vaidya. 'Exploring Constructs of Intellectual Disability and Personhood in Haryana and Delhi', *IJGS* Special Issue Vol. 15, No. 2, 2008, pp. 317–40.

Morris, J. 'Creating a Space for Absent Voices: Disabled Women's Experience of Receiving Assistance with Daily Living Activities', *Feminist Review*, 51, Autumn, 1995, pp. 68–93.

Rastogi, P. and Y. Mukesh. 'Issue of Consent for MTP by Orphan, Major and Mentally Retarded: A Critical Review', *Journal of the Indian Academy of Forensic Medicine*, Vol. 32, No. 3, 2010, pp. 267–74.

Sunder Rajan, Rajeswari. 'Beyond the Hysterectomies Scandal: Women, the Institution, Family and State'. In *The Violence of Normal Times*, edited by Kalpana Kannabiran. New Delhi: Women Unlimited, 2005.

Supreme Court of India 28 August 2009. Suchita Srivastava and Anr vs Chandigarh Administration. http://indiankanoon,org/doc/1500783

Thomas, Carol. 'The Baby and the Bath Water: Disabled Women and Motherhood in Social Context'. In *Disability and Society: A Reader,* edited by Renu Addlakha et al. New Delhi: Orient Black Swan, 2009.

TARSHI. *Sexuality and Disability in the Indian Context*. Working Paper, 2010.

Tilley, Elizabeth, Jan Walmsley, Sarah Earle and Dorothy Atkinson. 'The Silence is Roaring: Sterilisation, Reproductive Rights and Women with Intellectual Disabilities', *Disability & Society*, Vol. 27, No. 3, 2012, pp. 413–26.

Vaidya, Shubhangi. *Disability, Sexuality and Motherhood* (Unit 2, Block 1 Course MWG004, MA in Women's and Gender Studies). Indira Gandhi National Open University, School of Gender and Development Studies, 2013.

Forum for Women's Health (1994) *In the guise of Human Dignity*. Retrieved on 11 November 2014 http://www.unipune.ac.in/snc/cssh/HumanRights/07%20STATE%20AND%20GENDER/12.pdf

At Peace in Shirur, Site of Mass Hysterectomies, The Indian Express report in *The Punekar*, 22 January 2008. Retrieved on 11 November 2014. http://www.thepunekar.com/at-peace-in-shirur-site-of-mass hysterectomies/2008/01/)

'Her Story' Frontline, 7 February 2014. Retrieved on 11 November 2014. http://www.frontline.in/social-issues/general-issues/her-story/article5601365.ece?homepage=true

7
Mapping the Mother in France and India: Discursive revolutions*

We have previously commented on the inadequacy of Oedipal narratives, from a cross-cultural as well as a feminist perspective, in achieving a revised understanding of motherhood (see Chapter 2). Through a studied critique of Freudian and Lacanian psychoanalytic models, French feminist theory has played a significant role in advancing novel perspectives on maternal subjectivity. Here we ask if this critique may be of relevance in the quest for alternate ways of approaching the maternal in the Indian context, and in so doing, seek to map the latter onto a broader international canvas.

Whereas both psychoanalytic and sociological feminist trajectories offer significant critiques of motherhood ideology, we take into account the former's reliance on transformative discursive strategies to achieve cultural transformations as a useful trope in the context of contemporary discourse on motherhood in India. Motherhood has been both reified in French psychoanalytic discourse as well as rejected by critiques of

---

*This chapter is a revised and expanded version of a previously published article, 'Mapping the Mother in France and India: Cross-Cultural Applications of Psychoanalytic Theory' which appeared in *Mothering & Psychoanalysis* (Ed. Petra Bueskens), Demeter, 2014, pp. 391–410.
A preliminary discussion of a few, selected ideas pertaining to French feminist theory also appeared in a chapter contributed by the author for self-learning material for the MAWGS programme and published by Indira Gandhi National Open University, 2013 ('The Body in French Feminist Theory & Psychoanalysis', MWG 004, Gendered Bodies & Sexualities, pp. 229–46).

such positions from a Marxist feminist perspective. Both of these positions, contradictory as they may be, share certain underlying paradigms of womanhood and the maternal that are derived from western interpretive feminist theory and its related emphasis on the ability of discourse to shape reality.[1] This chapter will follow the limited trajectory of a few of the inferences drawn from Judith Butler's critique of Monique Wittig's and Julia Kristeva's work, within the specific context of the socio-cultural discourses around motherhood in urban India, delineated with the help of dominant Hindu socio-cultural registers, which have been referenced in previous chapters. We suggest that it is time to make room for interpretive approaches alongside empirical ones, and argue against an unqualified relegation of all psychoanalytic and interpretive approaches as inadequate in the context of an analysis of motherhood in India. In so doing, we explore the possibility of cross-cultural alliances through vigilant readings of potential impasses and coalitions made possible by feminist dialogue.

Mapping the Maternal across Cultures

It would be prudent to begin any cross-cultural critique with the caution that the export of ideas and theories across cultures is susceptible to uncertain effects of assimilation, especially in a post-colonial context. As noted by Christiane Hartnack, Freud himself openly wondered about the transportability of his theories in another climate[2] and 'expressed a premonition that psychoanalysis would not travel easily.' (Hartnack 2008, 7) While Freud's hesitation may serve as a forewarning about the potential difficulties of ferrying French psychoanalytic theory to India, the history of psychoanalysis in India is not without early examples of the willingness towards blending western and Indian models. For instance, Girindrasekhar Bose was among the first to test the employability of Freudian psychoanalysis in the Indian context.[3] More recently, as we have seen in previous chapters, Indian psychoanalytic theorists like Sudhir Kakar have freely combined Freudian and post-Freudian (Eriksonian) approaches with cultural insights on the Indian family in examining issues of gender, sexuality and motherhood. (Kakar 1981, 1989)

On the other hand, reified cultural differences may easily lead to the construction of us/them binaries, which do not necessarily hold up under close scrutiny, thus rendering the other unfathomable. It may also result in an unequivocal west/east divide as in the work of cultural critics such as Ashis Nandy, where there emerges a polarization of the west's focus on 'conjugality' and the Indian exaltation of 'motherhood'. (Nandy 1998, 34–43) In this context, Uma Narayan's warning that 'culture essentialism' (Narayan 2000, 81) may be as pernicious as gender essentialism may be instructive in avoiding a paralysis in the process of looking for global feminist contiguities and coalitions. For instance, a commonly held view about western theories of motherhood is that these may have limited applicability in India due to the 'individualistic' culture prevalent in the west. Such views are reinforced by overarching statements such as Sudhir Kakar's 'where and when tradition governs, an Indian woman does not stand alone; her identity is wholly defined by her relationships to others' and 'this is singularly true of Indian women.' (Kakar 1981, 56) Although it may be true that traditional Indian culture emphasizes relational identities at the expense of individual ones, it is equally difficult to point to any one homogenous tradition which would sustain this view over competing ones in contemporary times, given the advent of capitalism, globalization and swiftly transforming economies and cultures. The individual/collective debate may therefore, turn out to be an unexamined and over-simplistic binary trap which, in attempting to isolate cultural difference in absolute terms, may end up homogenizing all Indian women as 'relational' mothers. As observed by the authors of 'The Study of Gender in India', the unease of scholars who reject a feminist epistemology may arise because a 'sharp distinction is assumed to separate the individual from any collectivity' in countries like the United States, even though, as they state, 'such dichotomization is unacceptable to many Indian scholars.' (Purkayashta 2003, 506) The difficulties of individual vs. relational theories have also been pointed out by Seshadri-Crooks (Seshadri-Crooks 1994, 193–94) and Jane Flax (2004, 910). While many feminist scholars, including Chandra Mohanty, Chilla Bulbeck and others, have previously engaged in considered ways with the enduring sameness/difference debate,[4] as far as ethnographic psychoanalysis is concerned, it may be more productive, as suggested by Ranjana Khanna, to look towards 'a transnational feminism informed by a reconfigured psychoanalysis.' (Khanna 2003, 30)

The relative cultural emphasis on Indian relational values seems to suggest that those aspects of French feminist theory that are deeply embedded in questions of the individual psyche may well have to be combined with class-based theories as well as any others that speak to the complex identities of women as mothers in India (see previous discussion on relationality in Chapter 2). In this regard, Gayatri Spivak's uneasiness about 'the use of psychoanalysis in cultural critique' in contrast to her sympathy for the use of Marxism as well as feminist psychoanalysis because the latter is 'so actively contestatory' (Spivak 1993, 18) seems to sum up Indian feminist reservations and comforts about cross-cultural critique. But it is interesting to note that while Kakar, Nandy and others may view the relational aspects of Indian society as a defining feature which must be considered in developing culturally apt psychoanalytic models, in western feminist accounts, 'relationality' has been emphasized as an aspect which carries the potential to give new political dimensions to the maternal. For instance, in her discussion of Nancy Fraser's work, Patricia Boling notes that Fraser's work proposes relationality as a way of connecting the private to the public: 'Instead of focusing on the personal or individual dimension of concerns with the "concrete other"... Fraser tries to envision the political ethic that might arise from taking seriously the collective dimension of the relational concept of identity.' (Boling 1991, 619) Object relations theory is built on an inherently relational emphasis, as pointed out by Mary Caputi: 'according to these scholars, the subjects they study do not create their object but, from the beginning, find themselves enmeshed within a relationship to that external being.' (Caputi 1993, 311) An overview of the western objects relations theory as well as the work of many feminist theorists would immediately lead us away from a hurried, decidedly essentialist position in distinguishing cultures on the basis of 'individualistic' and 'relational' aspects. Consequently, in exploring possible cross-cultural alliances, we may benefit from vigilant readings of French feminist theories in looking for commonalities across cultures, without necessarily rejecting outright western perspectives purely on the basis of homogenized cultural identities.

Motherhood and Feminist Discourses in India and France

To say, at the outset, that there is no one, unitary view of women or of motherhood within the complex historical and multi-cultural collage, with its heterogeneous range of ethnic, class, caste and religious differences that together comprise 'India' would be mandatory, and perhaps, an understatement. Within India, feminist scholarship has tended to approach, with some amount of misgiving, any attempts to relate theoretical positions grounded in western cultural traditions to the situation of women in India. Ania Loomba notes, in fact, that 'a huge variety of feminists are invariably chastised for being influenced by Western modes of thought.' (Loomba 1993, 271) Thus, predominantly textual and theoretical feminist analyses of motherhood may tend to be viewed as somewhat supplementary to the 'real' work of ameliorating the unequal position of women by activists and scholars alike.[5] For instance, Sharmila Rege has voiced her concern that the celebration of motherhood in psychoanalysis may be the result of a postmodern focus on difference and its alliance with the 'New Right'. (Rege 1998, WS 40)

The predominantly 'rights'-based approach of the Indian women's movement may be better understood in the historical context of 19th-century debates concerning gender inequalities, which engaged many of the social reform movements of the time. Chitra Sinha observes that the struggle for legal rights for women remained a part of the dominant discourse of the early 20th century, leading 'women's organizations and liberal forces' to see this as 'an opportune moment in history to put India in the path to become a progressive, modern and egalitarian nation.' (Sinha 2007, 50) In this initiative to redefine women's changing status, motherhood became a focal point of debate. As argued by Sinha, the evolution of the Hindu Code Bill in the mid-20th century centred around the contested notion of motherhood, with women's organizations playing a critical role in the effort to win legal rights for women and mothers:

> The Hindu Code Bill provided a platform to achieve a consensus on motherhood in Indian society—and contributed towards transforming the Indian mother from its domestic confines with an exclusive focus on childbearing and rearing towards a somewhat broader role with presence both in the domestic and public spheres. (Sinha 2007, 57)

The ongoing scepticism of rights-based Indian feminism towards what are largely perceived as western, postmodern theoretical positions can thus be traced back to a moment in the historical evolution of the women's movement when the struggle for legal rights was an immediate and urgent concern, with perhaps little patience for discursive explorations and deconstructions of gendered identities. Such scepticism also results at least partially from the complex anti-imperialistic and post-colonial history of nationalism alongside which the Indian women's movement has continued to evolve, at least until the 1970s.

The women's movement made significant strides during the freedom struggle due to its coalitions with class- and caste-based political movements and groups. Thus, much of feminist scholarship in India rightly locates gender as an inter-sectional category within materialist analyses of inequalities of caste, class, nation, region and ethnicity (see Akerkar as well as Purkayashta).[6] Recent years have witnessed the flagging of some of the dangers of mainstreaming the woman's question at the expense of issues concerning the oppression of lower-caste women or Dalit feminism (see Rege 1998), alternative sexualities (see Sharma 2009; Shah 2008), among others. With the growing diversity in feminist scholarship, the earlier tendency of perceiving all western theoretical positions as culturally exclusivist, elitist or irrelevant is losing the currency it held in the 1980s and 1990s, as observed earlier by Ania Loomba and others.[7]

However, the historical emphasis on empirical studies, which formed the theoretical bedrock of the grassroots women's movement, has led to a general trend of combining academic scholarship on motherhood with empirical studies within the domain of the social sciences, and a distrust of theory per se, thus restricting the potential benefits of links between interpretive discourse and lived realities. For instance, Ashis Nandy, in one of his early works, complains that 'an uncritical disciplinary culture... equates theoretical work with wool-gathering.' (Nandy 1974, 10) More recently, Seshadri-Crooks observes that 'psychoanalysis in India has been supplanted by a quantifying psychology of neurological or sociological phenomena.' (Seshadri-Crooks 1994, 177) Interestingly, similar discontent has been expressed by western feminists like Robyn Wiegman, who takes exception to the dichotomization of theory and real feminism, and to the representation of 'theory as the interloper in a contemporary context that tends to wager the symbolic against the real.' (Wiegman 1999, 117)

Within French feminist discourse, on the other hand, a serious reservation about empirically oriented approaches can be discerned. As contended by Caputi, 'French feminism reproaches more empirically oriented feminist undertakings for actually harboring a hostile sentiment toward feminist sensibilities and toward women.' (Caputi 1993, 325) Rather, according to Caputi, the French feminists are much more interested in the 're-evaluation of the metaphorical implications of the maternal to uncover its subversive qualities.' (Caputi 1993, 325) This is not to suggest that French feminist discourse on the maternal is limited to the post Lacanian psychoanalytic school. Sociologically informed critiques of the institution of mothering in the tradition of

Simone de Beauvoir have continued to enjoy popularity, as for instance, evidenced by Elizabeth Badinter's work in the 1980s, which draws on trans-historical links between culture, power inequity and gender roles to call for a contemporary revolution in the practice of mothering (see *L'Un et l'Autre, L'Amour en Plus*) In fact, two distinct bodies of feminist work—one arising out of sociologically oriented perspectives, such as Badinter's, and the other out of psychoanalytic models, such as those of Cixous, Kristeva and Irigaray—have co-existed in France. Such a split also mirrors a larger dual impulse in feminist scholarship in general, as well as one within feminist psychoanalysis. Marking out a similar distinction, Julie Rodgers identifies the work of Elizabeth Badinter and Lisa Baraitser as exemplifying 'two main trends in circulation in the field of motherhood studies.' (Rodgers 2012) The first approach 'considers the idealization of mothering and its impossible standards of perfection' as 'deeply injurious to the subjectivity of the mother.' The second account (exemplified by Baraitser) 'endeavours to articulate the potential within maternity for new and generative experiences as opposed to positing the experience of becoming a mother as the inevitable annihilation of the self.' (Rodgers 2012) Petra Bueskens locates the 'conundrum' of the 'psychic/social schism' within 'the heart of the psychoanalytic project' itself and links it to a central question which defines 'feminism's relation to psychoanalysis', that is, 'how to integrate the "discovery" of the unconscious and of sexuality with the external realities of women's lives under patriarchy.' (Bueskens 2014, 9) The conundrum explains why, for instance, despite their discrete impulses, both sociological and psychoanalytical approaches continue to seek each other out in support of their own contentions.

Elizabeth Badinter's work on motherhood in the France of the 1980s clearly falls within the former (sociologically oriented) approach, although Badinter does not hesitate to recognize the important influence of Freud's 'holy scriptures' on femininity without which 'it is impossible to understand fully contemporary questions regarding mother love.' (Badinter 1981, 262) Within French feminism, Badinter's approach represents a concerted effort towards exploding the myth of a naturalized 'maternal instinct' and of the provisional nature of 'mother love'. The latter, she argues, is 'only a feeling and, as such, essentially conditional, contingent on many different factors' (Badinter 1981, 327) and that 'motherhood is not always the first and instinctive concern of the woman.' (307) In *L'Un et l'Autre* (Badinter 1986) she builds an argument about the shifting nature of feminine power and maternal roles throughout history by tracing the existence of an originary *'puissance féminine et maternelle'* (feminine and maternal power) to the Neolithic period. (Badinter 1986, 67) Based on ancient-Middle-Eastern and Indian iconographies of the Mother Goddess, Badinter points to the co-existence of archaic notions of bisexuality and feminine power, both of which become casualties of the division of labour under subsequent stages of patriarchy. This Mother Goddess, according to Badinter, points to the very real power wielded by women in ancient times: *'La Déesse-Mère n'est ni un myth, ni une légende, ni meme un symbole. Il suffit d'observer les nombreuses statuettes de pierre qui ornent les musées pour etre convaincu de l'extreme importance des valeurs féminine et de leur réalité historique.'* (1986, 67) (The Mother-Goddess is neither myth nor legend nor symbol. It suffices to view the numerous stone statues which decorate museums to be convinced of the extreme importance of feminine values and their historical reality.) (Translation mine) Here and in *Mother Love*, her historiographic appraisal of the evolution of motherhood in French history leads her to conclude that femininity and motherhood have coalesced over time to define women's roles in terms of passivity, masochism and subservience under an increasingly rigid patriarchy. In seeking to dissociate femininity from maternity, Badinter focuses on the efforts of 20th-century women who made incursions into the previously exclusive domains of knowledge and power. In *Mother Love*, she develops this idea along a historical axis, showing how the Enlightenment period did little to change ideology as far as women were concerned. For instance, Freud's normalizing of a certain kind of feminine at the turn of the 20th century did not depart radically from the image of the 'ideal woman' created by Jean Jacques Rousseau in the 18th century. (1981, 206–207) Badinter argues that despite Freud's recognition of an inherent bisexuality in the human psyche, the association of self-sacrifice and masochism remains inextricably tied to the female body in his work due to the central importance assigned to the mother in infantile psycho-sexual development. (1981, 206, 216) Neither does Jacques Lacan's subsequent highlighting of the symbolic father bring about a successful rupture in the fast hold of paternal law in the metaphorically oriented work of Lacanian psychoanalysis. According to Badinter, it is the 'new feminine discourse' of contemporary feminists which has 'rendered null and void the theory of the naturally devoted martyr-mother.' (1981, 293) Optimistically, she surmises that 'an objectively revolutionary situation' (294) has been brought about by a feminism which is propelling us towards androgynously inspired futuristic models such as that of the 'Father-Mother'. (322) Her vision of 'unisexism' as 'the royal road to bisexuality' leads her to pointedly ask: 'what's to stop the man and woman of tomorrow from re-creating this paradise lost?' (329) Although a search for lost origins and futuristic rewards may seem teleological from a post-structuralist perspective, Badinter's work stands in continuity with the affirmative tradition carved out from Simone de Beauvoir to Nancy Chodorow, feminists who have worked persistently towards a freeing up of women's identity from oppressive definitions of femininity and motherhood by turning their attention onto the role of fathers in 'mothering'. Such work has been invaluable in bringing about ongoing interrogations and dissociations of terms such as 'woman', 'femininity' and 'motherhood', consequently presenting a potential common ground between sociological and psychoanalytic approaches, especially those adopted by poststructuralist feminist theorists. For the latter, the Lacanian symbolic work on the unconscious acts as a springboard towards bringing about revolutionary transformations of the maternal in and through language.

In the light of the above, what, we may ask, is the possible relevance in India of a French feminist discourse that relies heavily on psychoanalytic and interpretive strategies in wrestling with issues related to motherhood? While the materialist analyses of institutionalized mothering enabled by Badinter and others may appear, at first instance, to be more amenable to a political alignment with the empirically oriented discourse on motherhood in India, the generation of a cross-cultural dialogue through the introduction of *dissimilarities* seems to us, at this moment, more productive. In this, we are persuaded by Jude Browne's proposal of an 'aesthetic model of dialogue' because, as Browne notes, 'there is more room for both identity and difference in politics when contrasting interpretations and understandings are considered in aesthetic terms.' (Browne 2007, 121)

Consequently, the lens of a post-Lacanian psychoanalytic model has been chosen in a deliberate attempt to 'interrupt' the empirical bent of Indian feminist discourse, through the introduction of hybrid elements, in an effort to disengage the maternal body from its negated representations in hegemonic Indian discourses. Moreover, the incisive poststructuralist interrogation of the 'mother-as-lack' metaphor at the basis of the psychoanalytic approach may be a particularly useful trope for enabling a parallel feminist critique of the notion of the 'deficient' maternal body. We have seen in previous chapters how the disembodied maternal occupies, in India, the place of a cultural deficit, whether through devaluation, commodification, desexualization, or in the shape of the disabled maternal body. Following the cue afforded by Patricia Elliot, who asks why the work of Lacanian-inspired feminists 'be considered apolitical or non-feminist?' (Elliot 1995, 42), we suggest that the discursive strategies unravelled by French postmodern constructionism, if explored alongside existing materialist modes, could open up possibilities of transforming and living differently the construct of motherhood in India.

Mapping Motherhood in India

Any scholarship on motherhood in India must, of course, contend with the female-woman-mother contiguity so deeply embedded in national and religious symbols and imagery. We began this book with a backward glance at ancient mythopoeic iconography and religion, in an attempt to trace the influences of mother-goddess representations on contemporary constructions of motherhood. Here, we revisit some of our earlier observations to draw up a grid which will allow for linkages between the cultural mapping of the maternal in contemporary India and French feminist psychoanalysis.

One way of identifying predominant representations of motherhood is to locate these at the level of wide-ranging cultural registers which I will term as the celestial, the national, and the familial. These descriptions are in no way meant to be either completely independent of each other, or an all-encompassing overview of motherhood discourse (given the vast cultural and regional differences between urban and rural locales, classes, castes, ethnicities, religions, etc.); rather, all three impinge upon each other to construct a compendium of cultural ideals which dominate, or may be opposed by, the many complex configurations of Indian motherhood.

Owing to the sustained importance of mythological and religious imagery and symbolism in mainstream cultural discourse, routine lessons drawn from ancient religious texts like the *Ramayana* and the *Mahabharata* continue to exert relevance in daily life. As noted in Chapter 1, despite its ancient origins, Hindu mother-goddess iconography persists in influencing contemporary constructions of motherhood. It finds concrete expression in ubiquitous images of Devi in her myriad forms, whether as the divine mother in her full and formidable powers (for instance, as the destructive Kali), or in her more circumscribed role as the consort of one of the major gods of the Hindu pantheon, namely,

Shiva, Vishnu or any one of his incarnations. In this form, she appears either in epic and mythic proportions, or in the form of the lesser-known religious iconographies. In the epic form, she finds her most enduring representation in the *Ramayana*, as the subservient, docile, husband-worshipping and chaste Sita, the wife of the lord Rama. Sita, as has been previously noted, embodies the life-surrendering devotion of the mother-wife, willing to risk all to prove her unwavering fidelity to the husband as an individual, and to patriarchy as the larger social structure to which she owes allegiance. However, other contrasting images of the formidable mother-goddess, for instance, in Kali's empowered but terrifying form as Durga (in Bengal), or more eroticized images of the goddesses Parvati or Radha, equally abound to capture more repressed aspects of the cultural imaginary, and offer culturally sanctioned alternatives to the self-sacrificing images of Sita, Sati and Savitri. The cultural significance of mother-goddess imagery in the context of gender relations and motherhood discourse has been extensively discussed both by feminist scholars (Bhattacharji 2010; Ramaswamy 2001 b) and by psychoanalysts (Kakar 1989). Kakar, in fact, suggests that 'certain forms of the maternal feminine may be more central in Indian myths and psyche than in their western counterparts' (131), while Ashis Nandy describes divine matriarchy as a burden that women have to live up to. (Nandy 1998, 24) In Indian (male) psychoanalytic discourse, the mother-goddess is predominantly seen as an annihilating force, to be deified, defied or atoned. (Nandy 1998, 35–39)

We have previously examined the iconographies of Vac and Kali (see Chapter 1) in the context of the cultural construction of the maternal metaphor. For some Indian feminists, such as Vrinda Dalmiya, 'the iconography of the Goddess Kali from India comes as a dramatic relief in our search for alternative constructions of femininity and motherhood.' (Dalmiya 2000, 125) Although she does not claim that 'Kali in India *is* a feminist principle', Dalmiya proposes 'an alternative encashing' of the 'spiritual phenomenon' made possible by Kali worship. (128) Through her reading of poems from the corpus of Ramprasad Sen's *Kali-bhakti*, Dalmiya envisions 'an alternative model of self-construction and of self-other relationship' which 'comes very close to the "relational self" of some western feminists.' (129) The dance of Kali becomes for Dalmiya 'an important metaphor' which suggests 'playfulness and light-heartedness' as well as 'change'. (136) Further, recalling the mother-goddess' identification with nature or *prakriti*, Dalmiya concludes that 'a relational self modeled in and through a dialogue with Kali-as-nature thus becomes an ecological self.' (143)

Dalmiya's emphasis on the 'relational self' made possible through devotional poetry draws us, once more, close to the 'relational maternal' emphasized in the works of various western feminists. Yet, the maternal metaphor in India is constructed not just at the level of the divine. The complexity of celestial configurations is rendered meaningful only once these are placed alongside other cultural constructions of the maternal, especially within the spatial registers of country and home.

The celestial register finds its direct reflection in nationalist discourse, transmogrifying the mother-goddess into the nation-as-mother. Here, in her metaphorical renderings as Mother India and *Bharat Mata*, the virginal and powerful nation-mother demands complete devotion from her sons and her daughters (especially the former), and her chastity is projected as an inspiring ideal for women. This was the repository of images most prevalent and most effectively used during the period of the freedom struggle, despite divergent interpretations of *Bharat Mata* by the nationalists and the peasantry.[8] In contrast to the imperialist, villainous and foreign assaulter who might pillage and plunder the nation-mother, the heroic sons of the soil must fight to the finish to protect her *izzat* (honour), with the unflinching support of their wives and mothers. The mother-as-nation imagery has been variously commented upon by Indian feminists such as Tanika Sarkar, Charu Gupta and Susan Abraham. Abraham is quick to remind us that 'the form of devotion addressing the nation as mother morphs into the current virulent politics of *Hindutva* in India' such that 'the devotee expresses his *bhakti* ideally by becoming a "demon slayer" in the manner of the Goddess by waging war on Muslims'. (Abraham 2009, 160) Gupta observes that mapping the mother onto the geographical contours of India 'served to define a loyal political citizenry, devoted in the service of the nation'. (Gupta 2001, 4292) As pointed out by these scholars, mother-nation iconography conceals within it the very present dangers cloaked under the co-option of the maternal idea by right wing, communalist and anti-feminist agendas. That these dangers are widespread is made evident by similar instances from diverse regions of the country. Sumathi Ramaswamy notes that in different parts of India, and especially in the south, the Hindi speaking and chaste *Bharat Mata* is rivalled by a regional Tamil mother-goddess, Tamilttay, whose various forms further complicate any unitary projection of the nation-as-mother.[9] (Ramaswamy 2001a, 108–30, chapter 2) In general, however, paternalistic nationalistic discourses ensure that the contradictory and diverse aspects of ancient goddesses are smoothened to fit the contours of the predominant earth-mother/mother-nation palimpsest that psychoanalysis must contend with.

The mother-nation symbolism is further reinforced by the identification of the 'mother-nation' with a 'mother-tongue' imposed from above with the help of state machinery which recognizes, in a multilingual nation, the superior significance of only one standardized language. As Charu Gupta comments, in late colonial India, 'the Hindi language itself was personified as a Hindu mother.... An indifference to the Hindi language was like disregarding your own mother.' (Gupta 2001, 4293)

> The language of motherhood evoked various reproductive relationships, while being simultaneously disembodied and limited in meaning. The maternal metaphor was constantly evoked for designating the nation, even if it often remained a bodyless and a wordless feminine body, taking the shape of maps, masculine gendered words or statistical figures. (4297)

As Gupta's study illustrates, the hegemony of a certain kind of upper-caste Hindi and the consequent marginalization of less prestigious forms such as Urdu, as well as of other Indian languages became the subject of ongoing language debates in the country. This, according to Gupta, led to a gendered dichotomy in which certain languages or dialects, such as Khari Boli, came to be identified with masculinity or '"mardon ki boli" (language of men)' (4295), while others such as Urdu and Braj Bhasha were feminized and eroticized: 'Khari Boli thus introduced a "symbolic order", whereby the nation was to be distinguished from a past in which the language of erotic and "feminine" was Braj.' (4295) In such a process of severance, Urdu came to be considered as 'so bad and erotic that its knowledge had to be denied to respectable Hindu women.' (4293) An evaluation of the process of appropriation, hierarchization and gendering of languages goes to show the crucial impact that discursive control has had on the construction of women's identity and women's rights in India. As far as the construction of maternal identity is concerned, if a 'pure' Hindi was identified with the mother (tongue), the Hindu (Hindi speaker) became the citizen-son, completing the masculine fantasy of the mother-son dyad at the expense of the exclusion of the 'polluted' feminine (Urdu, Braj or any other language considered inferior to Hindi).

In the light of the above, Indian feminism must perforce take into account the ongoing co-option of the discursive domain by right-wing, anti-feminist forces, and adapt its strategies to counter such moves. The co-development of revolutionary discursive strategies alongside empirical approaches is critical to such an enterprise. Feminist psychoanalytic discourse, informed by post-Lacanian French perspectives, as

I argue in a subsequent section, provides one possible avenue of such discursive incursions by opening up the possibility of multiple maternal subjectivities and interpretations.

The maternally loaded metaphors of *Bharat Mata* and *matri bhasha* have particular consequences for women's private lives. At the domestic level, patriarchally conceived roles of wives and mothers reflect some of the complex archetypal and traditional paradigms of motherhood discussed above. In our discussion in Chapter 5, we have already seen how the gradual shift, especially in urban areas, from the patriarchal extended family structure to the more recent nuclear family endorsed by industrialization, capitalism and the media, ensures that the traditional patriarchal family structure adapts to a modern one without disturbing an essential gender hierarchy, while sustaining a maternal contract assimilated to the service of patriarchy. Depending upon class, caste and other social differences, the multitasking housewife or the working mother may be perceived as an invisible economic support to the husband, and/ or the domestic guardian of moral and spiritual values. In an increasingly consumerist culture, the urban upper middle-class mother often combines elements of traditional Indian motherhood, modern career mothers, westernized 'helicopter moms', as well as global icons of fashion and style, seamlessly and without any apparent contradiction.[10]

One common thread that seems to run across these various registers is that of a fiercely preserved honour associated with women's bodies, which hearkens back to more ancient patriarchal traditions of equating the female body with territory, as well as to colonial Victorian values superimposed on the former. It finds its contemporary reflection in the association of sanctioned heteronormative motherhood with an incontrovertible social respect derived from adherence to the image of the de-sexualized mother. In lieu of the apparent lack of agency they may wield as individuals, the elevated status and privilege of motherhood promises to bestow on women 'compensatory' domestic and social powers, and varying degrees of control over the family and its resources. As Partha Chatterjee observes, 'the image of woman as goddess' serves to erase female sexuality. (Chatterjee 1989, 249) At the same time, the gap between exalted mother-goddesses and real mothers sustains the justification of patriarchal oppression in terms of what Sukumari Bhattacharji refers to as the 'tragedy of motherhood'. (Bhattacharji 2010, 6–7).

That such incongruities persist globally is evidenced by the observations of feminists across cultures.[11] The emphasis on virginity and chastity, and the suggestion, in religious terms, of other worldly powers to be obtained through these, are not limited to the patriarchal culture in Hindu India, and may find cross-cultural reflections in the Christian tradition, as identified in Julia Kristeva's discussion of the maternal feminine in 'Stabat Mater'. Paradoxical representations of motherhood across cultures invite obvious parallels as well as an exploration of potential feminist alliances.

From France to India: Contiguities and impasses

The etymology of 'psychoanalysis' reveals, in the cleft between 'psyche' and 'analysis', a merger of knowing and doing, with potential links between the two. In arguing against the language/culture opposition, Diana Fuss reasons that 'the claim that a concentration on language ignores material culture misinterprets the materiality of language and the semiology of culture.' (Fuss 1989, 86) Given the uneasy relationship between language, the maternal, and cultural transformation in French feminist theories,[12] two broad contours can be identified: first, the materiality of language and its relationship with culture, previously highlighted by feminist scholars across cultures,[13] and second, given the significance of the former, the possibility of performing motherhood in substantially different ways, beyond mere discursive, parodic subversions. Since the materiality of the body is decoded through a prism of discursive representations, a critique of cultural discourse that posits women as naturally attuned to motherhood and privileges mothers of male progeny may augur new ways of thinking about, and living, motherhood. The impact of such a critique, especially that of 'son-preference', in Indian academic and public discourse, is already evidenced in various public programmes and policies aimed at benefitting girls and women, especially in the realm of education and reproductive freedom. As pointed out previously, the jumbling up of Hindu nationalist fervour with Hindi language pride is evidence of the pre-existing co-option of the discursive sphere by anti-feminist agendas. The discursive analysis of traditional paradigms of motherhood and its gradual percolation into cultural discourse is thus a necessary step in the transformation of Indian women's roles as mothers. In the specific context of Indian psychoanalytical discourse, the significant rapport between language and materiality offers a manner of filling a substantial lacuna (an exploration of the maternal at the level of the textual, the interpretive, the imaginary and a countering of the maternal as 'deficit'), despite some inherent limitations. In the next section, we draw out some aspects of Judith Butler's critique of French feminist theory to work through its implications in such an enterprise.

Butler, Wittig and the Question of Maternal Identities in India

Using a Marxist-feminist approach, Monique Wittig refutes the search for an explanation of gender differences based on biological factors, locating it in the context of trans-historical power relations between men and women within capitalist economies. ('The Straight Mind'; 'One') To end the historical oppression of women as a class, she calls for the ultimate disappearance of this class through the undoing of economic, political and social inequalities. Arguing that any feminist glorification of the 'feminine' can only be a dangerous, essentialist trap ('One', 104–105), she unequivocally rejects the category 'woman'. Instead, she offers recourse to the term 'lesbian' as a way out of compulsory conformity to heteronormative structures. Thus, motherhood, conventionally seen as the 'natural' role of women, is viewed by Wittig as 'forced production' ('One', 104), alongside other economic activities which sustain heterosexist capitalist patriarchy.

In a move similar to Wittig's, Judith Butler (*Gender Trouble*, also 'Performative Acts') troubles the settled notion of biology as an a priori foundation of gender identity by showing how culture determines the way we construct sex, gender and sexuality at the level of biology itself. In *Gender Trouble*, Butler notes that Wittig's 'lesbian' represents a third oppositional category (Butler 1999, 143–44) in a larger effort to create a shift within heterosexual paradigms by introducing nominal categories invested with transformative powers. Butler, however, raises doubts against Wittig's faith in the ability of language to shape reality and questions her insistence that women must (or can) speak themselves out of gender (and thus, their oppression). In Butler's view, this would amount to a usurpation of authoritarian positions earlier occupied by heterosexual subjectivities, and a replication of existing power structures. (158) In disagreement with Wittig's radical polarization of two sexualities, Butler proposes a more nuanced understanding of sexualities through a redeployment of all categories of identity to render them much more complex, such that elements of heterosexuality and homosexuality are acknowledged as permeating both gay and straight identities, neither of which remains 'pure' or unmarked by its other. This understanding leads Butler to argue for the articulation of 'multiple sexual discourses' at the site of 'identity'. (155–63) If we agree with Butler about the porous frontiers that separate heterosexual and homosexual practices, and which are co-dependent for their very definitions, it becomes incumbent to question Wittig's proffering of lesbianism as an unequivocal rejection of heterosexuality, and by association, of heterosexual motherhood.

Butler's redeployment of sexual identities gains significance given the pervasive metaphors highlighting the 'tragedy of motherhood' in the trajectory of Indian psychoanalytic discourse, traced from the early work of Bose to contemporary theorists such as Kakar and Nandy. Here, one of the dominant trends has been to pursue the cultural links between the repercussions of woman's culturally assigned role as mother (especially of sons) and the female psyche, in a discourse replete with images of the castrating mother,[14] leading scholars such as Christiane Harnack to view the mother-son relationship as 'perhaps the most interesting aspect of the work of Indian psychoanalysts on the family drama.' (Hartnack 2008, 940) Given the abundance of mother-son stories in Hindu religion and mythology (Sita and the twins, Luv and Kush; Yashoda and Krishna; Kunti and Karan; and Parvati and Ganesha/Skanda, to name a few)[15] and a glaring absence of mother-daughter narratives, it is not surprising to see a similar imbalance reflected in cultural and psychoanalytic discourse. The relentless focus on mother-son relationships can be evidenced most palpably in Kakar's and Nandy's work, as in that of Stanley Kurtz. While Kakar's and Nandy's analyses are valuable in examining the impact of a skewed religious and cultural repository on women, one does end up with the disconcerting impression that these are masculinized narratives, more about sons than mothers, and that the embedded voices of women as maternal subjects have yet to be ferreted out (see Kakar 1981, 52–112; Nandy 1998, 14, 37) Wittig's defiant question, 'Who gave psychoanalysts their knowledge?' and her exasperation against the 'unrelenting tyranny' of psychoanalytic discourses towards women may well have been asked of Indian psychoanalysts, just as much as of Lacan. ('Straight Mind', 52–53)

Butler's careful attendance to the question of fluid identities may offer us an important cue by shifting the focus away from the mother-son dyad to the performance of maternal roles within a larger community of mothers. In a culture where acceptable homosocial conventions enable other possibilities of bonding between women and mothers at a variety of familial and social levels, 'sisterhood' (in its less obviously politicized connotations, but not necessarily precluding, and equally at variance with Robin Morgan's popularizing of the term) may more aptly replace Wittig's 'lesbian' as the subversive figure in dealing with an oppressive patriarchy that nominates the virgin-wife-mother as the only possible destiny for women. We have already seen in Chapter 2, how Bracha Ettinger's emphasis on matrixial connectivity and compassion proposes an alternate model of the maternal beyond its oppressive definitions. In this context, a strategic feminist move may be afforded by the subversive re-construction of the idea of community and relationality between women, which results from Indian patriarchal kinship structures, by uncovering empathetic currents in western models of fluid gender identities and maternal relationality as suggested by Judith Butler and Bracha Ettinger.

As persuasive and inclusive as Butler's approach may be against the much more stark design of Wittig's more absolutist landscape, what seems to get elided in both Wittig's and Butler's arguments is the figure of the biological mother. In proposing the lesbian as a utopic alternative and the only viable category for undoing the oppression of women as a class, Wittig occludes not only all heterosexual relations, but also any identification of women with reproduction and biological motherhood which she sees as oppressive and punitive. Wittig's worldview so completely collapses motherhood with normative heterosexuality that it forecloses any 'conception' of lesbian motherhood, in an effort to proffer the lesbian non-mother as the happy alternative to the oppressed heterosexual mother. Recognizing the lacuna accorded to heterosexuality in Wittig's work, Butler sees the construction of exclusionary identities as a 'tragic mistake'… 'as if the excluded were not, precisely through their exclusion, always presupposed and, indeed, *required* for the construction of [the normative] identity.' (Butler 1999, 163) However, the *requirement* being indicated by Butler is clearly one inspired by postmodern sensibilities, where nominal categories *require* their epistemological opposites in order to have any present meaning. Although Butler is thus impelled to posit the difference of 'heterosexuality' as the necessary qualifier for 'lesbianism', the figure of the biological mother is lost in her critique. One may wonder, then, why the mother is consigned to silence. The question leads us to speculate whether postmodern constructionism and a central trope of performance, unwilling to risk the slippery terrain of identity formation, impede the figure of the mother from emerging. The presence of the mother, however, persists in the form of an unspoken backstage anxiety since Butler, like Wittig, fails to account for 'real mothers' in western culture as well as in cultures beyond the west.

Here, Shelley Park's comparison between the lesbian and the adoptive mother, bonded in their 'queerness' may be particularly illuminating. Park suggests that both the lesbian and the adoptive mother interrogate and invert the idea of procreative motherhood: 'Like the term lesbian (a woman who has sex, that is, intercourse, with another woman), the term adoptive mother is oxymoronic.' (Park, 203) Adoptive motherhood, like queer sexuality, is according to Park, a way of resisting 'reprosexuality and repronarrativity' (217) through the posing of an 'epistemological' difference. Further, the lesbian and the adoptive mother, in as much as they are 'bodies marked as deviant in some fashion' (221), resist the 'medical language of "fertility" and "infertility"' and of 'compulsory motherhood'. (210) In contrast to Wittig's establishing of the biological mother and the lesbian non-mother as antagonists, Park's juxtaposition of the adoptive mother and the lesbian 'queers' the pitch of normative motherhood by clearing up a space for a variety of ways in which biological and non-biological motherhood can be lived by lesbian and straight women. It draws attention away from the sexual identity of the mother to the multiple possibilities afforded by mothering as practice. In identifying the notion of deviancy as one which flows out of centred heteronormative definitions of motherhood, Park exposes the binary which marginalizes non-normative mothering. Further, by siting the adoptive maternal body 'on the borderlands of maternity' (221), she shows how it is possible to dissociate motherhood from the maternal body, thus liberating it from its normative and oppressive limitations. Extending this notion enables the possibility of multiple sites of identity at the locus of the maternal.

However, whether the maternal is conceived in biological or non-biological terms, the question of biologism remains a central problematic in motherhood discourse. Diana Fuss had, in a timely way, reminded us that the troubling question of biology will not just simply go away and that 'this is a question which poses something of a stumbling block for anti-essentialists.' (Fuss 1989, 64) The slippage between biology and biologism, we might add, appears to be equally problematic for anti-essentialists, as it is for those French theorists like Kristeva, Irigaray or Cixous,[16] who have explored the territory of a feminine discourse linked to the body. Whether or not we agree with Butler on the issue of maternal desires being the product, rather than the cause, of patriarchal heteronormativity, it may still leave us to wonder about the exclusive scripting of such desires or instincts onto anatomically female bodies. The question of what specifically is the relationship between anatomical differences and their identification with cultural constructs, such as motherhood, remains an unanswered one in Butler's work, as perhaps in feminist discourse in general. In the context of India, the suspended question mark becomes even more significant given the exaggerated symbolic connections between mother-earth, mother-nation and mother-of-sons made out in cultural and psychoanalytical discourse, such that 'femininity is inextricably linked with *prakriti*, or nature, and *prakriti* with *leela*, or activity.' (Nandy 1998, 35) Given that the complex question of the body remains unresolved, and given its centrality in Indian discourse on motherhood, issues surrounding motherhood must continue to be addressed. We suggest that, rather than occluding the question, or seeing biology only as an obstructing force, it may be strategically gainful to conceive of motherhood in ways other than oppressive. The 'pleasures' afforded by French theory, as for instance in the work of Julia Kristeva, may provide a vital counterpart to existing materialist analyses of oppression.

Kristeva, Butler and Maternal Pleasures across Cultures

In a direct contrast to Wittig, Julia Kristeva constructs a psychoanalytic framework within which the 'feminine', earlier represented as either repressed (Freud) or as a figurative presence marked by its own lack (Lacan), now finds its apparently rightful place as the subversive force which can threaten to disrupt the realm of the symbolic, and make its 'presence' felt. (Kristeva 1984, 43–89) Kristeva takes a fresh look at the story told by Freud and Lacan, and writes a counter-narrative to the phallocentric one of 'castration' by spotlighting the process of the infant's separation from the mother's body. (48–51) Kristeva's semiotic 'chora' presumes a certain order of pre-symbolic communication through distinct signifiers, escapes total repression, and is carried forth into the realm of the symbolic in the form of a semiotic residue. Marked by its intimate connection to the symbiotic stage of plenitude with the mother's body, the semiotic is distinctly 'feminine' in that sense. Kristeva thus foregrounds the role of the 'maternal chora' (51) in undermining the repressive effects of the phallic law as codified through symbolic language, and re-writes psychoanalytical theory from the perspective of the repressed aspects of femininity previously ignored in Freudian and Lacanian theories.

In Kristeva's theory of motherhood, as pointed out by Lisa Cosgrove, 'entry into the symbolic does not only (or even primarily) involve pain or violence' but is equally associated with pleasure. (94) Kristeva's unveiling of specific maternal pleasures through religious iconographies invites rich comparisons with Indian narratives replete with empowering and laughing mother-goddesses, such as Kali or Durga in Bengal, whose links with the maternal have already been discussed by various scholars. (see Ganesh 2010)

Such a repressed feminine appears in very different forms in the work of post-Freudian/Eriksonian psychoanalysts in India. While Sudhir Kakar discusses the role of Devi and the maternal-feminine in terms of a 'hegemonic narrative' (Kakar 1989, 131–35) and Nandy speaks of the creative feminine in men (Nandy 1998, 38–39), the subject of their discourses is either the male child or the male adult, overwhelmed by an engulfing feminine, and desiring to be one with it. Kristeva's effort to dissociate the maternal chora from any strict application to an essentialized female body, by referencing representative male avant-garde writers (Kristeva 1974, 88) offers an interesting contrast to Kakar's and Nandy's isolation of the feminine and its link with creativity and bisexuality in men. In Nandy, especially, the feminine functions primarily to allow men to defy, or atone to the feminine maternal (Nandy 1998, 38–39) but the feminine imaginary, from the point of view of women as subjects, is largely ignored. Interestingly, feminist scholars like Akerkar, in contrast, suggest that women take the category 'woman' as an 'imaginary' to reach 'a realm of freedom'. (Akerkar 1995, 21)

Where Wittig impels us to move forward, and away, from an oppressive socio-cultural history, Kristeva invites us to turn inwards (if not backwards), into a pre-linguistic personal her-story, to salvage the maternal metaphor as a locus of pleasure. Critical of the association of a 'pre-cultural reality' (Butler 1999, 103) with a reified maternal body in Kristeva's work, Butler chides her for not being able to escape the Freudian psychoanalytical trajectory against which she writes. Notably, links between the worship of female goddesses and primitive cultures in Freudian theory have also been interrogated by feminist scholars.[17] While Butler's reservations would caution us against an over-dependence on traditional and religious imagery in re-defining motherhood, especially in the context of dominant Hindu culture, where the feminine-maternal metaphor is over-determined by cultural and religious iconographies, Kristeva's unravelling of maternal pleasures enables an imagining of the maternal beyond the oppressive narratives of penis-envy and womb-deification.

Thus, it may invite us to explore alternative and contradictory currents within dominant theological models, while remaining alert to the dangers of what Susan Abraham calls 'anthropological essentialism'. (Abraham 2009, 157) The 'entry into the symbolic' as proposed by Kristeva, with its attendant pleasures carried forth from the maternal chora, and Kristeva's attempts at resurrecting in Catholic theology an internal undercurrent of a resounding maternal energy may be metonymically linked with archaic speech-goddesses in other parts of the world. In Chapter 1, we have already looked at the iconography of the primordial discursive goddess Vac, the source of *akshara* (words, speech). The threat of the father's decapitating logos is more than matched by the re-construction of a cross-cultural feminist tradition which bridges time and distance in the narratives of Vac and Julia Kristeva's theological forays, and invites women to revolutionize the symbolic with the help of semiotic incursions from within. (Bhakti poetry, with its confounding of multiple selves, as we have already seen, may offer another such revelatory point of entry).

In *Gender Trouble*, Butler is equally critical of Kristeva's projection of childbirth as a re-identification with an idealized mother through 'the incorporation of maternal identity.' (Butler 1999, 110) Turning Kristeva's cause and effect proposition on its head, Butler argues that instead of seeing woman's body as naturally attuned to motherhood (represented as a privileged, culturally sanctioned activity), it may be more useful to see motherhood as an 'an *effect* of culture' (103), thus making the entire basis of positioning motherhood in terms of its subversive potential somewhat suspect. Moreover, noting that motherhood appears in Kristeva's theories as a displaced homosexual desire sanctioned within the larger discourse of heterosexuality, Butler faults Kristeva for failing to take into account the constitution of lesbian experience other than as a psychotic, unintelligible alternative. (110–11)

Astutely noting the occlusion of heterosexual women in Wittig's arguments and that of lesbian women in Kristeva's theories, Butler interrogates their deep faith in the revolutionary potential of nominal categories (the lesbian non-mother, or the pleasureful maternal 'feminine') to bring about radical transformations in our commonplace understanding of gendered categories. Of course, Wittig and Kristeva are not alone, amongst contemporary French feminist theorists (consider Irigaray and Cixous), in their insistence on the power of language to bring about real, material changes in the lives of women. Third-world feminists such as Gayatri Spivak have interrogated the cross-cultural relevance of a discourse which depends so entirely on a dense textuality, and language's purported ability to bring about real, material change in the lives and conditions of women. Spivak points out that the search for a woman's discourse may be 'an activity that is more politically significant for the producer/writer than the consumer/reader' (Spivak 1987, 142), in ways reminiscent of Judith Butler's critical stance.

We may note, however, that Butler's own dependence on deconstructive textual strategies to look beyond the world of the text perhaps keeps her from emphasizing that in both Kristeva and Wittig, women's passage to liberation remains tied to the isolation of the reified 'feminine' as a nominal category. If we agree that performative acts such as motherhood, framed within patriarchal social structures, can no more escape the identity conundrum and are as susceptible to being frozen into reified nominal essences, as are so-called 'natural' identities, the advantages of substituting constructionism for identity, as Butler intends, may not be that clear, unless radical transformations at the level of performativity have a considerable bearing on 'real' identities. Such possibilities open up the question of excavating maternal subjectivities at the level of discourse across cultures.

Although Wittig and Butler describe motherhood primarily as a forced disciplining of women's bodies, both stop short of interrogating the limits of the (patriarchal) structures which posit the maternal on the side of the punitive. This understandably gives rise to a broad scepticism of those positions, such as Kristeva's, that are seen as risking the conflation of the feminine and the maternal. However, such a perspective forces one to ask whether the singular destinies of discipline and oppression, in the Foucauldian sense, are the only ones available for motherhood. Early warnings, such as those by Sara Ruddick, who reacts against the association of the maternal with 'images of powerlessness' (Ruddick 1980, 344), remind us that accounting for motherhood only in terms of its pain can itself be oppressive.

While Butler side-steps the question of biology by reading the body as performance, by doing so, she at the same time opens the door for the subversion of biological roles including motherhood. The debate between Martha Nussbaum and Robyn Wiegman over Nussbaum's criticism that Butler 'prefers the sexy act of parodic subversion to any lasting material or institutional change' (Nussbaum, 10) urges us to wonder about what bearing, if any, the subversion of discursive performances of motherhood has upon the 'real' performance of motherhood. Against the 'narrow vision for the possibilities of change' (7) that Nussbaum accuses

Butler of, Kristeva's discursive performances of maternal pleasures, suggest a larger and freer landscape. (See 'Stabat Mater') This is, perhaps, where French postmodern constructionism may be most gainfully employed in the theatres of lived realities—in upsetting received categories not just through parodic, subversive performances of motherhood, but in re-claiming, through discursive revolutions and, to use Freud's term, cathexis, other pleasureful identities in deliberate acts of agency and empowerment.

Thus, an interrogation of the performance of motherhood and the maternal pact in India, as well as of the discursive constructions which uphold these performances (such as that of *matri bhasha* and *Bharat Mata*) may help us effect transformations at the level of the real. As Susan Abraham suggests in the context of feminist theology, the latter 'must critically assess tropes such as motherhood rather than mobilize them as presupposed or idealized special sources for theological anthropology.' In a reference to the 'politics of meaning' (originally proposed by Elisabeth Schussler Fiorenza), Abrahams suggests that we take into account this politics 'which constructs the meaning of such words as *woman* and *mother*.' (Abraham 2009, 161) Keeping the trope of motherhood in a constant state of tension through discursive re-evaluations and interrogations is essential in averting any impending freezing over of the maternal in such a 'politics of meaning'. Rhetorical constructions of motherhood effect very real controls on women's lives, as we have previously seen. If the way maternal lives are performed in the theatre of patriarchy is inevitably dependent on the discursive constructions upholding the dominant ideology of motherhood, discursive revolutions may equally bring about shifts in how the maternal is understood and experienced.

The weight of the dominant feminist imperative to focus exclusively on narratives of pain and oppression at the expense of other narratives of pleasure, and thus be seen as acting for others, rather than acting for the self, offers a narrow and artificial dichotomy to choose between. In the Indian context (and perhaps in many others), such a restricted choice also skirts dangerously close to the self-denying Sita-Sati-Savitri compendium of images that women have been bound to live up to for centuries. As noted earlier, since caste-class matrices operate as fundamental features of Indian feminism, inter-sectional sociological analyses of oppression tend to take precedence over investigations of individual repressions and satisfactions, perceived largely as elitist, western concerns. One finds, in recent Indian feminist discourse, an attempt to move beyond maternal narratives of oppression to encompass certain types of mothering practices as a site of empowerment and resistance. Sangha and Gonsalves, for instance, point out that 'cultural constructions of motherhood, despite being embedded in patriarchy, do not preclude mothers' attempts to assert power or agency.' (Sangha and Gonsalves 2013, 4) Rachana Johri similarly argues that 'the politics of feminism requires an interrogation both of the oppression in women's lives and their struggles to resist these.' (Johri 2013, 18) The dominant and overwhelming ideology of oppressive patriarchal motherhood, however, tends to contain such attempts within a dichotomy of oppression/resistance; at the same time, it also blocks them from transgressing beyond to embrace alternative subjectivities of pleasure that may be derived from altered understandings of the maternal as invoked through discursive strategies discussed above.

Here, it may be expedient to ask why, in feminist discourse, pleasure should be associated only with the self, pain only with the other; why talking about one should displace the other; and why the two cannot be invoked together considering they do co-exist. As Bueskens points out, 'the question for psychoanalytic *feminist* theorists, then, is this: how can we salvage what is revolutionary in both the conceptual and the political sense in psychoanalysis from what is reactionary and oppressive?' (Bueskens 2014, 9) Buesken's question impels us to emphasize that the above discussion, by no means, is a call to abandon analyses of motherhood in its oppressive aspects, which must remain crucial to feminist discourse; rather, it is an attempt to bring into the ambit of the feminist lens those ways of approaching motherhood which may have been previously neglected by predominantly masculinized subjectivities and constructions, such as those suggested by mythopoeic resources or within feminist psychoanalytic discourse. Keeping in mind the suggestion made by Seshadri-Crooks (1994, 209) for a revised psychoanalysis through historicization, it must be emphasized that structures such as class, caste, region and religion would undoubtedly impact and shape the definitions of such maternal 'pleasures' in the Indian context, since they construct broad and complex frameworks for the understanding of the role of motherhood, in contrast to the incisive semiotic excavation of gendered consciousness made possible by French theory. Notwithstanding, we may pause for thought before too quickly recounting narratives of motherhood as either always oppressive or always pleasurable, in terms of class, caste or other social structurations,

We begin and end on a cautionary note—despite the affirmative possibilities of cross-cultural alliances that have been mapped out above, some caveats may be necessary.

Butler's reservations should remind us that faith in the transformative capabilities of discourse needs to be accompanied by work at the level of culture. In India, this would imply that the cultural parameters within which maternal identities are performed need to be made more permeable to change through advances in educational opportunities and economic independence for women and mothers. Thus, rather than locating activist and academic agendas, and feminist empirical research and theory, as competing for the same goals, they can be seen as complementary, mutually advancing and equally necessary. Discursive subversions carried out at the level of psychoanalytic discourse offer vast possibilities of radicalizing cultural constructions of the maternal; however, these would need to be adapted to specific cultural considerations for any effective re-definitions of maternal identities in India. En route the revolutionary potential of French feminist discourse, the 'deficit' that is the maternal body can be invigorated by new maternal subjectivities through our attentive listening to the light-footed music of Kali's dance, or the silence-shattering words of Vac.

Notes

1. The faith in the transformative capabilities of language, and its empowering abilities, may be evidenced in a range of works by Hélène Cixous, Monique Wittig, Julia Kristeva, Luce Irigaray, Chantal Chawaf, Marguerite Duras, among others.
2. In her discussion of Freud's personal views on the relevance of his theories in India Christiane Hartnack cites an interesting anecdote: 'Yet he noticed that the "Freudian Orient", namely the wholesale reception of psychoanalysis in India, was not what he had hoped for. Despite his public stance, Freud intuitively sensed the importance of cultural differences. On the occasion of his seventy-fifth birthday, the Indian Psychoanalytical Society sent him an ivory statue of Vishnu along with a Sanskrit poem. Not only did his letter of thanks not reveal any interest in the symbolism of the gifts; he dubbed it his "trophy of conquest". When the statuette later developed cracks, he made the following entry in his diary: "Can the god, being used to Calcutta, not stand the climate in Vienna?"' (Freud, as quoted in Hartnack, The Diary of Sigmund Freud, 1929–1939. A Record of the Final Decade, Trans. Michael Molnar, London: The Hogarth Press 1992, 115.)

3. For a detailed discussion of Bose's work on psychoanalysis in India, see Hartnack, 2008.
4. See, for instance, Chandra Mohanty, who emphasizes the significance of conducting research at the level of the local while building coalitions across borders, based on 'a belief in the local as specifying and illuminating the universal' (224), and Chilla Bulbeck who describes coalition work as 'the product of accepting differences between women as well as similarities, and, hardest of all, working out which is which at any one time.' (233) Similar discussions can also be found in Akerkar, Narayan, Bhavnani, and Khanna.
5. See Supriya Akerkar's discussion of sectarian tendencies, and the divide between theory and practice in the women's movement in India.
6. For a discussion of the dominant trends in feminist scholarship in India, and the debate between the foregrounding of gender/intersectionality, see Bandana Purkayashta, et al.
7. Ania Loomba's essay 'Tangled Histories' provides a forceful commentary on the Indian/Western dichotomy in the women's movement. Lamba, for instance, points out that 'in a not-so-surprising continuance of nationalist or left-wing paradigms, to be Indian is to be more concerned with, say, poverty, than, say sexuality.' (275) She also observes that 'even though Marxists were themselves accused of being aliens on Indian soil, they in turn treated any unwarranted focus on gender as practically a conspiracy of Western feminists to lure their Indian sisters away from the Indian working class!' (273)
8. Supriya Akerkar cites an interesting incident from Jawaharlal Nehru's memoirs: During the days of the freedom struggle, Nehru repeatedly questions the peasants about the meaning of Bharat Mata, and is amused and struck by the differences between his own understanding of the term, and theirs. While the peasants associate Bharat Mata with the soil of the country, for Nehru the goddess stands for an 'imagined community' of people. (Akerkar, WS12)
9. Sumathi Ramaswamy's essay 'Maps and Mother Goddesses in Modern India' (*Imago Mundi* 53, 2001: pp. 97–114), provides a detailed discussion of the complex relationships between mother-goddess imagery and its recuperation by Indian nationalists during the freedom struggle. She also focuses at length on the different configurations of a similar mother goddess in Tamil India: 'From the 1890s, the claim of Mother India to the affections of her potential citizen-subjects was challenged in the Tamil-speaking parts of colonial India by another goddess of polity, Tamilttay (Mother Tamil), the Tamil language personified as goddess, mother and maiden.' (108)
10. For a detailed discussion of some of the paradoxes and contradictions caused by tradition and modernity in the lives of middle class urban women in India, see Phadke, 2005, 67–81.

11. The paradoxical ways in which motherhood gets represented and lived have been noted by Seshadri-Crooks 209, as well as Sara Ruddick, Maternal Thinking, 343.
12. Among many other works on the relationships between discourse, gender and sexuality, Bucholtz and Hall, for instance, provide an interesting discussion on this subject. Other essays include Brooks 1997; Akerkar 1995; Ede et al. 1995.
13. See for instance, Wittig, 1990, 55, Nair as quoted in Jane Flax, 911, and Brooks, 1995, 73.
14. See for instance, Nandy's description of the 'aggressive, treacherous, annihilating mother' which is the 'ultimate authority in the Indian mind.' Nandy believes that this feminine authority is propitiated by the Indian male 'through symbolic or real aggression against his own self.' (Nandy, 36)
15. For analyses of myths related to various Hindu gods and goddesses, including Krishna and Yashoda, see Doniger 1975.
16. In one of my earlier essays on Hélène Cixous' work, I have discussed such a slippage between the feminine as discursive construct and the female body: Aneja 1992, 17–27.
17. See, for instance, Seshadri-Crooks' essay (1994, 198) in which she points to an association between primitivity and matriarchy in Freud.

References

Abraham, Susan. 'Strategic Essentialism in Nationalist Discourses: Sketching a Feminist Agenda in the Study of Religion', *Journal of Feminist Studies in Religion*, Vol. 25, No. 1, 2009, pp. 156–61.
Akerkar, Supriya. 'Theory and Practice of Women's Movement in India: A Discourse Analysis', *Economic and Political Weekly* Vol. 30, No. 17, 1995, WS2–WS23.
Badinter, Elizabeth. *Mother Love: Myth and Reality*. (Translation) (Originally published as *L'Amour en Plus*, 1980). New York: Macmillan, 1981.
———. *L'Un est L'Autre*. Paris: Odile Jacob, 1986.
Bueskens, Petra (ed.). 'Introduction'. In *Mothering & Psychoanalysis: Clinical, Sociological and Feminist Perspectives*. Bradford: Demeter Press, 2014, pp. 1–72.
Bhattacharji, Sukumari. 'Motherhood in Ancient India', *Economic and Political Weekly*, 20–27 October. 1990, pp. 1–7. Also published in *Motherhood in India*, edited by Maithreyi Krishnaraj. New York: Routledge, 2010.
Bhavnani, Kum-Kum. *Feminism & 'Race'*. New York: Oxford University Press, 2000.
Boling, Patricia. 'The Democratic Potential of Mothering', *Political Theory*, Vol. 19, No. 4, 1991, pp. 606–25.

Brooks, Ann. 'Psychoanalytic Theory, Semiology and Postfeminism', *Postfeminisms*, London: Routledge, 1997.
Browne, Jude. *The Future of Gender*. New York: Cambridge University Press, 2007.
Bucholtz, Mary, and Kira Hall. 'Theorizing Identity in Language and Sexuality Research', *Language in Society* Vol. 33, No. 4, 2004, pp. 469–515.
Bulbeck, Chilla. *Re-orienting Western Feminism: Women's Diversity in a Postcolonial World*. Cambridge: Cambridge University Press, 1998.
Butler, Judith. *Gender Trouble*. New York: Routledge, 1999.
———. 'Performative Acts and Gender Constitution: An Essay in Phenomenology and Feminist Theory', *Theatre Journal* Vol. 40, No. 4, December, 1988, pp. 519–31.
Caputi, Mary. 'The Maternal Metaphor in Feminist Scholarship', *Political Psychology* Vol. 14, No. 2, 1993, pp. 309–29.
Chatterjee, Partha. 'The Nationalist Resolution of the Women's Question'. In *Recasting Women*, edited by Kumkum Sangari and Sudesh Vaid. New Delhi: Kali for Women, 1989, pp. 233–53.
Cosgrove, Lisa. 'Feminism, Postmodernism, and Psychological Research', *Hypatia* Vol. 18, No. 3, 2003, pp. 85–112.
Dalmiya, Vrinda. 'Loving Paradoxes: A Feminist Reclamation of the Goddess Kali', *Hypatia* Vol. 15, No. 1, 2000, pp. 125–50.
DiQuinzio, Patrice. 'Exclusion and Essentialism in Feminist Theory: The Problem of Mothering', *Hypatia* Vol. 8, No. 3, 1993, pp. 1–20.
Ede, Lisa, Cheryl Glenn, Andrea Lunsford, 'Border Crossings: Intersections of Rhetoric and Feminism', *Rhetorica: A Journal of the History of Rhetoric*, Vol. 13, No. 4, Autumn 1995, pp. 401–41.
Elliot, Patricia. 'Politics, Identity, and Social Change: Contested Grounds in Psychoanalytic Feminism', *Hypatia* Vol. 10, No. 2, 1995, pp. 41–55.
Fuss, Diana. *Essentially Speaking*. New York: Routledge, 1989.
Ganesh, Kamala. 'In Search of the Great Indian Goddess'. In *Motherhood in India*, edited by Maithreyi Krishnaraj. New York: Routledge, 2010.
Gupta, Charu. 'The Icon of Mother in Late Colonial North India: "Bharat Mata", "Matri Bhasha" and "Gau Mata"', *Economic and Political Weekly* Vol. 36, No. 45, 2001, pp. 4291–299.
Hartnack, Chriastiane. 'Colonial Dominions and the Psychoanalytic Couch: Synergies of Freudian Theory with Bengali Hindu Thought and Practices in British India'. In *Unconscious Dominions: Psychoanalysis, Colonial Trauma and Global Sovereignties* edited by Warwick Anderson, Richard C. Keller, Deborah Jenson. Duke University Press, 2008 (accessed online).
John, Mary. E. and Janaki Nair. 'Sexuality in Modern India: Critical Concerns', *Voices for Change* Vol. 3, No. 1, 1999, pp. 4–8.
Johri, Rachana. 'From *Parayi* to *Apni*: Mother's Love as Resistance'. In *South Asian Mothering: Negotiating Culture, Family and Selfhood*. Bradford: Demeter Press, 2013.

Kakar, Sudhir. *The Inner World: A Psychoanalytic Study of Childhood and Society in India*. 2nd edn. Delhi: Oxford University Press, 1981.

Kakar, Sudhir. *Intimate Relations*. New Delhi: Penguin, 1989.

Khanna, Ranjana. *Dark Continents: Psychoanalysis and Colonialism*. London: Duke University Press, 2003.

Kristeva, Julia. 'The Semiotic Chora', pp. 25–30 and 'The Thetic', pp. 43–45 in "The Semiotic and the Symbolic'. In *Revolution in Poetic Language*, New York: Columbia University Press, 1984.

Kristeva, Julia and Arthur Goldhammer. 'Stabat Mater', *Poetics Today* Vol. 6, Nos. 1/2, 1985, pp. 133–52.

Loomba, Ania. 'Tangled Histories: Indian Feminism and Anglo-American Feminist Criticism', *Tulsa Studies in Women's Literature* Vol. 12, No. 2, Autumn, 1993, pp. 271–78.

Mohanty, Chandra. *Feminism Without Borders*. Durham: Duke University Press, 2003.

Nandy, Ashis. 'The Non-Paradigmatic Crisis of Indian Psychology: Reflections on a Recipient Culture of Science', *Indian Journal of Psychology* Vol. 49, 1974, pp. 1–20.

Nandy, Ashis. *Exiled at Home*. New Delhi: Oxford University Press, 1998.

Narayan, Uma. 'Essence of Culture and a Sense of History: A Feminist Critique of Cultural Essentialism'. In *Decentering the Center*, edited by Uma Narayan and Sandra Harding. Bloomington: Indiana University Press, 2000, pp. 80–100.

Nussbaum, Martha. 'The Professor of Parody', *The New Republic*. http://www.tnr.com/index.mhtml.

Purkayashta, Bandana et al. 'The Study of Gender in India: A Partial Review', *Gender and Society* Vol. 17, No. 4, 2003, pp. 503–24.

Ramaswamy, Sumathi. 'Virgin Mother, Beloved Other'. In *Signposts*, edited by Rajeswari Sunder Rajan. New Brunswick: Rutgers University Press, 2001, pp. 17–56.

Ramaswamy, Sumathi. 'Maps and Mother Goddesses in Modern India', *Imago Mundi* Vol. 53, 2001, pp. 97–114.

Rege, Sharmila. 'Dalit Women Talk Differently: A Critique of "Difference" and Towards a Dalit Feminist Standpoint Position', *Economic & Political Weekly* Vol. 33, No. 44, 1998, WS39–WS46.

Rodgers, Julie. Review. 'Exploring the Unexplored and the Unexplorable in Lisa Baraitser's Maternal Encounters.' *Gender Forum*, Issue 38, 2012. www.genderforum.org Accessed 20 July 2015.

Ruddick, Sara. 'Maternal Thinking', *Feminist Studies* Vol. 6, No. 2, Summer, 1980, pp. 342–67.

Sangha, Jasjit K. and Tahira Gonsalves. 'Introduction'. In *South Asian Mothering: Negotiating Culture, Family and Selfhood*. Bradford: Demeter Press, 2013.

Seshadri-Crooks, Kalpana. 'The Primitive as Analyst: Postcolonial Feminism's Access to Psychoanalysis', *Cultural Critique* Issue 28, Autumn, 1994, pp. 175–218.

Shah, Chayanika. 'Alliances and Dalliances', *Himal,* March 2008. http://www.himalmag.com/component/content/article/5007-alliances-and-dalliances.html. Accessed 20 August 2012.

Sharma, Jaya. 'Reflections on the Construction of Heteronormativity', *Development* Vol. 52, No. 1, 2009, pp. 52–55.

Sinha, Chitra. 'Images of Motherhood: The Hindu Code Bill Discourse', *Economic and Political Weekly* Vol. 42, No. 43, 2007, pp. 49–57.

Spivak, Gayatri Chakravorty. 'French Feminism in an International Frame'. In *In Other Worlds.* New York: Methuen, 1987, pp. 134–53.

Spivak, Gayatri Chakravorty. 'Echo', *New Literary History* Vol. 24, No. 1, Winter, 1993, pp. 17–43.

Weigman, Robin. 'Feminism, Institutionalism, and the Idiom of Failure', *Differences: A Journal of Feminist Cultural Studies* Vol. 11, No. 3, Fall 1999, pp. 107–36.

Wittig, Monique. 'The Straight Mind', In *Out There: Marginalization and Contemporary Cultures,* edited by Russell Ferguson, Martha Gever, Trinh Minh-ha and Cornel West. New York: New Museum of Contemporary Art, 1990, pp. 51–57.

Wittig, Monique. 'One is Not Born a Woman'. In *The Lesbian and Gay Studies Reader,* edited by Henry Abelove and Michele Aina Barale. New York: Routledge, 1993, pp. 103–109.

Further Reading

Ahmed-Ghosh, Huma. 'Writing the Nation on the Beauty Queen's Body: Implications for a "Hindu" Nation', *Meridians* Vol. 4, No. 1, 2003, pp. 205–27.

Amos, Valerie and Pratibha Parmar. 'Challenging Imperial Feminism', In *Feminism & Race,* edited by Kum-kum Bhavnani. New York: Oxford University Press, 2001.

Butler, Judith. 'Performative Acts and Gender Constitution', *Theatre Journal* Vol. 40, No. 4, 1988, 519–31.

Cavallaro, Dani. *French Feminist Theory.* London: Continuum, 2003.

Ferguson, Ann. 'Motherhood and Sexuality: Some Feminist Questions', *Hypatia* Vol. 1, No. 2, 1986, pp. 3–22.

Flax, Jane. 'What is the Subject? Review Essay on Psychoanalysis and Feminism in Postcolonial Time'. *Signs.* Vol. 29, No. 3, Spring 2004, pp. 905–23.

Hirsch, Marianne. 'Mothers and Daughters', *Signs* Vol. 7, No. 1, Autumn 1981, 200–22.

Krishnaraj, Maithreyi. *Motherhood in India: Glorification without Empowerment?* New Delhi: Routledge, 2010. (See esp. Kamala Ganesh 'In Search of the Great Indian Goddess: Motherhood Unbound', pp. 73–105).

Kristeva, Julia. 'Semiotique et Symbolique', In *La Revolution du Langage Poetique*. Paris: Editions de Seuil, 1974.
Meaney, Gerardine. *(Un)Like Subjects: Women, Theory, Fiction*. New York: Routledge, 1993.
Meyers, Diana Tietjens. 'The Rush to Motherhood-Pronatalist Discourse and Women's Autonomy', *Signs* Vol. 26, No. 3, 2001, pp. 735–73.
Miller, Nancy K. 'Our Classes, Ourselves: Maternal Legacies and Cultural Authority'. In *Borders, Boundaries, and Frames*, edited by Mae G. Henderson. New York: Routledge, 1995, pp. 145–70.
Mitchell, Juliet. 'Procreative Mothers (Sexual Difference) and Child-Free Sisters (Gender)'. In *The Future of Gender*, edited by Jude Browne. Cambridge: Cambridge University Press, 2007, pp. 163–88.
Okin, Susan Moller. 'Is Multiculturalism Bad for Women?' In *Is Multiculturalism Bad for Women*, edited by Joshua Cohen et al. Princeton: Princeton University Press, 1999 (Originally published in the *Boston Review*, Princeton University Press, 1999)
Phadke, Shilpa. 'Some Notes towards Understanding the Construction of Middle-Class Urban Women's Sexuality in India'. In *Sexuality, Gender and Rights*, edited by Geetanjali Misra and Radhika Chandiramani. New Delhi: SAGE Publications, 2005, pp. 67–81.
Trask, Haunani-Kay. 'Love-The Return to the Mother'. In *Eros and Power*. Philadelphia: University of Pennsylvania Press, 1986, pp. 103–30.
Trebilcot, Joyce (ed.). *Mothering: Essays in Feminist Theory*. Maryland: Rowman & Littlefield, 1983.
Visweswaran, Kamala. 'Histories of Feminist Ethnography', *Annual Review of Anthropology* Issue 26, 1997, pp. 591–621.
Volpp, Leti. 'Feminism versus Multiculturalism', *Columbia Law Review* Vol. 101. No. 5, 2001, pp. 1181–218.

Index

Aashiqui 2, 84
Abhimaan, 84
ableism, 178n1
abstract glorification of mother goddess, 2
agency, 171–77
ahimsa, 93
Ahuja, Naman P., 3
Amar Akbar Anthony, 95
Amar Chitra Katha, 10
Anand Math (Bankim Chandra), 88
anatomy is destiny, xvii
ancient fertility idols, 4
ancient mother-goddess, 1, 3–7
 iconography, 2
 nation-as-mother during colonial times, 10
ancient river-goddesses, 29
Annadurai, C. N., 87
anpu, 57
anthropological essentialism, 202
art-house cinema, 77
Aurat, 90
autism/autistic child, xxi–xxiii, 107, 109–13, 130–31
 case studies, 125–29
 challenges and contestations for mother during child, 113–16, 119–20
 as a diagnostic category, 108
 mother as the voice of, 123
 and motherhood, 116–19
 parents voices on emerging discourse about, 108
 precedence of needs of, 123–24
 redefining personhood and agency of mother, 129–30
 sacrifice by mother, 124–25
Azmi, Shabana, 55

Bachchan, Amitabh, 84, 93, 99, 102
Baghban, 99
benevolent patriarchy, 97
Bengali mother mythicization, 88–89
Bharat Mata, 43, 89, 143–44
biological family, 139
blacks, South African, 38
Bollywood, global, 97–101
Bose, Mandakranta, 2, 7
Bose, Subhash Chandra, 10
Brahmanical tradition, 2
Brahminical culture, 5
Brahminical Hinduism, 5
Brahmins, religious myths of, 5
British Raj, 63
Burman, S. D., 77

capitalism, 134, 147, 152
capitalist economy, 136
capitalist labour process, 135
capitalist patriarchy, 138, 147

caste-based values, 2
Chopra, Aditya, 98
Chori Chori Chupke Chupke, 142
Christianity, 40
cinema, xix–xx, 134
  anticipation of mother dreams through, 41–64
  cultural resource for Indian generations, 75
Cixous, Hélène, 35
class-based values, 2
coalitions, 64–66, 70, 182–83, 186, 207n4
Cocktail, 84
constant mothering, 124
consumerism, xxiii, xxiv, 89, 135, 152
Convention on the Elimination of All Forms of Discrimination Against Women (CEDAW), 161
creativity, 22, 66, 76, 152–53, 201
cultural anthropology, 1
cultural deficit, 189
cultural influence, xv, xx, 1, 16
cultural positioning of mother, 35

dark continent, 37–39
Deewar (Yash Chopra), xxi, 84, 90, 93, 95
Demeter-Persephone complex, 60
Demeter-Persephone myth, 66
desexualized mother, 36–37
Devi, 7–9, 37
  dominant narrative of, 39–41
Devi (Satyajit Ray), 45–50
Dilwaale Dulhaniya Le Jayenge (Aditya Chopra), 99
disabled/disability(ies), xxv–xxvi, 156. *See also* Femininity
  definition of, 157–59
  discrimination faced by women with, 157
  and feminism, need for productive engagement, 159–62
  institutionalized women, case studies of, 171–77
  mothers, 166–71
  sexuality and female body, 162–66
displacement, 64
Doniger, Wendy, 3, 16
Doordarshan, 89
Doosri Dulhan, 142
Dravida Munnetra Kazhagam (DMK), 87
Durga goddess, xix, 2, 10, 33, 60

embodiment, 156
empowerment, 125–29
empty-womb identity, xxiv
English Vinglish, 100
entrapment, 125–29

familial contract, 151–52
female/feminism/feminist discourse/femininity(ies), 23, 56, 60, 69. *See also* Motherhood
  delineation of oppression, 65
  disability and, 159–62
  in India, 184–90, 195–96
  power, 67
  psychoanalytic and sociological trajectories, 181
  sexual, 138
  sexuality, 5, 38
  transgressive, 97
  transnational, 65
feminization of care, 109
fertility goddesses, 3–5. *See also* Ancient mother-goddess; Mother-goddess
Filhaal, 142
Fire (Deepa Mehta), 55–56, 59, 61–62, 69
France/French feminist discourse, 35, 184–90, 195–96
Freudian Orient, 206n2

Freudian psychology, 38
Freudian theory, 33–34

Gandhi, Indira, 93, 97
Gandhi, Rajiv, 97
Ganesha, 37
gender, 79–86, 150
gender performativity, concept of, 136
globalization, 134, 136
goddess-inspired Hindu feminism, 8
Graves, Robert, 5

Harappa civilization, 3
heterosexuality, 63
Hind Devi, 11
Hindi film/cinema industry, 76–77
    mother and motherland in, xx–xxi, 90–97
    produced during national movement, 78
Hindu child or family homogenization, 57
Hindu Code Bill, 185
Hinduism, 7, 41
Hindu mother-goddesses, 8
Hindu psyche, 39, 56
Hindutva mobilizations, 97
Hindu woman, 53, 77, 81, 83
Hindu mythology, 18, 55, 60, 141
Hindu myths, 2, 18, 26
homelessness, 64
homosexuality, 63
Hooke, S. H., 5
housewife, 100, 125, 147, 194
Hum Aapke Hain Kaun (Sooraj Barjatya), 98

iconographic resemblances, 5–6
idealization of motherhood, 36
Inanna goddess, 33
Indian Psychoanalytical Society, 206n2
individual source of the fantasy, 40

Indus Valley civilization, 2, 7
Ishtar goddess, 33
Isis goddess, 33

Jayalalitha, J. (Amma), 88
Johar, Karan, 98

Kabhi Khushi Kabhi Gham, 98–99
Kali goddess, xix, 2–3, 10
Kapoor, Shashi, 94
Karan Arjun, 95–96
Khan, Aamir, 76, 101
Khan, Salman, 76
Khan, Shahrukh, 76
Kramer, Samuel, 5

labour, mothers working as, 145–48
Lajja Gauri, 4–5, 7
Lakshmi, 8–9
literature, xix–xx, 1, 134
    anticipation of mother dreams through, 41–64
    lived experiences of mothering/mothers, xxi–xxiii, 109, 112, 116–19, 130, 156, 169, 177
love, 57–58

Mahabharata, 7, 9, 82, 96
Mahatma Gandhi, 10
mainstream, 75
male fantasy, 40
Margarita with a Straw, 102–3
marketability, 76
A Married Woman (Manju Kapur), 61–62, 66, 69
maternal, xvii. *See also* Femininity; Mother
    aesthetic, 66–69
    contemporary re-imagination of, 2
    exploration of, 42
    identities in India, 196–200
    incongruence, 26–28
    mapping across cultures, 182–84
    metaphor, xviii–xix, 3–7

modern and ancient
representations, link
between, 2–3
pleasure, 66–69
pleasures across cultures,
200–6
representation in urban Indian
cultural discourse, 2
sexuality, 37–38
subjectivity, xix–xx, 39, 59,
66–69, 181
matrixial space, 66
matrixial subjectivity, 67
Mesopotamia, 7
Modi, Narendra, 104
Mohabbatein, 98
Mohenjodaro civilization, 3
mother-blaming discourse, 107
mother-daughter relationships, 64
mother dreams anticipation through
literature and cinema, 41–64
mother-goddess. *See also* Ancient
mother-goddess
in contemporary India, functions,
2
cultural significance myths, 39
evolution from vedic to post-vedic
times, 7–8
feminist perspectives on
dependence, independence and
discursive escapes, 16–18
goddess as attribute, 24–26
motherhood and creation myth,
18–24
re-imagining maternal, 28–29
influence of iconography, 1
Mother India, 14, 89, 92, 95, 100,
103, 143–44
Mother India, xxi, 43, 90
mother/motherhood/mothering,
xv, xv, xxi–xxiii, 134–35,
156–57, 181–82
body, 86–90
burden of, 49

constructs of, 79–86
deconstructing motherwork across
caste and class, 148–51
de-sexualized, 144
desire of, xvi
emergence to hegemonic discourses of masculinity,
101–3
and familial contract, 151–52
faulty, 108
good and bad, 108, 170
ideal/idealization/idealized, xxvi,
36–37, 144, 166–71
ideology, xvi–xvii, 26, 34, 74–75
in India and France, xxvi–xxviii,
184–90
investiture of, 44
love for child with disability,
122–23
mapping in India, 190–95
middle-class, 146
and myth creation, 18–24
pact, xxiii–xxiv
patriarchal, 52
performing on private and public
stage, 135–38
perspectives during children
disabilities, 120–22
self-centred, 107
as ultimate identity of Bengali
women, 49
mother-nation pact, 143–45
multinational corporations (MNCs),
137
Mumbai film industry, 76
My Name is Khan, 102
myth(s), xxii, 18, 29, 37, 39–42, 79,
81, 125, 167, 187, 191,
208n15
ancient, 5, 53
creation of, 18–24
of mother-daughter love, 40
of motherhood, 112
religious Brahmins, 5

naihar (the matrixial home of childhood), 63
national identity, 86–90
National Museum, New Delhi, 3
nation-building, notion of, 147
nation-mother, 10, 143, 192
Nehru, Jawaharlal, 207n8
non-Brahminical culture, 5

Object Relations theory, 34
Oedipal myth, 34

Paa (R. Balki), 102–3
parenting system, 70n4
pativrata-dharma ideal, 81
patni, 82
patriarchy system, 40, 64
personal freedom, 62
personhood, 171–77
Piku (Shoojit Sirkar), 85
PK (Rajkumar Hirani), 76
positive maternal subjectivity, 35–36
prakriti, 80
psychoanalysis, xv, xv, xvi, xix, xx, xxiv, 34, 36, 38, 41–42, 59, 111, 195, 205, 206n2
  cultural criticism, use in, 184
  ethnographic, 183
  feminist, 184, 187
    critique of, 60
  Freudian, 182
  in India, 186
  infantalization of artist in, 67
  Lacanian, 188
  Marxism, 184
psychoanalytic theory, 34, 67
psychology, 2, 186

queer theory, 66

Ramachandran, M. G. (MGR), 87–88
Ramayana, 7–8, 55, 81–82
Ray, Satyajit, 43, 45

refrigerator mother, concept of, xxii, 108–13, 121. *See also* Autism
relationality, notion of, 59, 67
religion, xvi, xxiv, 2–3, 5, 15, 29, 43, 79–80, 89, 134, 141, 190, 197, 205
religious
  iconography, 33
  pantheons, 5
renunciation, 57–58, 65
reproductive contract, 138–43
reproductive rights, 161
Roja (Mani Ratnam), 90
Roy, Nirupa, 94
Roy, Nirupama, 43

Saptamatrika (Seven Mother Goddesses), 4
Saraswati river-goddess, xix, 4, 7–8
Sati-Savitri-Sita model, 15
sexual/sexuality, 79–86, 156–57, 207n7. *See also* Femininity
  abuse, 174
  disable women and, 162–66
  identities, emergence of, 143–45
  middle class, 137
  relationships, 161
sexuation, 61
shakti, 80
Shakti cult (female power), 3
Singh, Bhagat, 10, 13
Sita, 8, 81
Skanda, 37
snake goddesses, 3
sociology, 1, 117
Stanadayini (The Breast-Giver), 50–54
sure-footed grasp of the topography of desire, 42
surrogacy, 138–43. *See also* Femininity; Motherhood
Swami Vivekananda, 78
systematic empathy, 61

Taare Zameen Par, 77, 101
Tagore, Rabindranath, 43
Tamil nationalism, xxi
Tamilttaay, 15, 22
Tamil womanhood, 87
third-world feminists, 202–3
traditional Hindu India barrier between child and mother, reason for, 60
traditionalism, 147

United Nations Convention on the Rights of Persons with Disabilities (UNCRPD) 2006, 161, 176
untouchable castes in India, 38
urban Indian, xvi, xxiii, 2, 8, 26, 69, 109, 135, 142, 146, 148, 151–53, 163, 182
 cultural construction of motherhood in, 122
 maternal identities in, xxvi
 middle classes, 69
 oppression of women in, xxiv
 public and private spaces in, 135
urban motherhood/mothering/mothers, xxiii, 2, 18, 150–52

Uttar Ramayana, 82

Vac Devi, xix, 3, 7, 68
vairaagini, 9, 15
virginity, 15, 22, 194
virgin mother, 15

Wolkstein, Diane, 5
womb, mother/woman, 9, 87, 140, 142, 146, 148, 152, 157, 171–73, 201
women/womanhood, 2, 49, 56, 62, 78–79, 83, 87, 91–92, 134, 147, 182. *See also* Disability; Femininity; Motherhood
 devaluation of procreative activity, 135
 ideal, 78
 liberation to, 134
 mutual relations, 59
 propagated by religious systems, 79
 relational capacities of, 59
 role of Hindu right, 150
 as symbol and agents, 89

Yama/Bharat Uddhaar, 12

About the Authors

Anu Aneja is currently Director of the School of Gender and Development Studies, Indira Gandhi National Open University, New Delhi, where she coordinates postgraduate programmes in women's and gender studies. She has previously taught comparative literature and women's studies courses at Ohio Wesleyan University, Ohio. She holds a PhD in Comparative Literature from Penn State University, Pennsylvania and a BA in French from Jawaharlal Nehru University, New Delhi. Her current research interests are in the areas of contemporary feminist theory, motherhood studies, and distance education and feminist pedagogy. She has published widely in the area of French and francophone feminist literature, and on postmodern and postcolonial writers. Her other interests include clay sculpture and creative writing.

Shubhangi Vaidya is a sociologist by training and teaches at the School of Interdisciplinary and Transdisciplinary Studies at the Indira Gandhi National Open University, New Delhi. Her research interests are in the areas of disability studies, gender studies and culture. Parent of a young adult with autism, Shubhangi combines research and teaching with advocacy for the rights of persons with disability and their families. She has published research articles and chapters in edited volumes on gender and disability, and presented papers at national and international conferences. She enjoys writing for newspapers and magazines and is an avid reader of fiction and a movie buff. She lives with her two sons in New Delhi.